IDEALISM AND THE ABUSE OF POWER

Law, Ethics and Governance Series

Series Editor: Charles Sampford, Director, Key Centre for Ethics, Law, Justice and Governance, Griffith University, Australia

Recent history has emphasised the potentially devastating effects of governance failures in governments, government agencies, corporations and the institutions of civil society. 'Good governance' is seen as necessary, if not crucial, for economic success and human development. Although the disciplines of law, ethics, politics, economics and management theory can provide insights into the governance of organisations, governance issues can only be dealt with by interdisciplinary studies, combining several (and sometimes all) of those disciplines. This series aims to provide such interdisciplinary studies for students, researchers and relevant practitioners.

Recent titles in the series

Integrity Systems for Occupations
Andrew Alexandra and Seumas Miller
ISBN 978-0-7546-7749-9

Promoting Integrity
Evaluating and Improving Public Institutions
Edited by Brian W. Head, A.J. Brown and Carmel Connors
ISBN 978-0-7546-4986-1

Protracted Displacement in Asia
No Place to Call Home
Edited by Howard Adelman
ISBN 978-0-7546-7238-8

Governing the Heroin Trade
From Treaties to Treatment
Melissa Bull
ISBN 978-0-7546-7121-3

Islam Beyond Conflict
Indonesian Islam and Western Political Theory
Edited by Azyumardi Azra and Wayne Hudson
ISBN 978-0-7546-7092-6

Idealism and the Abuse of Power

Lessons from China's Cultural Revolution

ZHUANG HUI-YUN
Griffith University, Australia

Routledge
Taylor & Francis Group
LONDON AND NEW YORK

First published 2010 by Ashgate Publishing

2 Park Square, Milton Park, Abingdon, Oxfordshire OX14 4RN
52 Vanderbilt Avenue, New York, NY 10017

Routledge is an imprint of the Taylor & Francis Group, an informa business

First issued in paperback 2020

British Library Cataloguing in Publication Data
Zhuang, Hui-yun.
Idealism and the abuse of power : lessons from China's Cultural Revolution. -- (Law, ethics and governance series)
1. Abuse of administrative power--China--History--20th century. 2. Rule of law--China. 3. Idealism, Chinese--History--20th century. 4. Power (Social sciences)--China--History--20th century. 5. China--Politics and government--1949-1976. 6. China--History--Cultural Revolution, 1966-1976
I. Title II. Series
340.1'1'0951-dc22

Library of Congress Cataloging-in-Publication Data
Zhuang, Hui-yun.
Idealism and the abuse of power : lessons from China's Cultural Revolution / by Zhuang Hui-yun.
p. cm. -- (Law, ethics, and governance)
Includes index.
ISBN 978-0-7546-7208-1 (hbk)
1. China--History--Cultural Revolution, 1966-1976. 2. China--Politics and government--1949-1976. 3. China--Social conditions--1949-1976. 4. Power (Social sciences)--China--History--20th century. 5. Abuse of administrative power--China--History--20th century. 6. Idealism, Chinese--History--20th century. 7. Communism--China--History--20th century. 8. One-party systems--China--History--20th century. 9. Law--China--History--20th century. I. Title.
DS778.7.Z49 2010
951.05'6--dc22

ISBN 13: 978-0-7546-7208-1 (hbk)
ISBN 13: 978-0-367-60267-3 (pbk)

Contents

Preface

The central idea of this book is to establish a principle of 'power check'. It identifies a need to reject the form of power totality in a socialist state such as China, and affirms a necessity to keep state power checked by the means of law. To this end, the Constitution of the People's Republic of China (hereafter PRC) should play a major role in providing both the principle and the legal framework for imposing limits and mutual checks on the state apparatus as public power. However, due to the current totality of power structure, the law lacks the independence and authority required for this task. There is, therefore, a need for a structural change through the Constitution.

This book takes a position that there is no justification for such a power totality in Marx's vision, and argues that, contrary to some common beliefs, it is in fact a serious abuse of Marxist basic democratic values and the principle of people's sovereignty over any political parties. It is therefore a betrayal of the purpose and the principle of a Marxist revolution to legitimize such a power totality, such a totality having been rejected by both Marx and Engels as the politicalization of feudal power. The consequence of this was a total submission of the people to an absolute power that had total control over every aspect of society, from law-making and law-keeping to controlling the very lives and thoughts of the citizens as individuals. Yet, at the same time, the power holders were immune from the force and justice of the law, with a type of legal privilege that is traditionally associated with an arbitrary feudal power structure.

The book then goes on to argue that this problem of total power structure has persisted even after the adoption of the rule of law as a national policy. In fact, law has become supplementary, without any authority of its own. This situation must change if China is to have inherent stability: the people must be given greater protection, some choice in the state officials who are their representatives and greater scrutiny over officials' abuse of public posts.

This position is based on the belief that no state power should be free of constraints, to rule by the virtue of its own authority without check. Such a path leads to arbitrary rule and inherent instability because such power cannot correct its own corruption without a system of multi-levelled checks and balances. This historic advancement in power check from the previous feudal system should apply to all political ideologies and classes, with socialism being no exception. Law, as a legal forum, should have an important role to play in this power check process.

The book then examines the Constitution of the PRC itself, to see how it can be used to implement this principle, and finally makes some proposals on how to combat the problem of power abuse.

Chapter 2 identifies the problem of power totality and its relationship with law and with the people. It first identifies that this is a problem because it contradicts the basic values in Marx's ideology and his vision for a civil society after a revolution. Marx rejects the total power structure and affirms a principle of state power being under the people's authority and the law. It recognizes that the problem is also based on cultural values and other factors *beyond* the law.

Chapter 3 examines how the legitimacy of this power totality has been developed in some socialist theories, in the name of socialist legality; and how some of Marx's basic concepts were abused as a means to justify this power totality. The reality of mass movements has confirmed, rather than rejected, this feudal power structure. This problem has persisted to the present day, in spite of the official adoption of the rule of law in China.

Chapter 4 examines the role that law can play in this challenge. It is based on the legal philosophy that power must be checked as a fundamental principle in a civil society. Law can facilitate the checks and balances of state power in due process. China should establish the principle of power check in the belief that public power should be under public scrutiny and that no political power should be left unchecked or above the law. To this end, an independent judiciary is essential for the task – to keep power in check and to protect the people.

Chapter 5 examines the Constitution as a framework for such a power check mechanism. It argues that the Constitution in China has an important role to play. It should endorse the power check in principle and provide structural changes to enhance the public supervision of state agencies and public officials. Finally, it proposes to expose corrupt officials and power abuse by an independent and legally binding office, directly under the Constitution and open to the public as the first step in breaking this totality. As stated earlier, such a process must of necessity be gradual but the principle itself should not be compromised.

The case studies used in this book are selected from a series published in the *New York Times*, examining the struggle in China over the creation of a modern legal system. The authors examined flaws in the system, the lack of legal protection in criminal and civil cases, and pressures faced by judges and lawyers who question the system.[1]

Hui-yun Zhuang (Peggy Krenn)

1 These articles are available at http://www.nytimes.com/asia. Articles as primary sources on the Cultural Revolution are rather limited, even after more than 40 years have passed, owing to restrictions on the media. To this day, Jicai Fang's *A Decade of 100 Personalities* (2004) still stands as the most substantial and comprehensive compilation of the life stories of that period. Hinton's documentary film *Morning Sun* is included in this study. Other non-Chinese sources such as BBC's documentary on the topic are rare.

In memory of my loving parents

Chapter 1
Introduction

The issue of state power raises the question of how it should be used in theory, and how it has been used in reality. The problem is raised because it is widely acknowledged that power can be easily abused when it is not constrained by law, and is concentrated in the hands of a few, either as individuals or as the leaders of a ruling party. It is a concern because this power, with its claimed legitimacy, is not constrained as a principle, and is not checked or sanctioned by law when it is abused. In other words, the problem identified here is a power held by individuals who are unaccountable to the rule of law and the legitimacy of ordaining authority by virtue of one's own power as a ruler. This problem of power concentration is not new. It was officially recognized by Chinese leaders such as Deng, who said: 'First of all, it is not good to have an over-concentration of power. It hinders the practice of socialist democracy and of the Party's democratic centralism … Over-concentration of power is liable to give rise to arbitrary rule by individuals at the expense of collective leadership, and it is an important cause of bureaucracy under the present circumstances' (Deng 1981: 426).

This power was further consolidated by virtue of its own authority without being subjected to the will of the people, thus gaining an unquestionable supremacy that could not coexist with contrary ideas or organizations. It has the power to imprison its opponents, as it has the privilege of being the sole truth holder and cannot be challenged. The problem with this kind of authority is that it places itself above the society and above the law and converts any opposition to its own views through means of persuasion – often involving criminal offences. In this situation, people's basic rights and their livelihoods are seriously threatened or violated. As a result, it leaves no room for alternative views and is a serious violation of the people's general rights to freedom.

People need protection against arbitrary power, and they need it by an authority such as the law that overrules arbitrary power when necessary. However, the problem identified, as identified in this introductory chapter, shows that law itself has no such authority while under the spell of a totalized power structure. Kant once said that 'law is the totality of the conditions under which the arbitrary will of one can co-exist with the arbitrary preference of another according to the general law of freedom', yet a state under a power totality suggests that, contrary to Kant's 'general law of freedom', there is another type of control conditions that justifies totality of power within a society (Curzon 1979: 75).

To many, this can be justified by the theory of Marxism, which is still the main doctrine of the PRC. However, Marx never envisioned a workers' state with an unconstrained power monopoly. His theory of dictatorship of the proletariat, although being used as a justification for the power monopoly, was never intended to endorse an authoritative state without legal limitation by the people's will expressed in the Constitution. In other words, Marx's theory in this regard has been seriously abused, and his belief in power limited by law and allowing free expression was largely discarded in favour of a total control by the ruling party.

Some argue that the power monopoly has suppressed or sidelined the role the law plays in relation to the state and the protection of individuals. Even today, the principle of the rule of law does not impose any restraints on the rulers (Potter 1991, 1994). Others see law deriving its 'validity' from its cultural uniqueness in order to reject other views. For example, Tumanov, writing in 1969, believed that Soviet jurisprudence had a unique character with nothing in common with Western legal philosophy and that Marxist ideology cannot coexist with Western legal philosophy (Curzon 1979: 179). The current Chinese slogan of 'Socialism with Chinese characteristics' echoes this concept of legal validity. However, this concept of unique characteristics fails to explain why ordinary people are left unprotected and why people must be content with fewer basic rights in a socialist state. A socialist state is supposedly, as Vyshinsky claimed, 'the most advanced class' of all, so this should include the concept of law being defined as a right for all. In Kant's words, 'law carries with it the right to coerce him who seeks to interfere with it' (Vyshinsky 1948: 75). This should include a person's liberty and freedom, which must be protected.

The problem is that power monopoly, by its nature, is opposed to people's basic rights and is unable to protect these rights. The purpose of identifying the problem of power monopoly is to prevent the accumulation of power in a few hands with the authority of individuals unrestricted by law. The fact that many political scientists and lawyers in China have been removed from their posts due to their endorsement of Western liberalism (Peerenboom 2002: 64) raises the question: Must a person's freedom as a constitutional right be the price to pay for the rule of the state? Does the state or a leadership have the power to contravene the basic rights of the citizens without being sanctioned by law?

Such concerns about state power in China, in particular, have arisen out of an historic event – the Great Proletarian Cultural Revolution of the 1960s and 1970s – and, beyond that, from more recent debates about the rule *by* law and the rule *of* law by Chinese jurists (Peerenboom 2002: 64). State power came to be concentrated in the hands of a few executives, without any conditions or constraints by law or by the will of the people. This concentrated power was supported by a political network, as seen in the case of the 'Gang of Four', and by a political structure that totalized this power.

This book originated as a reflection on China's Cultural Revolution, following the author's personal experience of it, and has developed into a search for the cause of and a solution for an historic episode that is now some 40 years in the past. As a result of this search, the central theme that emerged was a concern with the use of the state power. Questions such as Who gave the authority for this power? and Can this ruling power be checked or limited by itself? have widened the search to embrace issues such as the principles of power monopoly and power separation; the structure and management of state officials; and the consequences of a total power state.

First, at a principle level, this book takes the view that the authority for ordaining power should rest with the people through their representatives and not in the hands of any individual or groups. This principle of power check should be part of the Constitution, which has supremacy over the dominance of any political parties.

Secondly, at a structural level, this book argues that a power totality as a form of monopoly should be rejected. This is because it is dangerous and repressive in that it denies people's basic rights as expressed in the Constitution; and it is regressive in that it maintains a feudal style of rule. After a study of the history of this power monopoly within the framework of Marxist theories, I argue that this power totality cannot be justified. I will, instead, point out that the practice of this power totality is in fact a gross abuse of the original intent and basic values of Marxism. This is because the power totality has stripped away the essential elements of Marx's vision for a new civil and democratic state of working people, in which people uphold their authority over the state executives and are entitled to democratic values and opinions by law. In other words, it is the will of people that should ordain power and not the ruling party or government.

This power structure entails another problem – state officialdom. How these executives are appointed and managed is a clear indicator of how state power is used or abused. This book takes the position that these public officials should be appointed by representatives of the people, but not by the ruling class. State officialdom has yet another dimension – that of cultural inheritance. This has manifested itself negatively in a form of legal privilege and political networking and has resulted in a tradition of mutual protection with or without the norms of law. As a product of the power totality, these state officials are both lawmakers and lawbreakers. Because of this legal culture of power monopoly, the use of what can only be described as thugs in state-orchestrated persecutions is but one example of the kind of criminal activity that Chinese society has tolerated up to the present day. This feudalistic legacy has presented enormous problems and challenges both to law and to wider society.

Thirdly, at a consequential level, the book will demonstrate that, both in the past and at the present, people's basic livelihood, work choices, freedom of movement, opinions and every other aspect of life have been ruthlessly crushed by power careerists who have taken the law into their own hands without any legal penalties. This suggests that, unless we reject the power totality in principle and in the form of government, ordinary people will have no real legal protection and are liable to be persecuted under any political ideology that the power-holders see fit to impose. Moreover, there would be no legal forum on which people can challenge this arbitrary power and voice their demands without being condemned or imprisoned. The obvious imbalance of there being too much power at the disposal of the ruling elite and too little for individuals' basic rights, such as the right for one's voice to be heard, or for a fair hearing or appeal, is a striking indicator of how far a state can betray its people and change its 'colours' from what it claims to be. It also shows that power cannot correct itself without an independent and separate mechanism of law.

Background

This book is based on personal observations and experience of the Cultural Revolution. This period forms the focus of this study, because its impact on the people was extremely painful, and yet the official account of it is extremely brief and recollections and accounts of it have been largely suppressed in the media, even 40 years on. More importantly, however, the Cultural Revolution raises many questions such as the arbitrary use of state power to suppress ordinary people and the abuse of Marxist theories. To my knowledge, such issues have not been systematically investigated or publicly debated in China. Four decades is an instant in history but a long time in a person's life. For those who experienced it, the so-called the Great Proletarian Cultural Revolution of the 1960s and 1970s still weighs heavily in the memory. Citizens and families were profoundly and irreversibly affected by this occurrence, regardless of their social and political rank or role. To write about the event is to recall the lost lives of thousands of people in every corner of China, and one of the most dramatic and massive state persecutions of the last century.

There has been a steady and substantial growth in legal studies, both in Europe and in China, on the role of state and law, from a perspective of Marxist theories and practice. The instrumental role of law is widely acknowledged in assisting state dominance, regardless of the political system. There are also critical views of law in both capitalist and socialist states. What makes the rule of law debatable in a country like China is that it serves a dual legality: one role of the law is to serve the ruling party, and its other role is to serve the justice system.

'Dual legality', writes Amire Arjomand in an important article published in 2003, marked an 'ideological constitution-making of the intervening [i.e. post-communist] era' (2003: 7–32). In the wake of the collapse of communism in 1989 in Soviet and other former communist states in Europe, the article puts the constitutional reconstruction into an historical perspective. It considers the 'new constitutionalism' as the novel feature of the post-1989 transition to democracy, as contrasted with the old constitutionalism and the classic idea of the rule of law. It highlights the role of constitutional courts as the typical institution of the new constitutionalism. The concept of 'constitutional politics' is developed to focus on the process of political reconstruction, and the variation in its interface with the law is considered, ranging from the 'judicialization of politics' to the 'politicization of the judiciary'. The article considers the extent to which the powers of state executives enjoy a situation of 'dual legality' and the contribution of the legal institutions in the transition to democracy. In the case of China, the similarity is apparent in the 'dual legality' of the Party leadership over the state on one hand, and the judiciary and the rule of law on the other. The difference is that a constitutional court is yet to become a reality in the Chinese legal system, and the Chinese judiciary is not independent enough to keep state power balanced by legal and structural supervision and public scrutiny.

The main theoretical basis of this study is Marx's theory of class dictatorship, which Lenin developed into a state theory with power concentrated in one party. Law has played a secondary role in supporting and justifying this monopoly of power up to the collapse of the former communist nations in the late 1980s and the official adoption of the rule of law in China. The need to abandon this monopoly of power, with the use of the law, can be argued from many aspects. Law now plays a new role in reconstructing the power balance within the legal framework of the Constitution. Although law has existed in China since ancient times, the notion of the governance of law over those with power is still a relative rarity today. This study argues that, in the case of China, the theory of law is relevant only to the point that the law, in its formation and implementation, can effectively serve to protect people and withstand the power vested in individuals. In the struggle for law, the rule of law thus entails a change of legal culture and a notion of civil protection. This is a change that goes beyond the legal norms and institutions. It has become a challenge to the power that vetoes the law. Because of this, and because of Chinese history and its culture of the 'rule of man', law – in its 'pure' sense in the Western legal tradition – has not been given a top priority in this study; instead, it sets out to challenge the power that hinders the due process of the law, which I consider to be a more pressing concern. This study argues that a power totality has abandoned the essence of Marx's theory and that his theory of class struggle and dictatorship has been abused. It should be made clear that it is the power concentration and power abuse that need to be checked and rejected; but not the Marxist basis.

Apart from Marx's theory of law, other theories and methodologies crucial to my argument include the natural law of human reasoning (Aquinas); the rule of law in England (Hobbes); the separation of power (Locke and Montesquieu); constitutional studies (Pan); constitutional supervision (Lin Feng); critical legal studies (Hunter) and Weber's sociology of law (Beirne and Quinney). I have marshalled all of these perspectives to argue how a power totality should be replaced by a principle of power check, regardless of social and political orientations.

The significance of this book lies, first, in its focus on the state and the extent to which its power can be misused and justified. The state claims, in the context of Marxism and the theory of state by Lenin, that power concentration is legitimate for the interests of the people. It is against a contradictory reality that the claim is examined and rejected. This study rejects the legality of the state and the logicality of power concentration. It has the potential to clarify the original intent in Marx's vision, and to restore that vision by rejecting both its critics in the West and its distortion in China. This has significant implications for state ideology as a form of power abuse within a socialist framework. More importantly, it brings the question of historic stages to light as to whether a feudal power structure can be replaced by economic advancement by means of law; and whether this transition of power by the forum of law is part of a gradual but inevitable process of social and political transformation.

Secondly, this study intends to re-instate the study of law within the context of social experience. The purpose of this study is not for the pure pleasure of academic argument; instead, it calls for social responsibility and asserts the relevance of the law for the suffering of millions of people over decades in China. It pioneers a comprehensive investigation of an historic event in China, as an example of how this responsibility has been lost, and seeks a legal remedy that should create practical improvements in reality.

Thirdly, this study warns against dogmatic readings of Marxist theory on revolution and power that provide radicals, extremists and powerful states alike with visions or aspirations to justify their anti-humanistic actions. The study rejects this arbitrary legality as a criterion for war.

It is difficult to destroy an old order, but it is even more difficult to create a new and better one in the name of law. This requires a complete break away from the old, arbitrary values. We need to reconstruct the logicality of Marx's vision without losing sight of its original intent. It is clear that the true Marxist vision has never endorsed a power concentration unconstrained by law and the people.

The social context of this book is also significant. Readers of Western legal philosophy may easily take it as commonsense to empower an independent judiciary or a legally bound government with a minimum degree of liberty granted to the members of a civil society. It still presents a serious challenge in a largely rural economy with a vast, less educated population; and it also signifies a fundamental shift of power in a culturally autocratic society such as China.

Chapter 2
Identifying the Problem

Introduction

The issue in question is the use of state power – how it should be used in theory, and how it has been used in reality. This question is raised, to a large extent, as a review of an historic event in China that saw incredible suffering endured by the people under a state power that claimed to be the servant of people, but enjoyed a monopoly that was both buttressed by and above the law. This phenomenon is referred to as 'power totality', the definition of which will be given later in this chapter. Power totality is a problem for several reasons. There are many theoretical criteria we can use to indicate that power totality is problematic. The first such criterion is Marx's vision in Marxist theory, which clearly challenges a state power without constraints. The second criterion used in this argument is the individual's right to reason and protection. The lack of such protection leads to the next question of law: can or should law protect people in a socialist state? It is sometimes argued that law became a part of the problem rather than the solution because it lacked the authority required under the system of power totality. There were other factors besides the law that contributed to the debate about power monopoly: as an historic underdevelopment of power check and human rights; as a cultural concept of authority in a feudal tradition, and as an economic necessity for a centralized government.

Marx, Power and Law

To explore the notion of power check, we first need to examine Marx's position in regard to power check in a civil society after a Marxist revolution. Marxism, as one of the four cardinal principles in China, is important to China both in theory and in practice; and the issue of power check is at the heart of the power use, or abuse, as envisioned by Marx and Engels for a socialist state after a Marxist revolution. This study will demonstrate that Marx's vision confirms the principle of power check rather than rejecting it. The same vision also confirms people's democratic rights and the positive role the law plays in rejecting a feudal style of power structure where power is totalized or concentrated in the hands of a few as rulers or Party elites. In this section, the principle of power check will be examined in the light of Marx's vision, and the absence of this check of power shown as problematic in the use of state power.

There are three elements in Marx's vision, namely 1. that people should be respected and protected by law; 2. that we need a radical break from the feudal structure of power – so that total power lies with the people; and 3. that state power should be restricted by the means of law and the Constitution of the new state.

Before proceeding to Marx's vision of civil society, we need to clarify the position of law in Marx's theory. Contrary to his many critics, Marx believed that law was needed in society. Even though Marx was an uncompromising critic of existing bourgeois society and law, he insisted, nonetheless, that law is indispensable. As a trained lawyer, Marx engaged in and took the law seriously, especially issues such as parliamentary democracy, voting and elections, suffrage, trials, human right declarations and concepts of rights. He also argued political questions from a 'legal' perspective, as revealed in one of his texts, an outline for an unpublished book on political questions. It shows a concern with the law and the state that is still pertinent today. Marx's original outline for this unpublished work was as follows:

> 1. The genetic history of the modern state or the French Revolution
> – The overweening presumptuousness of the political sphere – confusion with the state of antiquity.
> Relationship of revolutionaries to civil society.
> Duplication of all elements in the domain of civil society and of the state.
> 2. The Proclamation of the rights of man and the constitution of the state
> – Freedom, equality, and unity.
> The sovereignty of the people.
> 3. The state and civil society.
> 4. The representative state and the Charter
> [program of the British Chartists]
> The constitutional representative state.
> The democratic representative state.
> 5. The separation of powers
> – Legislative and executive power.
> 6. The legislative power and the legislative bodies.
> Political clubs.
> 7. The executive power
> – Centralization and hierarchy.
> Centralization of political civilization.
> Federal system and industrialism.
> State administration and local administration.
> 8(a) Judicial power and law
> 8(b) Nationality and the people
> 9(a) Political parties
> 9(b) Suffrage
> The struggle for the abolition of the state and civil society.
> (Draper 1978: 187ff.)

Such an outline speaks to, and arises from, what might be called Marx's 'legal imagination' – his jurisprudential vision. I want to, as my first task, explore Marx's vision, addressing the democratic values within it.

Marx sees the people as the legislative body. He wrote of 'the voters, that is, the people who make the legislative body' (Draper 1978: 294). Later, Marx pointed to the Paris Commune's system as a triumph of democratic achievement. This is because the Paris Commune minimized and thoroughly subordinated executive power, placing, for example, the control of the courts, as well as the army, in the power of the people. Marx was, however, against the separation of power, and was in favour of unity of power, with executive and executive legislature combined (Draper 1978: 316).

The danger of power is omnipresent in all systems, whatever kind they may be – political, religious and legal. Marx realized this danger and dismissed the mere overthrow of one rulership by another: 'The mere overthrow of an oppressive rulership by its (untransformed) victims does not necessarily "transform circumstances" at all' (Marx and Engels 1966: 426). On the contrary, a common historical pattern has been that of the 'servant become[ing] master', who, as Marx noted in another connection, may be even more obnoxious than the traditional ruler. Others before Marx had called it 'the slave on the throne'.

Freedom of expression, and in particular a free press, is, in Marx's words, the 'heart of one concerned with civil society' and 'a citizen concerned with the state' (Marx cited in Draper 1978: 65). So rights – especially a right to free speech – stood at the core of Marx's understanding of the law. Freedom of expression is not the only right; there is the right of the people to 'give themselves a new constitution unconditionally', 'for the constitution becomes an illusion as soon as it ceases to be the real expression of the will of the people' (Draper 1978: 92). This was the real meaning of political emancipation (from the old feudal relations) and from the political restraints imposed by a feudalist state on the people.

Marx never fully discussed his vision of civil society as a specific topic or separate theory as such; but he mentioned it in many places in his writings, such as his *Critique of Hegel's Philosophy of Right.* Civil society was inaugurated, for Marx, by the French Revolution, which 'abolished the political character … it unchained the political spirit. Political emancipation was at the same time the emancipation of civil society from politics … Feudal society was dissolved into its foundation, into *man*' (Draper 1978: 118–19). A picture or view of civil society begins to emerge here. What does civil society look like?

First, civil society is a 'rational' state, involving a just and ethical harmonious relationship among the sectors of society. It is an *ideal* against which existing states are to be measured. 'The extent to which it "really" is a state depends on its closeness to the ideal.' It is the 'great organism in which juridical, ethical, and political freedom has to achieve realization' (Draper 1978: 32). So the law is fundamental to civil society. But what role does this law take? In a workers' state, Marx expected to see the following elements (Marx 1859 cited in Draper 1978: 301):

- The Constitution should limit the executive's power;
- The People's Assembly (or Congress) is the sovereign of the people;
- The society has the legal means to protect the civic realm;
- The people must have the knowledge and understanding of this equal relationship;
- The people possess the democratic values and protected freedom.

The second element is to reject the total power structure based on class or party supremacy. After the revolution, the proletariat becomes the ruling class and abolishes the condition for class distinctions, therefore abolishing its own supremacy. This is the principle that all are the same, regardless of class origin, as Engels stated: 'The revolution which modern socialism strives to achieve is, briefly, the victory of the proletariat over the bourgeoisie, and the establishment of a new organization of society by the destruction of all class distinction' (Engels cited in Tucker 1978: 665).

Marx noted that, in terms of power and state, feudalism differed from capitalism in its totality over people and the society as a whole. Marx's point is that by virtue of its ownership, the landowning aristocracy is also *automatically* the political ruling class. This fusion of law, politics and economics under feudalism renders power as the basis of law, and the basis of the 'rule of man'. As Draper noted, 'the baron *is* the state, for all in his demesne; the state is not some juridical independent executive committee, which acts on his behalf. *L'état c'est Lui*. Economic power is political power directly' (Draper 1978: 118). This is Marx's notion of politicization, which covered all aspects of civil society under feudalism:

> The old civil society had a *political* character in a *direct* sense; that is, the elements of civil life, such as ownership or the family or the kind and mode of labour, for example, were elevated into elements in the life of the state, in the form of the manorial system, social estates, and corporations. In this form they determined the relation of the single individual to the *state as a whole,* that is, his *political* relationship, that is, his relationship of separation and exclusion from the other components of society. (Marx cited in Tucker 1978: 44)

This politicization also witnessed the disappearance of the divide of one's civil life and political life. So individuals sank into a state of insignificance.

The process of transformation from a feudal society to a modern one involves a change in people's attitudes to authority and to law. This process eliminates the old servile mentality, a residue of the feudal society. The so-called 'sheep and saviours' mentality was opposed to the free will of modern man. People were divided between those whose leaders posed as messiahs and saviours and those who were engaged in seeking a messiah-saviour. 'Marx was especially sensitive to the German pattern that he labelled *obrigkeitliche Sinn*, the mentality submissive to authority on high.' He commented: 'For the German working class the most necessary thing of all is for it to cease conducting its agitation under the by-your-leave of higher authority. Such a bureaucratically schooled race must go through a complete course in "self-help".' His passing remark is: 'Germans are by nature very submissive, excessively obedient and deferential' (Marx cited in Draper 1978: 156).

The same could be said of the twentieth-century Chinese. But with a difference – for them, submission to authority is not residual; it is their very mode of being, precisely because they inhabit a sphere that is doubly politicized – as both feudal and socialist. To differentiate this feudal socialism from a modern democratic state, the old power structure would have to be changed by means of a power check that subjects the ruling state organs and executives to the rule of law.

It is clear, then, that the violation of man's dignity and lack of protection for the people are the corollary and the result of a total and totalizing power structure, cloaked in the 'legitimacy' of state ideology. This is an abuse of the Marxist theory of dictatorship of the proletariat, as well as an abuse of Lenin's theory of the Party as a 'vanguard of the proletariat'. Instead of acting on behalf of the proletariat, the power of the 'vanguard', when divorced from the people it claims to protect, ultimately betrays its original purpose for the revolution. This monopoly of power is unable to eliminate its own legal privileges within the law; or to prevent those careerists who seek and maintain their own personal power without any commitment to Marxism or to the people. This is a departure from Marx's vision and the socialist principle that power should be repositioned with the proletariat. I will argue, therefore, that a countermeasure must be put in place outside of, and in opposition to, the ruling party's own system. This task falls on the Constitution – in spite of there being some problems within the Constitution itself in regard to the total power structure (this will be examined in Chapter 5).

The third element – to limit the power of the state executive – is closely related to the second element, the power structure. History shows that certain levels of the state executive are untouchable by law, in contrast to the heavy measures placed on ordinary people. What has emerged here is a 'new' class using their public posts as 'capital' for their own benefit, for control of public resources.

To Marx, it is vitally important to limit executive power. For example, in 1853 he analysed the provisions in the new draft constitutions for Schleswig and Holstein. There he saw the Constitution as a means to curb power abuse, and he believed that one of the major functions of the Constitution was to reduce the state executive's power to a minimum. He advocated every possible means of minimizing the autonomous power of the executive. In 1859 he wrote an analysis of the Hessian Constitution of 1831, which he praised as 'the most liberal fundamental law ever proclaimed in Europe', except for its undemocratic method of electing representatives. The reason for this? 'There is no other Constitution which restrains the powers of the executive within limits so narrow, makes the Administration more dependent on the Legislature, and confides such a supreme control to the judicial benches' (Marx cited in Draper 1978: 301).

To Marx and Engels, the role of executives in a modern state is mainly managerial rather than dictatorial. Engels once stated that 'it is the executive which forms the "managing committee" while other state agencies are its arms', and that 'the modern state-power is but a committee which manages the common affairs of the whole bourgeois class' (Marx cited in Draper 1978: 469). In the *Communist Manifesto*, it is stated that 'the executive of the modern state is but a committee for managing the common affairs of the whole bourgeoisie' (Tucker 1978: 469).

In the view of Marx and Engels, there would be a process of transformation in the new workers' state after the revolution, but with two conditions: one is that all public posts should be elected by universal suffrage, and that people have the right to recall these posts and executives at any time; and the other condition is that all officials should be paid the same as other workers without privileges. This is to banish careerism and to bind executives to delegates of representative bodies. Marx expressed this view in *The Civil War in France* in these words:

> Against this transformation of the state and the organs of the state from servants of society into masters of society – an inevitable transformation in all previous states – the Commune made use of two infallible means. In the first place, it filled all posts – administrative, judicial and educational – by election on the basis of universal suffrage of all concerned, subject to the right of recall at any time by the same electors. And, in the second place, all officials, high or low, were paid only the wages received by other workers. The highest salary paid by the Commune to anyone was 6,000 francs. In this way an effective barrier to place-hunting and careerism was set up, even apart from the binding mandates to delegates to representative bodies which were added besides (Marx cited in Draper 1978: 628).

In China, however, these two conditions are not met owing to the current structure of the state power under a single ruling party. Under this structure, there is a lack of power check, which means that the state officials are not subject to recall by the people and state officials also enjoy privileges that are available only as a result of this power totality. The issue of state officialdom has a long tradition, especially in China, and a widespread social network with power 'fused' into their personal syndicates. The inseparable network of lawmaker, law-keeper and the courts makes it a 'haven' for this power network, and ineffective in limiting the power of state executive. It can be even more devastating when all are united against the citizens. Law, in this sense, is powerless to protect people, unless a separate legal entity is set up to deal with this corrupt state officialdom, such as a special administrative court that is independent and has power equal to its opponents, directly under the Constitution.

Power Totality

The definition of 'power totality' as used in this book is a power structure that has totality over the people, the laws and the society as a whole. It is a form of power monopoly in a structure of power totalized in a few hands without legal limitation. Marx noted that this power totality was marked by a *politicization* of all aspects of civil society – in his words, 'the vital functions and vital conditions of civil society always remains political, even though they were political in the feudalistic sense'. This is also the point where feudalism differed from capitalism in its political character: the latter abolished this feudal political character and freed the society from such political totality (Draper 1978: 118–19). A characteristic of feudalism is the politicization of society, with the power structure, both political and military, in the hands of feudal lords. This structure vested power in the individual not in law. In fact, this was the basis of law in a feudal society.

Power totality is a problem for three reasons. First, it is against natural law, and in particular the principle of equality to reason; secondly, it offers no protection to the people in the form of basic rights, and thirdly, it is derived from its own authority without check or limit. I discuss each of these reasons below.

Rejection of Equality to Reason

Reason is one of the most important principles in the theory of natural law. Human laws are not valid at all if they conflict with those principles, which are morally binding. The Roman orator Cicero summarized classical natural law doctrine as follows:

> True law is right reason in agreement with Nature; it is of universal application, unchanging and everlasting; it summons to duty by its commands, and averts from wrong-doing by its prohibitions … It is a sin to try to alter this law, nor is it allowable to attempt to repeal any part of it, and it is impossible to abolish it entirely. Senate or People cannot free us from its obligations, and we need not look outside ourselves for an expounder or interpreter of it. And there will not be different laws at Rome and at Athens, or different laws now and in the future, but one eternal and unchangeable law will be valid for all nations and for all times … (Cicero cited in Hunter et al. 1995: 51).

The Dutch philosopher Spinoza sees reason as a part of man's actual nature. He believes that reason is of great importance in man's life, that only the individual who lives in accordance with reason is truly free. Accordingly, a society is most free when its laws are based on reason. So the idea of democracy, to Spinoza, is 'the most natural of all forms of government' (Curzon 1979: 67).

Wolff, a German philosopher, also believes in the power of reason as against approaches dictated by the senses alone. He sees that all phenomena, including the law, have adequate and knowable reasons for their occurrence. To him, law exists on the basis of moral obligation. There exist innate human rights and they are the same for all people; therefore these rights are equal because they are the very consequences of human nature. Furthermore, men are free only under conditions of security and peace (Curzon 1979: 69). His limitation on this point, however, is his equation of natural law with the ruler and the idea of liberty resulting from obedience to the ruler as if to natural law.

Others see reason as an important ingredient of human happiness, as the end to the common good itself. Aquinas, for example, takes this view that 'the rule and measure of human acts is the reason, which is the first principle of human acts, for it belongs to the reason to direct to the end' (Aquinas 1964: 205). Aquinas added:

> The law is not always directed to the common goods as to its end … But reason is the foundation not only of what is ordered to the common good, but also of that which is directed to private good. Therefore the law is not only directed to the good of all, but also to the private good of an individual … The first principle in practical matters, which are the object of the practical reason, is the last end; and the last end of human life is happiness (Aquinas 1964: 225 A4).

More importantly, in this law of reason Aquinas emphasized that there is equality in all men by reason. In his words: 'It is a universal right for all men that all their inclinations should be directed according to reason', and that 'it [the will] must direct all other powers to reason' (Aquinas 1964: 224). Plato, moreover, sees happiness as the basis for legal justice and legal reasoning. In his words: 'We call these legal matters just which are adapted to produce and preserve happiness and its parts for the body politics' (Plato 2003: 1129b 17).

However, in a society where total power is concentrated in the hands of a few individuals, this equality to reason as a means to man's happiness is not possible. This is because the view of the ruler is made indisputable and any contrary views are discouraged. More importantly, the media, under such a structure, would be under the tight control of the state. Thus, for example, only a few articles were published in Hong Kong to mark the fortieth anniversary of the Cultural Revolution in 2006, owing to the controversial nature of debate over this historical event. The Tiananmen Incident, even among the local Beijing residents, was hardly mentioned as recently as early 2005 and, in conversations with the writer, was referred to only as the 'revolt period'. The fact remains that many political scientists, such as Liu (Peerenboom 2002: 64), and many lawyers in China have been reprimanded or removed from their posts owing to their views being different or contrary to the official standard. This suggests that power totality works directly against the law of reason; and it has denied access to, and equality in, the reasoning of the public.

Equality to reason, however, is not merely a matter of opinions, but a matter of power dominion of one individual over another. Locke stated:

> for no man or society of men having a power to deliver up their preservation, or consequently the means of it, to the absolute will and arbitrary dominion of another, whenever any one shall go about to bring them into such a slavish condition, they will always have a right to preserve what they have not a power to part with, and to rid themselves of those who invade this fundamental, sacred, and unalterable law of self-preservation for which they entered into society (Locke 1690, 1924: 117).

Equality to reason, in Hobbes' term, became a fundamental right to self-preservation. To him, this right is a very important natural right of man. He sees that all men are equal in a state of nature, but no rules exist in a state of conflict with 'everyman against everyman'. To end these conditions, a measure of liberty is necessary, in that if a man should accept a measure of liberty against other men, he would allow them the same liberty against himself, bound by legal agreements entered into as a social contract. According to Hobbes' theory of social contract, a sovereign cannot act 'unjustly' because his rule is 'authorized' as a result of the covenant, and is constituted by the exercise of power on behalf of his subjects who cannot act unjustly towards themselves. He believes that the greatest liberty of subjects is not contrary to the will of the sovereign, and is with the silence of the law. Although the subject has the liberty to demand the hearing of his case, according to the law, in fact there is no action of law. This is because 'for all that is done by him in virtue of his power, is done by the authority of every subject, and consequently he that brings an action against the sovereign, brings it against himself'. 'On the other hand, if a monarch, or sovereign assembly, grant a liberty to all, or any of his subjects, and he does not provide for their safety, then the grant is void, unless he renounces or transfers the sovereignty to another' (Hobbes 1996: 146).

Hobbes believed in the powers of sovereignty and sees that the sovereignty is the soul of the commonwealth. At the same time, he believes that men have the right by nature to protect themselves in the covenant they made with the ruler. Although sovereignty is meant to be immortal, in its own nature it is subject to the violence, ignorance and passions of men. Hobbes' concept of the equation of sovereignty as the will of subjects, being equal to the will of the ruling class, is problematic; for when the monarch or the ruling body departs from the will of the people, or fails to grant liberty to the people, the sovereignty of the people may be voided, and hence unable to override the monarch or the ruling group.

It is necessary at this point to differentiate a total power structure from a general will as expressed in law. Rousseau explained how this concept of general will was made legitimate in a process from a natural form of freedom and equality to the natural rights granted by the society in the form of civil liberties. This general will is the will of a wider community as its sovereignty. Individuals are subject not to any other single person, but to the 'general will' of this community. Rousseau sees this sovereignty of the community's general will as absolute and inalienable, and capable of overthrowing government and laws. To him, legal norms bind only when people voluntarily participate in the lawmaking process, and those lawmakers will be bound by those norms. Thus, the general will entails a sense of authority that is not vested in the hands of a few leaders, but in the wider community. In Rousseau's view, natural law does not create individual rights, but it confers on the people as a whole an absolute and inalienable authority (Curzon 1979: 70). This is the people's general will, which is different from the will of a few individuals who have total power over the majority of the people. The general will, in this sense, is more than the mere sum of individual wills; it is the unalterable and constant will of the majority of the community.

Denial of Rights

Denial of rights is directly related to a power structure that is against reason in the natural law, and is itself separated from the general will of the people. The structure of a power totality means that an individual's life is subject to a special group that holds the power of the state, and that has an exclusive power to interpret what constitutes the definition of people and their basic rights, as well as the right to determine who deserves protection of their rights. Under this kind of arrangement, individuals' work units, their residential registration, their organization managers and local committee members and police – all of which are under the dominance of a single organization and its leaders – prescribe the movement and activities of the individuals.

Such a structure leaves people with no means to protect themselves and their families. The experience of life under such a power totality in China during the Cultural Revolution was both horrific and slavish without any protection for a person's freedom or basic rights. The details of this period will be found in the next chapter of this study, as an example of total power structure supported by state ideology. The fact that millions of ordinary people, seen in the stories of many lives recorded in Zhang's collection (see Appendix 2), had to suffer incredible ordeals, losing control over their lives in every aspect (including their career, education, livelihood and personal security) suggests that the system had failed to protect people and their basic rights. The fact that so many people lost their personal dignity and family life suggests a fundamental flaw in the nature of power totality, and questions the legality of such a power structure.

Power totality, then, betrays the trust the people give to the ruling body, but, thanks to the sovereignty of the people, such a trust can be forfeited and withdrawn. Locke believed that supreme power should remain in the hands of the people who have the right to remove or alter the legislative or the ruling class. He sees that all power is given in the trust of achieving an end and is limited by that end. Whenever that end is 'manifestly neglected or opposed, the trust must necessarily be forfeited, and the power devolve into the hands of those that gave it, who may place it anew where they shall think best for their safety and security'. And thus the community perpetually retains a supreme power of saving themselves from the attempts and designs of any body, even of their legislators, 'to lay and carry on designs against the liberties and properties of the subject' (Locke 1690, 1924: 116).

Derived Authority without Checks or Limits

Montesquieu sees law as 'the necessary relations arising from the nature of things' (Curzon 1979: 69). Law is in general human reason and is oriented to justice and should be judged by it. To him, the true purpose of political association is to prevent the power accumulation in a few hands. To achieve this, it is essential to have checks and balances against the concentration of power, especially in the hands of the lawmakers who should be bound by the legal norms. Power should not be concentrated in a few hands, but should be defined and checked separately. This is to maintain a people's liberty.

On the other hand, a power totality suggests that it is not bound by legal restrictions because the power has control of lawmaking and law enforcement without being subject to or limited by those legal measures. Such a power is limitless and cannot be challenged or removed by legal means without its own consent; for it is this ruling power that has the supreme power of legislation, not the law.

Accountability here is defined as responsibility with a clear boundary, subject to the specific rule of law in question. This includes the executives, who are responsible to their posts and subject to the law relevant to them. The danger of a power totality is that persons who are both lawmakers and law enforcers may suit the law to personal interests opposed to those of the rest of the community and contrary to the common good of society. Locke sees this danger and calls for the lawmakers to be subject to the laws they have made. In his words:

> For the same persons who have the power of making laws to have also in their hands the power to execute them, whereby they may exempt themselves from obedience to the laws they make, and suit the law, both in its making and execution, to their own private advantage, and thereby come to have a distinct interest from the rest of the community, contrary to the end of society and government. Therefore, the legislative power is put into the hands of diverse persons … a power to make laws, which when they have done, being separated again, they are themselves subject to the law they have made (Locke 1690, 1924: 115).

A power derived from its own authority is a ruling made without subjecting it to the will and interest of the people. The necessity of having a higher authority to restrain such a power is to ensure that the wishes of the people, as expressed in the laws, are carried out faithfully.

The People Unprotected – The Consequences of Power Totality

The Cultural Revolution in China in the 1960s, as examined here, is a good example of the consequences of a power totality and of life under an ideological state. It occurred when state power was totalized in the hands of a few leaders; where people were left unprotected and had no legal means to challenge the abuse of power. It was a revival of the feudalistic characteristics of a Chinese society that had not changed in terms of its power structure. Although in theory it was called a revolution, in reality it was more like an historical regression, in terms of people being unprotected and losing their basic rights. Historians estimate that of the more than 700,000 people who were persecuted during the revolution, about 35,000 were killed. Thousands more committed suicide after being harassed by Red Guards (*Current Events* 2005: A2).

Montesquieu made a comparison of features among republics, monarchies and despotic governments and said: 'In republican governments, men are all equal; equal they are also in despotic governments: in the former, because they are everything; in the latter, because they are nothing.' (Montesquieu 1731, 1949: Book VI, Ch. 2). For Montesquieu liberty is a kind of luxury – in his words: 'Luxury is therefore absolutely necessary in monarchies as it is also in despotic states. In the former, it is the use of liberty; in the latter, it is the abuse of servitude ... Hence arrives a very natural reflection. Republics end with luxury; monarchies with poverty' (Montesquieu 1731, 1949: Book VII, Ch. 4). Yet the true spirit of equality is as distant from that of extreme equality (as under a dictatorship or in a lawless society) as heaven is from earth. To reach this true spirit of equality we need law. In Montesquieu's words: 'In a true state of nature, indeed, all men are born equal, but they cannot continue in this equality. Society makes them lose it, and they recover it only by the protection of laws' (Montesquieu 1731, 1949: Book VIII, Ch. 3). His concept of government is based on whether it governs by law. Unlike Aristotle who based his concept of government on the virtue of the sovereign, Montesquieu based his on the concept of law. Therefore, the distinction between monarchy and despotism depends not on the virtue of the monarch, but on whether or not he governs 'by fixed and established laws' (Montesquieu 1731, 1949: Book II, Ch. 1). Each form of government has a principle, a set of 'human passions which set it in motion' (Montesquieu 1731, 1949: Book III, Ch. 1) and each can be corrupted if its principle is undermined or destroyed. In this light, the principle of the Cultural Revolution, which, in theory, was to give the people a say in the government, was, in practice, utterly undermined and destroyed by the ruler's concept of power over man's liberty, and power politics over the spirit of humanity.

The Rationale for the Cultural Revolution

There are many theories on the motives and reasons why Mao, as the state leader, launched the Cultural Revolution. From some of Mao's unpublished speeches, which were circulated in the capital city at the time, and from articles in the official state magazine, *Red Flag*, and the newspaper *The People's Daily* (1966a), the Cultural Revolution was about the impurity of the Party and how its power should be applied or corrected. Mao was concerned that the real danger for the nation lay inside the Party, and this could make or break the country in the long term. This concern is valid even today. However, as to the question of *how* to eliminate this danger from within the Party, and prevent it from 'changing its colour' (that is, changing its destined ideological direction), views varied. Mao's own view was to encourage young people to act under his command. His official line was:

> The heart of the Cultural Revolution has indeed been a struggle for power, a struggle over the control of state power ... but it has not been a struggle over power for power's sake ... It has been a class struggle to determine whether

> individuals representing the working class or individuals representing the bourgeoisie will hold state power. It has been a struggle to determine whether China will continue to take the socialist road and carry the socialist revolution through to the end, or whether China will abandon the socialist road for the capitalist road (Hinton cited in Pugh 2005: 33–43).

Mao's official directions were superficially clear:

> At the start of the revolution, Mao urged thousands of students, who came to be know as Red Guards, to destroy China's 'four olds – old customs, habits, culture, and thinking'. Red Guards raided homes, destroying remnants of traditional Chinese society, including books and artwork. They took over schools and offices, humiliating and torturing teachers, scientists, and anyone else they suspected of not being a true communist ... (*Current Events* 2005).

At a deeper level, however, the definition of a 'socialist roader' or a 'capitalist roader' was never clarified. This caused confusion and the situation became chaotic as people took the law into their own hands. Under Mao, society as a whole believed that people had the right to condemn and to punish whomever they saw fit – those they perceived as belonging to the wrong class background. Thus the country quickly sank into a lawless state.

Even at the time, however, others saw the Cultural Revolution as the result of an internal power struggle within the Party. Many of Mao's personal staff saw it as nothing more than a testing ground for Mao's personal dominance of power within the ruling party. The struggle was prompted by a development external to China itself. In 1956 Khrushchev's attack on Stalin threatened to undermine Mao's rule and to call China's own leadership into question. What Stalin was to the Soviet Union is what Mao was to China, so for Mao to agree to the attack against Stalin was to admit that it was permissible for him to be attacked as well. This 'Mao could never allow' (Zhisui Li 1994: 114). According to his staff, Mao was constantly alert to attempts to undermine his rule. He did not want any of his underlings becoming a 'Chinese Khrushchev', writing condemnatory reports attacking him after his death.

If Mao's idea of an internal cleansing process was based on the assumption that the Party is always above the people, then the Party could not be made subject to the people's will, or limited by the people and the law. This view poses problems about unlimited power and the relationship between the Party and the people. As a result, people would lose their authority and claim over the Party as their agent or delegation, but not as their master. Thus Mao's view did not solve the problem of power concentration, or the issue of people's authority over the ruling agent, and without the authority and sovereignty of the people, a people's state is illusive.

This power totality was both regressive and oppressive. In theory, the country's feudal characteristics should have been superseded by a fairer distribution of state power by the collective will of the community. This would have stemmed from new productive relationships, advancement of the economy, and an increased notion of citizens' rights and responsibilities in a new civil society within the rule of law. Under this new public ownership of state power, any public powers should have been subject to public scrutiny and to the limitations set by law. People and their delegations should have made decisions without the dominance of any organization. In the process law should have been a mechanism in this public ownership of power and provided a legal forum for protecting public will and voices against any form of power monopoly.

It is therefore argued that, in order to determine how to apply state power appropriately in a workers' state, we should set the limit on state power in any form. The limit and the task of checking should be set by the people's assembly or congress, but not by the ruling party itself. This should be what the Cultural Revolution *originally* set out to achieve, but it was completely missed in the historic event. Instead, it became a war against ordinary people who had no legal access to defend themselves against unexpected attacks of verbal and physical violence, political condemnation, and personal and social discrimination.

The following section will show the consequences of a state in total control and with unlimited power. First, people's basic rights were seriously eroded and many lives were destroyed by state power. People were ruled under a totality of power and every aspect of their lives and thoughts were thus dictated or condemned by the state. Secondly, there was a lack of the notion of basic rights of personal freedom in a modern and civil society, and, thirdly, there was no limit to this power abuse – those in power faced no legal constraints on their use of power and were not subject to any scrutiny from a higher order. Law, under such circumstances, had no authority and was powerless to protect people.

Revival of Feudalism – Dogmatism of Mind

As mentioned earlier, a characteristic of feudalism is the politicization of society, with power, political as well as military, resting in the hands of feudal lords. This structure vested power in the individual, not in the law, and was the basis of law in a feudal society. Persons had no value other than as the property of the masters or lords, for they could be killed or sold as their master wished – control was total. Feudal practice revealed itself in the Cultural Revolution, mainly in the events that unfolded between 1966 and 1976. The widespread violence among the masses revealed the lawless nature of the society, while the apathy of the cadres who cared only about pleasing their masters was by-product of this feudal power structure. The point to be made here is that, either as a state or as a people within this state, China has remained feudal both in its outlook and in its actions. Its modernity was found only in its revolutionary rhetoric and in an exercise of political power that perhaps even exceeded its feudal past in terms of its total control of an individual's movement, property and private life. More dangerously, it was able to dictate an individual's thoughts to such a degree that one accepted total self-denial or even took one's own life as a result of the mental abuse and torment. Yet the extent of the abuse is such that no one questioned the very nature of this power practice. With no accountability the state had unlimited power to suppress any of its citizens in the most inhumane fashion, while ordinary people had no rights and no choice other than to conform with state ideology if they wished to avoid prosecution. Free thinking was prohibited.

One example of this mind control was the suppression of the media. During the Cultural Revolution, in the late 1960s, the country was in a state of virtual anarchy – many prominent individuals were physically attacked and governmental agencies and schools were temporarily paralysed. For a short period there were some independent newspapers and unsourced leaflets were distributed in millions of copies. One of these free newspapers was *The Newspaper of Cultural Revolution in High Schools* (May 1967) which published a famous article entitled 'On family background' calling for equality for young people from accused 'class backgrounds' with regard to their participation in society and the revolutionary movement. The author of this article, Mr Yu L K, had studied Montesquieu's *Persian Letters* and noted in his diary (May 1966) that 'Montesquieu stated that "in order to love and conform to one's religion, it is not necessary to hate and persecute those who do not conform to it"'. Here the word 'religion' could easily be replaced by 'thought' or 'Marxism'. His diary, unfortunately, was seized in a raid and Yu was arrested on 5 January 1968 on suspicion of writing the news articles and holding dangerous ideas. Not only him, but all staff of the *Newspaper for High Schools* were questioned. Later the family was told that Yu had been shot and his father burst into tears on receiving the news. The response demonstrated nothing short of barbaric cruelty: 'You are supposed to draw a clear line between yourself and your son, why do you cry?' (Hinton et al. 2003: Video, Channel 10)

This inhumane indifference regarding human life was quite a common standard of the time: anyone could be accused and lives were destroyed like animals'. Even the President of the PRC, Liu Shaoqi, was beaten and assaulted repeatedly while trying to talk with a copy of the Constitution of the PRC in his hand. He later died of an illness, alone in a rural village, without any medical care and without any clothes on him. His whole family were also treated like animals. Liu, the elected president of the nation, thus died in the most destitute circumstances, without being giving any human care or dignity. The masses did not care which political debate or class theory was applicable to these tragic cases. Many simply enjoyed the sense of liberation and the power they had for the first time to be able to challenge the privileges of the state leaders. Both the state leaders and the masses did not have any concept of humanity. The mob became animals themselves and took the law into their own hands. In this situation, no one was immune from sudden brutal attack by others and no one enjoyed legal protection. There were no other rights for ordinary citizens except the right to join in this mass persecution.

Such dogmatism was accompanied by physical violence and crimes that borrowed from the old feudal system of punishment. Public display of the accused had been standard feudal practice for centuries – the pointed white hats, with the names written on them in black ink and with a huge red cross struck through each name to indicate a death sentence, were all too familiar to the Chinese mind. Nothing had really changed, except that it was now all done in the name of communist ideology. It was a practice that involved a deliberate humiliation of the victim in public and by the public, and prisoners, regardless of their guilt, were inhumanely treated. It was a culture of violence that turned young middle-class girls, for example, into thugs and murderers who delighted in beating strangers until the torturers themselves were exhausted. The only thing that had changed was the slogans used to goad people into persecuting others. Feng's book contains a great deal of detail on this kind of persecution (including graphic photographs; Feng 2004: 142), as does Hinton's archival footage (Hinton et al. 2003).

The use of thugs and rapists in prisons to torture political prisoners was common, as seen in the case of Zhang, a young Party member who cared to criticize the Party leaders and their policies during the Cultural Revolution. She was put in prison and, in order to break her spirit, the authorities rewarded her fellow prisoners with credit points if they raped her. They tormented her in every possible way, blindfolding her while others were being shot around her. Even on the day of her prosecution, they slashed her throat with a knife to cause maximum pain and to stop her from uttering her last words out loud (Jin 1993). There could be no better summary of the blackness of this repressive society than Zhang's case, and yet her only 'crime' was to criticize the Party authority. She was left at the mercy of criminals and social thugs, under the very party that purported to be the vanguard of the people. In reality, of course, the Party was behind the criminal activities, including the mass murders, and they regularly employed thugs to inflict physical harm and to issue threats, as they still do today. In Chapter 4, more recent cases are included to show how this barbaric practice has been used by local government officials and law-keeping agencies.

The power of the state was strengthened by the fact that it kept systematic records on individuals – records that state officials could use whenever and for whatever they saw fit. In the case of Li Cunxin, for example, when Li married and decided to stay in the United States, officials went to his native village and visited his family only two days after he had made his decision. 'Do you know what your son has done?' one of the officials growled at Li's mother. 'Your son has defected from his motherland for the filthy America! You, as his mother, should be ashamed to have brought up such a bastard!' His parents have lived in constant fear and despair even since. They had been prepared to go to prison and lose everything they had to defend his honour. Subsequently, his academy school officials burnt all Li's personal belongings. Some of his relatives and friends distanced themselves from Li's family, for fear of being implicated in the whole affair. Again when Li returned to China nearly a decade later, the Chinese secret police were waiting to see him: they wanted to know if anyone was involved or behind his defection. This was the epitome of what many people had to bear in life, largely beyond their personal control.

The abused were in a hopeless and powerless position. Their personal or private files, which they never saw or even knew about, were kept in secret government units, accessible only to those in charge at the time. These files could be added to, deleted, relocated or reopened without the knowledge of the individual in question. The individual's fate could be determined overnight simply on the whim of those in power, and the individual locked up indefinitely without further ado. In the name of the revolution, the feudal practice of the master having control over his slaves was developed into its modern version, as the individual was subjected to totalized power, comprising both physical and mental abuse and loss of control over every aspect of their life.

Moreover, there was no legal framework or legal protection for those individuals targeted or imprisoned, and they were therefore at the total mercy of those who held power, who believed they had the political, if not the legal, right to control other human beings – to determine whether they should live or die, where they should go, and what they should say and do, for the rest of their lives.

The Terror of the Total Political State – Marx Rejected

Marx, commenting on the Paris Commune, noted that, in terms of power and state, feudalism differed from capitalism, in its totality over people and the society as a whole. It was marked by a politicization of all aspects of civil society. The French Revolution abolished this political totality and freed the people's spirit.

During the Cultural Revolution, China became an ideological state in which people were ruled by the terror of political totality. This meant that they lived a life that was entirely dictated by the will of a few individuals with unlimited power over others. In this state, ordinary people lost control of their livelihoods, their jobs, their families or where they lived. Political purges continued and doubled the misery of those who had already being 'doomed' as 'rightists' earlier. Also included in the purges were those doomed during all previous political 'verifications' in the cities and political classifications in the rural regions – and their children and relatives were not immune. The real-life stories selected from thousands of autobiographical accounts in Feng's book are evidence of the terror that ruled people's lives and thoughts (Feng 2004). The country began a descent into turmoil and local fighting broke out everywhere as a result. The entire nation with its millions of people were directly involved in a top-down struggle against the country's invisible class enemy, once so eloquently described by the state media, and, without the protection of civil rights, millions of lives were affected profoundly by the unprecedented scale of political prosecution.

Several characteristics of this political state emerged during this period of turmoil. First, there power was concentrated in the hands of a few without any constraint. Leaders were praised and worshipped to the extent that could be matched only by worship of the Divinity. The Party leader, Chairman Mao, for example, was worshipped almost feverishly and his image was widely used by local leaders as a means of intimidating and controlling the masses, to the extent that individual fates could be determined by the image of Mao, as seen, for example, in one peasant's story (see Appendix 2). There were even many incidents where unfortunate individuals who had unintentionally damaged a picture of Mao were put to death unconditionally.

Secondly, a product of power totality was apathy. Special social circumstances produce a special breed of people. This was true during the period when everything a person did and said or thought was closely scrutinized and interpreted. This became a by-product of the political climate in a society where year after year there had been campaign after campaign. Many individuals educated in this climate were able not only to survive but to thrive, just as the henchman had in feudal times. They became bullies, living under the protection of their powerful masters. They were skilful in creating lies to please their superiors. They specialized in targeting innocent people and seeking out victims for persecution. In so doing they would meet the quota requirements for catching political 'class enemies' and thus be promoted or at least praised. They were talented in ingratiating themselves with the boss and gained merits by capitalizing on the misfortune of others. 'In China, the first to be observant and sensitive to others' moods are the political cadres not writers' (Feng 2004: 142). The prison superintendent in 'T''s case is another example of how apathy had led to a dearth in human compassion (see Appendix 3). Such apathy was especially rife within the prison system where torture, violence and personal tragedy were commonplace. All this suggests that a slave mentality existed – of a willingness to serve one's master, regardless of who they were, or however evil and bereft of compassion or conscience they might be.

Thirdly, there was no such a thing as a 'private matter' during the Cultural Revolution. For example, in T's case, it can be seen how prisoners were forced to use 'standard language' in order to pass the political censorship imposed by the superintendent of the prison – reflecting a use of jargon that was prevalent during that period. The letter started with the salutation 'Long live, and long, long, long live Chairman Mao!' and was only then followed by the normal greetings. A translation is needed to decode what the prisoner meant in the letter. He was arrested and imprisoned for ten years without any legal process, and yet he could not tell his family that he was in jail. To decode his letter, the sentences should be read like this: to say 'I am imprisoned' he wrote 'the revolutionary masses rescued me and put me into the Bureau to study there'; to say 'I was watched closely', he wrote 'everyday I studied under army supervision personally'; to say 'I won't give in', he wrote 'I will be reformed to be a new person again'. He had to repeat the study class before he could ask for some personal items to be brought into the prison.

Fourthly, humanity was the price paid under this system of power politics. Man's conscience and honesty, as part of his soul, were no longer valued. In this highly pressured political climate, fear turned people into liars and hypocrites – a phenomenon that prevailed during the Cultural Revolution. It became second nature as a survival strategy. 'For my survival and my family, I had to lie,' Mao's personal doctor Li observed, after seeing the turmoil that afflicted the lives of all the staff who worked around Mao (Zhisui Li 1994: 63). The Party required people to pledge public support for policies with which they did not agree. 'Life depended on constantly betraying one's conscience' (Zhisui Li 1994: 65). The final words of Li's book are:

> I write this book in great sorrow for Lilian and for everyone who cherished freedom. I want it to serve as a remainder of the terrible human consequences of Mao's dictatorship and of how good and talented people living under his regime were forced to violate their consciences and sacrifice their ideals in order to survive (Zhisui Li 1994: 638).

Humanity entails the spiritual nature of man manifested in his vision and faith. Marx recognized this spirituality in the dual nature of man. People as individuals have two roles – that of the '*citizen*, egalitarian, community-oriented and equal'; and that of the private individual in so-called '*civil life*' (Marx 1843 in Tucker 1978: 34). He called for a *political* emancipation for the people – the ability to participate officially in the government, to vote, to run for office etc. – as part of the long chain of social development towards a modern civil society. The deepest tragedy of the Cultural Revolution is rooted in the betrayal of faith, the faith that people had in the Party – a party that turned against the people and in so doing sacrificed the essence of humanity and dignity of life itself. In this sense, the masses became blind believers and also god makers.

It is clear, then, that the faith and devotion of the masses were abused by the power-holders. This can be seen in the similarity between the devotion shown by the millions of people during the Cultural Revolution and religious practice. The worship nationwide involved an absolute devotion and religious commitment of each soul, the divine and untouchable image of Mao like that of a perfect god; the harassment and persecution that followed if a person was found not holding Mao's *Little Red Book* (like holding the Bible in church) or not swearing by Mao's image; the self-criticisms to the group leaders (like the Catholic confession); the mutual fear and mutual surveillance; and the use of group pressure and massive numbers of people as proof of truth. The effect of all this was to put the leader on a pedestal like a god – a being who would never fail the people, never do them harm, never tell lies and who is absolutely and always in the right and cannot be doubted. This religious-like practice was in fact a betrayal of man's right to reason and a tool to maintain power, dominance and authority. This obviously had nothing in common with Marx's original vision.

This monopoly of the truth ensured the privilege of the chosen few. They had all the power to determine people's fate, leaving them with no rights at all. The leaders, who possessed state power in their hands, manipulated the vision of the masses to their own advantage. The abuse of Marx's humanistic vision was thus linked with the spiritual nature of man and mixed with revolutionary theories as inspiration – without a real understanding of man's value and rights.

The abuse of this inspiration is based on a cognitive confusion between the idealized vision on one hand and the interpretation of the reality on the other. Many young people were convinced by the empty rhetoric peddled in the media and by the official justifications prevalent in state propaganda; but more important was their conviction that their leaders would never let them down; that the leaders were morally truthful and honest and were true believers like the youths themselves and would not lie to the masses. Little did they know the complexity of the power struggle at the top level of the Party machine at the time; so the 'great leader' and vice president Lin Biao's air crash and his conspiracy to overthrow Mao came as a profound shock to many (Hinton et al. 2003: video). As Montesquieu reflected, republics end with liberty and despotic states with poverty and loss of equality. Society could recover liberty and equality only by the protection of laws and tolerance (Montesquieu 1731, 1949: Book VIII, Ch. 3).

It is undisputable that the Cultural Revolution was manipulated from the central office of the ruling party where the state was concentrated in the hands of a few individuals. The official media pronounced otherwise, of course – the mass movement was initiated from the grassroots and by the people. In theory, China was a republic, but in reality, the personal power of the ruler, Mao, was easily transferred to his wife, Jiang Qing, like a latter-day dowager empress. She not only believed in her personal power as in the olden days, but also made sure she exploited this feudal power to the full. And with her feudal position as Mao's wife, the empress demanded total loyalty and obedience from all those who worked for her. In this sense, China operated just as it had under the imperial court.

In the prison system, meanwhile, cases indicate that guards were violating the very laws they were supposed to be upholidng, with some even committing crimes such as rape or torture without being charged or even questioned. Many of those who broke the law were even promoted. In T's case, both the chairwoman of the revolutionary committee and the military representative in the factory, both of whom abused their public power in various ways (including a coerced divorce and causing physical harm), were soon after to be found in leadership positions in the factory. The fact that this situation has recurred in some more recent cases indicates that this problem of a lack of accountability has persisted, well after the Cultural Revolution. This is a key problem that the law faces today. Those beneficiaries of the political turmoil, who inflicted great suffering on others and who were masters of political rhetoric, showed contempt for human life and rights. This happened despite the fact that both policy and the law had been changed at the top level of the government after the Cultural Revolution.

How was the law implemented then? There were policies regarding the people who were wrongly accused of political crimes that they had not committed. The policies or directives were issued from the top level of the state. However, to issue a policy does not assure a corresponding implementation at the local level. Often a policy was met with strong resistance from local authorities and those beneficiaries who held the deciding power. For example, in T's case, T was released because of the change of policy that was meant to free those wrongly accused and imprisoned. However, T still had many obstacles to overcome and a long wait before the benefit of the law reached him. When T went to the housing management office for his accommodation, the office staff lied, saying they were not responsible for T's problem, when in fact they were. The housing problem T faced back then still remains unresolved to this day some 20 years later (see Appendix 3).

It is alarming that, no matter how well intentioned the law was, it could be easily frustrated by a local officer. This local officer might not hold a high position in society, and might not be highly paid for his job, and yet he was able to manipulate and to abuse his authority. He had no difficulty in denying his responsibilities and dared to challenge the policy or law as if he possessed some God-given right to deny the rights of others and the interests of those individuals whom the law was intended to protect. The evidence in this study shows that for the ordinary people the power of the law seemed ineffective.

The Authority of the Law

The authority of law is important to the rule of law, but the source of this authority is perhaps more important as a power of ordaining the law. But where does this authority come from? I will argue that the source of this ordaining power should come from a single source as authority of law: humanity. According to Kant, each one of us has an absolute worth and a *practical imperative* of acting 'to treat humanity, whether in your own person or in that of any other, in every case as an end withal, never as a means only'. To Kant, there is only one natural right – the independence of a person from the arbitrary will and coercion of another. This right belongs to each man by reason of his humanity (Curzon 1979: 75–6).

The authority of law can come either from a partial interest, such as the power of a few individuals, or from a common good that one may call humanity. The source of the ordaining power should not be by virtue of one's own authority, but from the will of the collective or common good. The Cultural Revolution showed that, under power totality, law had no authority to protect people or the common good. In fact, law was virtually abandoned as a state institution, as state power fell further into the hands of a few political opportunists and careerists who took the law into their own hands.

The lack of authoritative law means that the law is unable to limit the power of the state. Locke argued that it is important to limit the power of the state. For example, the state power, although supreme, should be limited in its powers in these ways:

1. It cannot rule in an arbitrary way – 'It is a power that hath no other end but preservation, and therefore can never have a right to destroy, enslave or designedly to impoverish the subjects.'
2. It cannot transfer the power of making laws to any other persons.
3. It cannot deprive a man of his property without his consent.
4. It is bound 'to dispense justice and decide the rights of the subject by promulgating standing laws' (Curzon 1979: 68).

Needless to say, to limit the power of the state, we need the authority of law. The Chinese experience during the Cultural Revolution, on the other hand, proved that, without the authority of law and without humanity as the source of the law, we couldn't expect to limit the arbitrary power of the state.

This lack of authoritative law has its roots deep in the Chinese history of a total power structure. From Pan's study of the history of China's constitutions, it is apparent that power totality has been the force that has undermined the authority of constitutional law.

Lack of Authoritative Law in the History of China's Constitutions

Although Dr Sun Yat-sen, the first president of the Republic of China, believed in the people's sovereignty and in the obligations of the administrative powers of the government, his vision of state power regulated by a proposed Bill of Rights was never realized due to a lack of authoritative law – in spite of the fact that there had been several Chinese constitutions in the past. Dr Sun's vision of people's rights to monitor state power by means of the law remains a vision still. Pan's study of China's historical constitutions shows that previous constitutions had provisions for the legal scope of responsibilities of state agencies such as procurators and the courts (Pan 1945). In reality, however, these constitutions meant little to ordinary people as the authority of interpreting and executing these laws lay in the hands of a few powerful individuals or military rulers. Chinese critics of the Republic bore witness to this phenomenon, recording how, despite the existence of certain laws, people's constitutional rights were in reality being stripped away. For example, according to Hu:

> In the Criminal Code of the Republic of China, of course, there is a clause making it a crime to interfere with the freedom of others, but all the illegal actions of which we complain, are committed in the name of the Government or the Party. So the people have no guarantee at all.
>
> Under present conditions, if a man is accused by a Party or Governmental organ of being a reactionary, counter-revolutionary or Communist, personal rights are denied to him, his body is assaulted, and he is deprived of his freedom, while his property may be sequestrated. Are these not illegal actions? Books and publications, which are suspected of being reactionary, are subject to prohibition. Is this not a menace to freedom? … [S]chools run by Chinese citizens which are accused of being academically cliques or reactionary, are liable to be closed up and sealed. Do these actions not also menace freedom? In all these matters, what kind of guarantee do we have? (Hu Shih and Lin Yu-tang 1945: 24).

I have another example. The principal of Anhui University had delivered some speeches, which aroused the anger of Mr. Chiang Kai-Shih (the top ruler), so he was put in prison for some time. He was finally released, but it was impossible, of course, to bring in a suit for illegal detention against Mr Chiang Kai-Shih in any court of law. This is government by caprice, not government by law (Hu Shih 1945 and Lin Yu-tang: 25). Another example of illegal detention (and indeed torture) was that of Mr. Yang in April 1929, reported in the Chinese newspaper *Ta Kung Pao*. In Yang's words, 'I have not an inch of skin left that is without a wound.'. All this happened exactly one week after the mandate guaranteeing the rights of man was issued by the government (Shih 1945 and Lin Yu-tang: 26).

When Dr Sun Yat-sen advocated the San Min Chu I (the Three Principles of the People – People's Sovereignty, People's Livelihood and People's Rights) he made democracy the final aim. If a people cannot look after their own interests, manage their own public affairs, and take an active part in the government, they cannot build up a strong nation. The most powerful and at the same time most stable nations in the world are founded on the will of the people, and the interests and policies of the government are identical with those of the people (Pan 1945: 142). The object of the Principle of the People's Sovereignty is to create a nation in which the government is 'of the people, by the people, and for the people'. However, this principle will not be protected if the law lacks the authority to check state power.

Dr Sun Yat-sen had always wanted a period of rule under the Bill of Rights as a transitional stage in which 'the rights and obligations of the people as well as the administrative powers of the Revolutionary Government' would be defined (S. Hu and Lin 1969: 31). With time, economic prosperity was to lead the way to people's rights. To pave the way for this transition from power totality to the rule of law that can check state power requires an authoritative law that is both independent and capable of sanctioning power abuse in its own right.

So, if law lacks the authority to check state power, who then does have this authority? Hu believed that in his time it was the ruling party who had this authority (S. Hu and Lin 1969: 31). A comparison may be drawn between power-holders in both the past and present in relation to the inability of the law to provide a power check mechanism in its own right.

The Party's Role in Law – Lack of Judicial Independence

It can be argued that the ruling party of China dominates the legal institutions and that this makes it impossible to check the Party as an independent legal authority. This is because almost all the judges are Party members, and only the Party and the Party-controlled government can issue lawyers' licences in China. This factor has given people the impression that state officials and the court staff can and will work together to protect each other (SBS 2008, *China's Court*). The general perception is that the people have little faith in the legal system because they know that state power is in the hands of the Party.

Evidence for a ruling party whose rule transcends the rule of law may be found as early as 1929, when Kuomintang (the Nationalist Party of China) delegate Mr Chen Te-cheng proposed to censure the judicial courts 'for being over-conscientious about obtaining clear proof when persons are charged' (S. Hu and Lin 1969: 24). Under Chen's proposal, any one found guilty of being a counterrevolutionary by the Party should be sentenced by the judicial court, or a similar legal organization, in conformity with the charge preferred against him by the Party headquarters. If the accused were not satisfied with the judgment he could appeal against it before a higher court, but the higher court in question must reject the appeal on receiving written evidence from the headquarters of the Central Party. Hu commented: 'That means that the court need not hold a trial in such a case and can find a person guilty merely on the strength of a scrap of paper produced by the Party. Is this not a fundamental denial of government by law?' (Hu's articles on Chen's proposal were subsequently suppressed.) Hu then asked the question: 'Now, why is a citizen not qualified or permitted to be responsible for the publication of a discussion of problems bearing on his own country? Is such an action not an arbitrary interference?' (Hu Shih et al. 1945: 24–5).

Similar evidence may also be found in the current state structure where the ruling party is in charge of the judicial decision-making process at the expense of the independence of the law, which contributes to the problem of power being unchecked or unsanctioned by law.

The Communist Party of China's involvement in legal cases can be decisive and positive, but can also work against the independence of the law. The Party has control of both the government and the judicial process, and thereby functions as the 'judge of the judges' in many conflicts between the courts and the procuratorates or the local governments. Peerenboom's study shows that the Central Organization Department has records of the appointment of all judges and that the People's Congress appoints judges after the Party's approval (2002: 305–6). The Party's involvement in the courts is especially significant in 'politically sensitive cases' that might have a big impact on economics. Government officials have two hats: government and the Party, and it is impossible to tell which is which. Judges are influenced both by the Party and government, while personal influence is also exerted by individual Party members (Peerenboom 2002: 308). Clearly, this kind of total control by a single party over both the government and the judiciary is both undesirable and dangerous. The dependent nature of the law in present-day China is discussed in more detail in Chapter 4.

Some critics see such a legal system as equating to no law at all. Lubman, for example, claimed that China does not even have a legal system. He sees that China suffers under a considerable fragmentation of authority because it lacks a unifying concept of law. More seriously, the fact that the law is made to serve the Party/state contradicts the very principle of law itself and undermines any claim that China must be governed by law and aim to attain the rule of law. For this reason, China's institutions and judiciary remain weak. In Lubman's words: 'Structural weakness, ideology, rigidity, entrenched interests, localism, and corruption limit the functions and autonomy of the courts and undermine their legitimacy … [T]he difficulties of the courts in applying Chinese law and enforcing their judgments raise an issue of the very capacity of the Chinese state' (Lubman 1999, 2002: 565). Others view the law as a challenge to political legitimacy with a choice of ruling either by power or by reference to the legal system. Potter, for example, in his study of law in relation to the Party's role in China, stated: 'By relying on the socialist legal system as a source of legitimacy, the regime also strengthens its ability to justify specific actions by reference to law' (Potter 1991, 1994: 325).

The regime has attempted to ensure that the legal system remains subservient to the political needs of the Party by aggressively disseminating its version of socialist legality and repudiating alternative versions. It has tried to make certain that popular notions about the law do not overreach its own view that the law should be merely an instrument of rule rather than a set of generally applicable principles that regulate the state as well as the people it governs (Potter 1991, 1994: 325–26).

The Legal Privilege of Officialdom

Officialdom is both the basis and a product of this power structure. There is a 'power culture', as I have argued in this study, that has been inherited from a feudal social structure and serfdom. The power culture operates in the interests of certain state officials, who, as in a feudal society, exploit their status and manipulate the law to their own advantage, as will be seen in the case of Xie in Chapter 4 of this study. Xie's final call is not for justice alone, but for the restoration of his family's reputation, a concern typical of Chinese culture. In studies of oriental despotism, many have observed how, so often, the 'tyranny' of the top bureaucrats is even stronger than that of the sovereign power itself, and how the 'reins of government' are often in the hands of viziers leaving the emperor 'profoundly ignorant of the domestic and political condition of his empire' (Bernier 1853 cited in Draper 1978: 643). Quesnay has argued that, often in the history of oriental despotism, the absolute power of the emperor is tempered by the de facto power of officialdom (Quesnay 1767 cited in Draper 1978: 643).

A feature of this type of despotism is the dependence of subjects on the state, given that all are equal under the power of the state. It aims to destroy all forces of countervailing influence other than the central state power, and to reduce all elements of the population to fragments of individuals dependent on the benefit of the bureaucratic state. The function of the state is, moreover, not only that of ruling the nation, but also that of remodelling the minds of the people and reshaping the mentality of the population using a predetermined model. As de Tocqueville wrote, 'In short, they set no limit to its rights and powers; its duty was not merely to reform but to transform the French nation – a task of which the central power alone was capable.' The state makes men exactly what it wishes them to be (Draper 1978: 645).

Hegel, too, noted this equality under despotism. In his lectures on *The Philosophy of the Spirit*, Hegel supported the right on which state power is based and the subordination of the authorities to law. In his words, 'it is necessarily true in China that the difference between slavery and freedom is not great, since all are equal before the emperor, that is, all are equally degraded.' Hegel distinguished despotism from sovereign power in that the latter wields force but itself is not merely a matter of force; whereas the former denotes in general the condition of lawlessness where the particular will of some counts as law, not counts instead of law (Draper 1978: 647–8). In this 'patriarchal despotism', Hegel writes, in his *History of Philosophy*, where the emperor runs everything in a 'fatherly' way, even the upper-class subjects are legally minors: 'No independent categories or classes have interests to protect for themselves, as in India, for everything is managed and superintended from above.' Thus 'in China the people are dependent on the laws and moral will of the emperor without distinction of classes', and 'this very equality is not a triumphant testimonial to a person's inner worth but to a low level of self-esteem that has not yet attained to recognizing distinctions' (Hegel cited in Draper 1978: 649). For Hegel, equality minus freedom equals despotism. Law, he argues, is in the hands of officialdom: 'the government proceeds exclusively from the emperor, who carries it on as a hierarchy of officials or mandarins' , together with its varieties, gradations, classifications and checks. After pages of detailed description of the bureaucracy, he concludes that 'the whole of this administration is thus covered with a network of officials lacking all autonomy with respect to the One Power above' (Draper 1978: 651).

The result of this legal culture of officialdom is official corruption. A famous Chinese writer, Hu Shi, once noted:

> In corruption, China certainly leads the world. Not only is there an open and organized sale of offices in the State, not only has there been for twenty-five years no system of examination for government posts, but there is also the universal habit of bribery in every branch of Chinese society … [w]hich in polite language is called 'dipping one's fingers', and in the common language 'rubbing oil'. Military officials take a percentage of their soldiers' rations; local officials scrape the skin off their community; whilst, in business, compradors add to their commissions.
>
> I remember that in the semi-official Shanghai weekly, the *China Critic*, there was once a leader whose thesis was that China had always respected honest officials, as evidenced by the habit of presenting a *pien*, or erecting a monument, in honour of an official who had rendered meritorious services. In civilized countries, however, an official is expected to be honest, so there is no need for special recognition. Corrupt officials should be sent to jail (S. Hu and Lin 1969: 15).

Law is invariably a balancing act between normative rules and the corrupt nature of power. This phenomenon has often been noted in Chinese culture as well. For example, there is a Chinese saying (its ultimate source is unknown) that describes the illegal gains of corrupt officials and judges as liquid water and the law as an iron gate barring the way to undesirables: 'The gate of the court is made of iron, but the magister is fluid as water' (SBS 2007a).

On the other hand, as Weber argued, the imperial administration and judiciary were irrational from a capitalist point of view, as modern development and industrial investment could not allow such operative uncertainty. China lacked the political prerequisites for the early emergence of capitalism that were so evident in the West. Weber's view was that internal conflicts were evident throughout Chinese history in comparison to conflicts between states in the West. He explained that the 'whole of Chinese history is replete with great and small feuds … there has been no rational warfare and … no armed peace during which several competing autonomous states constantly prepare for war. Capitalist phenomena thus conditioned through war loans and commissions for war purposes did not appear.' 'As in the Roman Empire, political competition for capital disappeared following the unification of the Chinese Empire' (Weber 1968: 103). Thus Weber concluded that:

> rational entrepreneurial capitalism, which in the Occident found its specific locus in industry, has been handicapped not only by the lack of a formally guaranteed law, a rational administration and judiciary, and by the ramifications of a system of pretends, but also, basically, by the lack of a particular mentality. Above all it has been handicapped by the attitude rooted in the Chinese 'ethos' and peculiar to a stratum of officials and aspirants to office. (Weber 1968: 104)

Importance of Culture in the Study of Law

Many argue that law is part of culture and should be examined in a local cultural context. The importance of a culture in the study of law is expressed in the way law reflects the society we live in, without which any philosophy of law would be irrelevant to the needs of the people. Gramsci, for example, believed that Marxism should be applied in local and historical contexts. He was concerned that revolution lent new life to older forms of control by redeeming old interests – it had to dance between fascism and Stalinism – and that 'state' as a form of organized political community was abandoned or controlled by a few individuals. The 'state' is not a single entity but many forms of organization. Narin observes that 'Any political theory is written in a specific historical context'; and with writers like Machiavelli, Lenin and Gramsci who focus on a national reality in order to change it, this context becomes particularly important. Gramsci, referring to the experiences of the Bolsheviks and the Russian Revolution, maintained that 'any political theory developed in one set of circumstances had to be "translated" for a new situation'. It could never simply be applied (Gramsci cited in Sassoon 1982: 168–70).

Gramsci also rejects the idea that revolution has to contradict almost every rational expectation and liberty, and has to succeed by sweeping everything before it. He studied various types of consolidation of ruling class hegemony after 1917 as well as the role of state and the expansion of social strata in the context of the general extension of state activities. He questioned the relationship between state and civil society, and between democracy and the building of socialism. This is a question that is being posed widely today, both by critics of socialism who reject it altogether and by socialist critics of traditional 'left' organizations. The idea of democracy is opposed to the concept of power monopoly, which means any ruling class that moulds a society. And this ruling class has to represent more than its own power interests: 'This is true of both the bourgeoisie and the proletariat' (Gramsci cited in Sassoon 1982: 10). Gramsci once used Edmond Burke's expression of 'passive revolution' to argue that society had to change in order to stay the same – that is, to preserve its most essential features. In this sense, historical changes were often initiated from 'high above'. He used the notion to describe a style of politics that preserves control by a relatively small group of leaders while at the same time instituting economic, social, political and ideological changes. For Gramsci, revolution must be understood as a process of social transformation. It is not a dramatic break after which the new society begins to develop from scratch, but is a process that begins within the old society and continues after moments of dramatic change. An old society will be destroyed in all its aspects only insofar as a new one is built and consolidated. In other words, a revolutionary movement, such as the establishment of his Italian nation-state, will be able to destroy the old only by building qualitatively new social values; and this notion of construction/destruction must be made by the mass of the population, not by a small elite.

Law in the Historical Context

Any political theory is written in a specific historical context, and Marxism is no exception. Marx's view is, as discussed earlier, a result of a rich German tradition of philosophy; a product of the nineteenth-century industrial revolution and the free trade economy; a well-established parliamentarian system and a history of liberal thought. The battle against feudalism in industrialized economies had been won and rule by feudal lords brought to an end. Thus, many features of modern democracy were achieved or granted by the laws in those countries – such as free speech and a free press, elections, petitions and public debates. These are the fruits of previous social and political struggles and are the more progressive reforms in historical development.

It is therefore expected that the later state in history, in Marxist terms – namely the socialist state – should inherit these social benefits and greater liberties. To reject this heritage and to dismiss the enlarged freedoms of the people as 'bourgeois law' is a dogmatic reading of Marxism and a denial of the basic democratic values and freedom of the Marxist vision. Moreover, to claim, as Stalin's theorists did, that without these 'bourgeois' values the state better represents the proletariats (who were the 'most advanced class in the world') is 'socialism' without substance and a mere self-deception. Thus democratic values are still being denied, and in China the battle against a feudalist mentality is still to be won. There is by no means a natural progression as suggested by some socialist theories. Indeed, the possibility of a regression is never really far away, as evidenced by the Cultural Revolution.

Historic Evolution of (Western) Legal Thought

As Gramsci suggested, any social transformation from a previous society, such as a feudal power structure, to the rule of law, is a fundamental but gradual process that will evolve over a long period of time. The legal tradition of the West was strongly influenced by Roman law, which began to develop in Europe in the tenth century. What I am concerned with here is not those legal rules developed in Roman times, but with the original concept of law and state as institutions. Although highly complex and abstract, the philosophy of law has evolved as principles guiding societies in a wide range of social and state relationships over a long period of time. The source of authority has thus shifted from the personal will of the monarch to an independent philosophy of law. Contrary to a power totality system, this autonomy in the structure and development of the law produced, as early as ancient Roman times, an independent role in the development of society as a whole (Huntington 1996: 33).

The fact that the history of Roman law did not cease with the fall of Rome but continued to be developed by jurists and scholars working in European universities from the eleventh century onwards demonstrates that the substance of Roman law has continued to be a part of the Western legal tradition. It might therefore be expected that in China, too, as an ancient nation, the rule of law would be able to continue to develop even after the fall of the various rulers. This is due to the fact that legal philosophy rests its sovereign power in the common will of the people, and that a monarch or a king is bound by the Constitution and law, and not by his personal rule, or party rule for that matter. It is also due to the highly respected status of law as a binding force to keep state power in check, without which the law would be ineffective.

A good example of this is in the text of the Magna Carta of 1215. This document was the product of a great deal of bargaining and was the work of many jurists as advocates of this legal philosophy. Scope for abuse in the feudal system at the time was great and had been the subject of complaint long before King John came to the throne. Moreover, abuses were aggravated by the difficulty of obtaining redress for them. In the Magna Carta the provision of the means for obtaining a fair hearing of complaints, not only against the King and his agents, but also against lesser feudal lords, achieved corresponding importance. About two-thirds of the clauses of the Magna Carta were concerned with matters such as these and with the misuse of their powers by royal officials. The significance of the Magna Carta lies in the fact that the people's complaints were addressed and the King was forced to make concessions – and that both of these two goals were achieved by means of law.

The significant role that law played in the Magna Carta as a legal forum can never be overemphasized. Although most of its clauses deal with specific grievances rather than with general principles of law, the Magna Carta signified the subjection of the King to law. What is lacking in China's case, on the other hand, is the strong bargaining power of England's barons, and the authority of law that can withstand the King's power against the modern 'feudal lords' and 'royal' state officials.

The similarities between the complaints made at the time of the Magna Carta and in China today are apparent. China, too, needs just such a legal forum to redress the complaints against corrupt officials. Another example of this redress can be found in the Habeas Corpus Act. Responding to the abusive detention of persons without legal authority, public pressure on the English Parliament caused the government of the time to adopt the Habeas Corpus Act in 1679. The significance of the Habeas Corpus Act has been to reconfirm the authority of law in the governance of the country. Although the key issue of the Act was specific (it was about detention), the general concept of a critical right was established as a legal consequence of this Act, one that was later written into the Constitution for the United States (online source: Habeas Corpus Act 1679).

The evolution of any legal philosophy lies in the fact that any change in the concept of power, and the idea of humanity, will also need a long period of time, as noted by Walter Bagehot:

> It took a long, long time after the art of printing had been perfected before we learned the priceless value, the sovereign dignity and usefulness of a free press.
>
> But these lessons have been taught and learned; taught for the most part by the prophets of our race, men living in advance of their age, and understood only by the succeeding generations. But you have the inheritance.
>
> Custom is the first check on tyranny; that fixed routine of social life at which modern innovations have, and by which modern improvement is impeded, is the primitive check on base power. The perception of political expediency has then hardly begun; the sense of abstract justice is weak and vague; and a rigid adherence to the fixed mould of transmitted usage is essential to an unmarred, unspoiled, unbroken life (Walter Bagehot cited in Landry 2004: 229–30).

The preservation of existing laws as represented by tradition and cultural rules – to early man, at least – was of greater concern than putting up with bad laws. Change was what men feared – change and its social upheaval was what brought on suffering and death. I quote again from Bagehot's work:

> In early societies it matters much more that the law should be fixed than that it should be good. Any law which the people of ignorant times enact is sure to involve many misconceptions, and to cause many evils. Perfection in legislation

> is not to be looked for, and is not, indeed, much wanted in a rude, painful, confined life. But such an age covets fixity. That men should enjoy the fruits of their labour, that the law of property should be known, that the law of marriage should be known, that the whole course of life should be kept in a calculable track, is the *summum bonum* of early ages, the first desire of semi-civilized mankind. In that age men do not want to have their laws adapted, but to have their laws steady. The passions are so powerful, force so eager, the social bond so weak, that the august spectacle of an all but unalterable law is necessary to preserve society. In the early stages of human society all change is thought an evil. And most change is an evil. The conditions of life are so simple and so unvarying that any decent sort of rules suffice, so long as men know what they are. Custom is the first check on tyranny; that fixed routine of social life at which modern innovations have, and by which modern improvement is impeded, is the primitive check on base power. The perception of political expediency has then hardly begun; the sense of abstract justice is weak and vague; and a rigid adherence to the fixed mould of transmitted usage is essential to an unmarred, unspoiled, unbroken life (Walter Bagehot cited in Landry 2004: 229–30).

Economic Factors – Geographic Size and Poverty

There are many economic factors that we need to consider when we discuss state power in China. These factors show a great degree of complexity in the state administration, and affirm a necessity of strong leadership for the unity and stability of the nation. These factors show a need for economic prosperity as the country's main priority and this has often obscured the issue of power abuse and been used to justify the power totality of the leadership.

China is still an agrarian society with many living below the poverty line. According to a CCTV report in May 2007, there are hundred of millions of Chinese still living below the poverty line (SBS 2007b, 2007c). The economic needs of these people as a priority are undeniable and have been the primary concern for the Chinese government. Without any doubt, this economic factor is of great importance when we consider any issues concerning China. The country has a huge population (1.3 billion); a geographic scale and physical size (9.6 million square metres) that is vast and extremely diverse, and a distinct culture that has persisted over thousands of years. This presents a real probability of there being local unrest, simply owing to the sheer size of the population and the geographic distances. In addition, there is a large population of mobile farm workers flowing in and out of the major cities daily. It is estimated that, to date, 150 million rural workers have migrated to the cities (SBS 2008). In addition, the literacy rate has been low and uneven across the country.

For the majority of those who are struggling on the poverty line, it is understandable that the idea of personal liberty and freedom is not a high priority. This is perhaps one of the reasons why the Tiananmen Square incident did not arouse a wider response outside the intellectual circles in the cities, or induce the nation to another civil war of 'revolution' for democracy.

China has undergone several stages of economic development. Prior and during the Cultural Revolution, between 80 and 90 per cent of the population in China lived in the countryside and life for them was a constant struggle against poverty and poor living conditions, as witnessed by the author of this study in a remote village in Shanxi Province. The political cliché of that time, that we lived in a near paradise, when compared with our dark past of suffering, hid a much harsher reality, based on a metaphoric misperception that, if the reality was to be perceived differently, then the reality would be different or much better than what it really was. Li's descriptions of life in his village made this reality evident (C. Li 2003: 225).

To provide a decent living for 1.3 billion people is in itself a remarkable achievement. It has fulfilled or is in the process of fulfilling the goal of providing for the basic needs of the majority of the population. Political freedom, the Chinese government argues, is not what the Chinese people need. This view, however, does not explain why people in China deserve fewer constitutional rights and less freedom; and why a socialist government must oppose these rights – in particular, the right to supervise and determine how state power should be exercised. Indeed, while economic factors, geographic size and population argue strongly for a centralized government, state power still needs to be limited by a collective check system. These are two separate issues that should not be considered as identical. A central power does not have to be arbitrary and dictatorial. The economic factors cannot justify a repressive state that can only rule by silencing the views of the people and which offers people no legal protection to redress their concerns or grievances against corrupt officials.

Cultural Factors: A Belief in the Harmony of State and Man

Undoubtedly, culture has played a decisive role in the development of Chinese law, via a concept of authority vested in the ruler, not in the law – as we have seen, in traditional Chinese culture the ruler was above all laws. There are many cultural differences between Eastern and Western social philosophy. For example, a concept of unity in the Chinese culture is more salient than its counterpart in the West. It emphasizes an ideal stage of harmony between the ruler and the ruled within the framework of natural law and justice of Chinese philosophy.

Chinese scholars noted that, traditionally, classical teaching has not focused on power vested in individuals. Instead, it has emphasized harmony in popular sovereignty and a faith in universal justice. In Pan's words,

> Popular sovereignty has always been the traditional belief and teaching of the Chinese people. The works of Confucius, Mencius, Lao Tzu-Mo tzu and numerous other political writers and philosophers and the Chinese Classics

> often reflected the thoughts of the Chinese people ... Mencius says: 'The people are the most important element in the nation'. (Pan 1945: 134)

This saying has in time become a popular Chinese proverb. Another old Chinese saying that 'The King is the boat, the common people the water: the water can support the boat or capsize it' depicts this relationship between the ruler and the ruled – tyrannical emperor and the people. The idea was also expressed by the Chinese philosopher Mencius: 'He who outrages the benevolence proper to his nature is called a robber; he who outrages righteousness is called a ruffian. The robber and ruffian we call a mere fellow. I have heard of the cutting off of the fellow Chau the name of a tyrannical emperor, but I have not heard of the putting a sovereign to death, in his case' (James Legge tr. Pan 1945: 135).

Pan too noted a family-like style between the ruler and the ruled:

> Traditionally, the emperor and his people were considered as composing one large family and the happiness and prosperity of the people were the criteria by which the emperor was to be judged. Should the emperor not administer for the common good of the people, he would be considered to have lost the mandate of heaven and cease to be emperor. As a result of this abuse of power, the emperor would be subject to removal or else the people would have the right to revolt against him. Thus, keeping up with this belief throughout all the Constitutions thus far proclaimed, the people are placed in the foremost chapters and their sovereignty recognized. (Pan 1945: 135)

Thus, traditionally the Chinese people have not believed in class distinction or in the inheritance of class superiority, a belief succinctly expressed by Confucius as 'Yu Chiao wu lei', meaning 'with education there is no class'. Thus, throughout the centuries there has grown up a deep-rooted tradition that officials are not born of any special class. This, as time went by, developed into the competitive examination system for the civil service, which was open to both rich and poor.(Pan 1945: 136). As Yen remarked:

> China has no constitution, if by a constitution one means a written instrument ordained and established by the people as that of the United States of America, or one granted nominally by a king as that of Prussia; but if by a constitution one means a body of customs, traditions, precedents, as that of England, China has one. As the Christians cherish the Scriptures; the English, Magna Carta; and the Americans, the Constitution; so the Chinese cherish the Confucian Classics (Pan 1945: 136).

This belief in harmony between the ruler and ruled coincides with the principle of natural law, which is based on human reasoning and ultimate justice. This view suggests a non-individualistic approach to the common needs of people, and a non-hostile stance towards the state. This position, however, should not be interpreted as being consensual to any tyrannical or arbitrary ruling including power in totality. On the contrary, harmony has a universal characteristic vested in humanity. In this worldview, regardless of differences in political or ideological systems, total power is not endorsed.

But how do we restrict this power? Traditional Chinese belief did not give guidance on this matter, and there was nothing on the subject in law either. Even legal reforms such as those introduced during the rule of the first emperor of China (221 BC) could not occur without the approval of the emperor. This shows a lack of legal means in restricting the ruling power in Chinese history, owing to the social and political structure of the times, and this in itself therefore poses a great barrier to legal reform today in the process of power check.

These differences between Chinese and Western cultures also indicate that the change will not only be gradual but will also require a social and cultural change beyond the legal norms. Transition to democracy will involve a process of change from arbitrary power to shared power. As the populace becomes part of the power-sharing arrangements, government will be open to greater public scrutiny and participation. The problem identified in this chapter shows that, at present, the people are not part of this process, as they are not able to exercise this duty by law.

This chapter also shows, on the same grounds, that the wholesale importation of the Western notion of liberty to an ancient state like China is inappropriate. This is because the idea of liberty, as so eloquently elaborated by Hayek, is based on the freedom of individuals – the idea that separates the citizens as individuals from the state as an alienated entity. This cultural differences between the two traditions would make a direct importation of the idea of individualistic liberty unworkable, unless the state leaders and the people are committed to it as an essential value in their lives. Some surveys show that individual liberty is not a priority for many Chinese people who are still struggling for a better livelihood and education (Peerenboom 2004: 137 and notes). Montesquieu also pointed out that democracy can be corrupted by the spirit of inequality, which arises when citizens no longer identify their interests with the interests of their country, and therefore seek both to advance their own private interests at the expense of their fellow citizens, and to acquire political power over them (Montesquieu 1731, 1949: Ch. 8). Historically speaking, therefore, there will have to be a gradual and slow evolution of thinking and values in China.

On the other hand, the traditional Chinese concept of harmony between the ruler and the ruled does not entail the acceptance of tyrannical rulers, nor does it endorse despotism that is structured by power totality. However, what is absent in this Chinese cultural concept is an independent legal philosophy that provides not only for the principle of a legal check on state power, but also a legal forum and structure that is independent and that will enable people to challenge and monitor that state power. A socialist or Marxist revolution, then is not simply a matter of overthrowing one form of government and replacing it with another; it is a question of all the powers of the state, irrespective of their ideological claims, being mutually regulated by the rule of law under public scrutiny by means of constitutional supervision and independent legal authorities.

Conclusion

In this chapter we have identified a form of power totality as the problem to be dealt with in this study. This power was established by virtue of its own authority without being subjected to the will of the people or to the law. It has an unquestionable supremacy and is without limit. This, as we have seen, has undermined the authority of law. It is a problem because it contradicts the Marxist vision it claimed to follow by denying people's basic rights. It is a problem because it rules by its own power without the authority of people. This form of power is a regression to the feudal past, placing totalized power in the hands of a few, and without constraint. It is a problem because it has failed to give the people the protection they need and has made law irrelevant in granting such protection. The result of this power totality is a continuation of the feudal style of officialdom in which legal privilege is enjoyed only by the club of power-holders. As a result of this, the people have suffered and have been unprotected. Neither can they hold offenders accountable owing to the lack of a legal forum. Despite the laws made through the history of China, power totality has the final ruling. Taking other non-legal factors into consideration, any challenge to this power totality will have to be a gradual process and its impact will go far beyond the law. The study of the cultural aspect of law is also important because the traditional lack of legal authority continues to be a barrier to power check today.

In this chapter I have identified the problem of power totality as the central issue of this study. I have examined the form, the reasons and the consequences of such a problem. Law is seen as a part of the problem, and as one of many factors contributing to the complexity of the problem. But these factors are not the main reason why power totality has developed and been justified. In the following chapter, I will argue from a theoretical viewpoint that Marxist theories have been grossly abused to justify this power totality.

Chapter 3
How Power was Justified

Introduction

This chapter examines Marxist theories in more detail. Marxism is still the official doctrine in many countries, including China, but was cruelly abused during the Cultural Revolution. This theoretical examination starts with some basic concepts of Marxism such as class struggle and dictatorship theory and how these concepts were developed and abused – as, for example, in the socialist legality theory developed in Russia. I will also look at some more recent theories along this line in China, such as the four cardinal principles and the notion of stability (at the expense of basic human rights), and how these have justified unlimited power being placed in the hands of a privileged group in society.

Marxist Theory

To understand what has become abuse[1] in the context of power monopoly, it is necessary to introduce some basic concepts of Marxism, namely Marx's view of history and of the economy as the basic structure. His theory of the dictatorship of the proletariat resulted in class struggle and his denial of the capitalist legal system affirmed the law as a power check against a totality of power structure after the revolution.

Marxist View of History

The greatest influence on Marx was Hegel's philosophy of history and its notion of historical change. The idea of historical change is based on the dialectical: that is, of conflicts and struggle of opposites within one entity. Despite these forces of change, Hegel, paradoxically, insisted that there is an unchanging supreme law, or the 'Idea of the Absolute' which, independently of human will governs nature, society and human beings. Hegel sees that the mental things (ideas and concepts) are fundamental to the world, not matter, and that material things are

1 In this study, abuse is not about the theory per se, but the way it is used for a purpose other than that originally claimed. The way abuse treats the theory is often dogmatic and even threatening. The essence of the abuse is to turn an idea into a doctrine that can control, threaten or incriminate the believer. It becomes an ideological tool –a justification for repression and the undermining of core human values.

merely expressions of ideas, in particular, of an underlying 'Universal Spirit' or 'Absolute Idea'.

Marx, to the contrary, argues that matter is fundamental and that ideas are but expressions of material necessity. In his words, 'revolution needs a material foundation. The degree to which a theory is realized in a nation, depends on the extent this theory is capable of meeting the nation's needs' (Marx 1844: 9). With this materialist conception of history, Marx sees the world as something separate from human activity, and therefore 'objective' – meaning that which is independent of human will and consciousness. This formed what Engels called the 'scientific' basis of Marxist theory (Engels 1892: 425).

From this point of view, history is seen as a continuous process in stages. It develops with various transitions, for example, from feudalism through a number of intermediate stages to capitalism. In this view, history is perceived not as an isolated event, but a process gradually moving towards a higher stage of human civilization. The final stage is one in which man's ultimate freedom is fully realized in a communist society. According to Marx, communism is a stage in which people will live at a higher stage of realization of true freedom with other men and with society as a whole. The transitional periods between the feudalist stage and the socialist stage (perceived as an initial step towards communism) were not elaborated in Marx's writing, as he expected the historical process would evolve naturally in the most industrially developed nations. However, as we will discover, the missing link between an undeveloped economy and capitalist economy is very important in terms of how law is perceived and applied in the name of Marxism.

According to the theory of historical materialism, the reason for the evolution of societies is the conflict between the forces of production and the relations of production, which brings about revolutionary ideas. Marx explained this conflict in the preface to his essay 'A contribution to the critique of political economy' (Marx in Tucker 1978: 4). There, he sees material circumstances as being vital to sustain even the most elementary forms of social life. People satisfy their needs for the development of the human species through the use of the available technologies and natural resources.

Base and Superstructure

The conceptual division of 'base and superstructure' has relevance for the law as we see it today. The base structure is the economic foundation of a given society – its mode of production and economic relationship of production. The economic relations are determined by the mode of production in which the factors of production such as land, labour and capital are organized. Rooted in this economic foundation is the 'superstructure', which includes ideas, ideologies, theories, philosophies, religion, ethics, art and so on. Part of this superstructure are the legal rules and institutions referred to as 'the law'. The bases of a system of law, its purposes and manifestations, must be understood in terms of their relationships with this mode of production and its economic relationships. This means that legal ideas and structure can have no meaning or significance outside a materialistic framework of analysis. Legal thought has to be interpreted in relation to the social fabric within which it was conceived and nurtured. There is no separate theory or discussion in Marx about the growth of theories of natural law or common law, but there is detailed discussion about the concept of right in the context of German philosophy and Hegel's philosophy of law. For Marx, it is the relationships embedded in the society's economy that determine the nature of legal ideology.

Class struggle and Proletarian Dictatorship

In *Das Kapital* Marx argued that the struggle between the proletarian class and the bourgeois class was inevitable. The struggle was clear cut, 'for one class to represent the whole of society, another class must concentrate in itself all the evils of society … for one class to be the liberating class par excellence, it is necessary that another class should be openly the oppressing class' (Marx 1844 in Marx and Engels 1966: 63). The result of this opposition has proved catastrophic. In his words, 'the antagonism between the proletariat and the bourgeoisie is a struggle of class against class, a struggle which carried to its highest expression is a total revolution' (Tucker 1978: 219). This leads to the concept of ownership by working people: 'Communism deprives no man of the power to appropriate the products of society; all that it does is to deprive him of the power to subjugate the labour of others by means of such appropriation' (Tucker 1978: 486). Tucker continues:

> The society will become a new form of association, in which the free development of each individual is the condition for the free development of all, by means of new mode of production. The ownership of property will always be Marx's leading concern, which is expressed in the last paragraphs of the Manifesto: 'In all these movements they bring to the front, as the leading question in each, the property question, no matter what its degree of development at the time'. (Tucker 1978: 500)

Marx sees that the leading class, in the process of *universal human emancipation*, should identify itself with the rest of society as the *general representative* of this society: 'Its aims and interests must genuinely be the aims and interests of society itself, of which it becomes in reality the social head and heart. It is only in the name of general interests that a particular class can claim general supremacy.' To be the 'head and heart' of the movement and to attain this liberating position, the leading class must be part of the society at large. It is because 'no class in civil society can play this part unless it can arouse, in itself and in the masses, a moment of enthusiasm in which it associates and mingles with society at large' (Tucker 1978: 62). That leadership, however, will cease to function once the transition to the classless society has been completed. In Marx's words:

> And now as to myself, no credit is due to me for discovering the existence of classes in modern society or the struggle between them. Long before me bourgeois historians had described the historical development of this class struggle and bourgeois economists the economic anatomy of the classes.
>
> What I did that was new was to prove: 1) that the *existence of classes* is only bound up with *particular historical phases in the development of production*, 2) that the class struggle necessarily leads to the *dictatorship of the proletariat*, 3) that this dictatorship itself only constitutes the transition to the *abolition of all classes* and to *a classless society*. (Tucker 1978: 220; italics in original)

Marx's View of Law and Revolution

Marx was very critical of bourgeois society and law as its superstructure, to the point that he argued for its total abolition by means of a radical form of revolution. This view is based on his theory of base and super structures of society. This total denial of existing legal systems has provided theoretical excuses for the later development of socialist legality of power monopoly.

According to Marx, the legal system is part of a legal and political superstructure that is part of an oppressive mechanism that protects the interests of the ruling class and oppresses the working class. Although it was the bourgeois class that he called upon to be overthrown, he included all its superstructures on the revolution list as well. This idea of overthrowing an old system because of its oppressive nature is not new or unique to Marxism, but unique problems arose when a revolutionary force took over power and itself became oppressive. Abuse occurred when working people, not necessarily the proletarian class, were oppressed by a new state in the name of a 'people's revolution' against oppression.

For Marx, from the standpoint of 'Ruthless criticism of everything existing' (letter from Marx to Arnold Ruge 1844 in Tucker 1978: 12), law, as a part of superstructure, is expected to be thrown out completely by the storm of the revolution. As stated in the *Communist Manifesto*, 'The proletariat, the lowest stratum of our present society, cannot stir, cannot raise itself up, without the whole super incumbent strata of official society being sprung into the air' (Marx 1844 in Marx and Engels 1966: 250).

The notion of 'class instrumentalism' that had significant influence on many European jurists of the twentieth century derived from this idea of superstructure and the concept of struggle. Ideas relating to the law – its content, theoretical basis and principles of legal institutions – are viewed in the context of the class interests jurists serve. Law, according to Marx, is an instrument of class domination, enabling the ruling class to control and suppress those groups that challenge its power. Behind the apparent legal system of 'justice' or 'reason' is the veiled purpose of the *protection and preservation of class interests.* For Marx, jurisprudential ideas are not to be viewed not as independent or disinterested ideas in themselves but as a rationale for certain ideologies and used as a weapon to safeguard those who hold power.

What is open to abuse, apart from class suppression, is the abandonment by the new working people's state of the old society and the concept of law. In the *Manifesto*, Marx states that some would argue that 'religion, moral, philosophical and juridical ideas have been modified in the course of historical development. But religion, morality, philosophy, political science, and law, constantly survived this change.' Their answer to this is that 'there are, besides, eternal truths, such as Freedom, Justice, etc., that are common to all states of society. But communism abolishes eternal truths, it abolishes all religion and all morality, instead of constituting them on a new basis; it therefore acts in contradiction to all past historical experience.' It is because 'the communist revolution is the most radical rupture with traditional property relations; no wonder that its development involves the most radical rupture with traditional ideas' (Tucker 1978: 489).

Law and State

Marx's theory of base and superstructure also leads to his concept of state and law. Law, in a sense, is perceived as 'super' law, which is beyond the normal scale of legal institutions. The state, its apparatus and ideology are perceived as a part of the general superstructure of society, reflecting its economic base. Marx's view of state started with an examination of the relation of state and law to property. He traced back the history of property development and saw a parallel function of state evolving with the process, from the early stage of state property, where tribes lived together in one town, and tribal property was conceived of as state property, to the modern pure private property of big business, where the state was cut out from any influence on the development of property. Modern private property has fallen entirely into the hands of big private owners. Through this movement private property has freed itself from the community, and the state has become a separate entity, beside and outside civil society (Marx in Tucker 1978: 160).

The function of the state, in Marx's view, is nothing more than the form of organization that the bourgeoisie necessarily adopts both for the mutual guarantee of its property and interests. There can be no independent state unless it is a country where the estates have not yet developed into classes, and where the estates still have a part to play – a state in which no one section of the population can achieve dominance over the others. State, in this sense, is seen as a group of individuals of a ruling class asserting their common interests, and mediating in the formation of all common institutions, so that the institutions thus receive a political form. In his words, 'the bourgeoisie has at last, since the establishment of Modern Industry and of the world-market, conquered for itself, in the modern representative State, exclusive political sway. The executive of the modern State is but a committee for managing the common affairs of the whole bourgeoisie' (Tucker 1978: 475).

Marx believes that it is an illusion that law is based on the will in its dealings, because the will is in fact divorced from its real *free* basis. Similarly, justice is in its turn reduced to the actual laws. Marx's logic is that this is because they are the laws of the private interest holders, whose interest is contradictory to the common and public interest. Marx sees that 'civil law developed simultaneously with private property out of the disintegration of the natural community' (Tucker 1978: 187). 'Modern industrial labour, modern subjection to capital … has stripped him [i.e. society in general] of every trace of national character. Law, morality, religion, are to him so many bourgeois prejudices, behind which lurk in ambush just as many bourgeois interests' (Tucker 1978: 482).

Marx sees that the old civil society as a whole should be abolished because its basic foundation was wrong, and his resolution was a radical and complete destruction of the old society. In his words, 'In the formation of a class with *radical chains*, a class of civil society which is not a class of civil society, an estate which is the dissolution of all estates, a sphere which has a universal character by its universal suffering and claims no *particular right* because no *particular wrong* but *wrong generally* is perpetrated against it' (Marx 1844 in Marx and Engels 1966: 13).

Marx's denial of existing political and legal systems was clearly demonstrated in one of his speeches:

> the immense and unresisted encroachments of that barbarous power, whose head is at St Petersburg, and whose hands are in every cabinet of Europe, have taught the working classes the duty to master themselves the mysteries of international politics; to watch the diplomatic acts of their respective Governments; to counteract them, if necessary, by all means in their power; when unable to prevent, to combine in simultaneous denunciations, and to vindicate the simple laws of morals and justice, which ought to govern the relations of private individuals, as the rules paramount in the intercourse of nations. (Marx in Tucker 1978: 519)

Again he stressed this denial of existing systems in the last paragraphs of the *Manifesto*: 'In short, the Communist everywhere supports every revolutionary movement against the existing social and political order of things' (Marx in Tucker 1978: 500).

How was this abolition of the old society to be achieved? The answer Marx gave is that 'the first step in the revolution by the working class, is to raise the proletariat to the position of ruling class, to win the battle of democracy', and then to use this political supremacy to wrest all capital from the bourgeoisie and to centralize all instruments of production in the hands of the state, that is, of the proletariat organized as the ruling class; and to increase the total of productive forces as rapidly as possible (Marx in Tucker 1978: 490).

The Abuse of Marxist Theory

There are three areas of Marxist theory that are open to abuse – namely contracted democratic values and diminished humanity; the class struggle to justify power oligarchy and class superiority; and the dictatorship theory used to justify power monopoly.

Marxist theories have been subject to various critiques as theories of totalitarianism opposed to democracy. To clarify where abuse relevant to this study has occurred, we need to identify two aspects of the theory – namely, class and dictatorship; and the totality of power structure. As will be discussed in this chapter, Marx's vision is based on, and not opposed to, democratic values. However, his class and dictatorship theory has been used by many as a means to consolidate rather than destroy class distinctions and class superiorities. The ruling class has used its power to oppress other human beings, and the old feudal view of man as a worthless and disposable being has persisted. This is a direct result of an abuse of Marx's class and dictatorship theory – without a change in its substance. Marx's call for a total change and total destruction of the existing order, by the radical means of revolution, has contributed to the sense of total denial of any progress in the previous social evolution and in the rule of law including the principle of curbing the arbitrary power vested in the state or Party officials. In this sense, law and state power cannot be simply classified as proletarian or bourgeois, for power has no class boundary and should not be sanctioned in any society without legal privilege.

Democratic Values

Marx expressed his democratic values in his writing about the future workers' state. First, this state is a civil society with a just and ethical relationship of harmony among the sectors of society. It is the 'great organism in which juridical, ethical, and political freedom has to achieve realization' (Marx in Tucker 1978: 32). He saw the state, after the revolution, as part of the law; but not above the law, and no individuals or political parties would be granted immunity from the law or given a power monopoly. Instead, Marx thought that the state would be the 'agent of the people' – and that its executives would be under the direction of the people. Marx wrote:

> The right of the democratic mass of the people to exert a moral influence on the attitude of the constituent assembly is an old revolutionary right of the people which, since the English and French revolution, could not be dispensed with in any period of stormy action. It is to this right that history owes almost all energetic steps taken by such assemblies. (Marx in Draper 1978: 290)

However, many see the idea of communism as either utopian or repressive. Some, such as Colin Wilson, maintain that communist regimes always seem to end in oppression and totalitarianism. In Wilson's words:

> Since those early days, the west has had the chance to see communism in practice in many countries in the world, and to observe that it always seems to result in oppression and totalitarianism. From the Stalin purges to the Vietnam boat people and the takeover of Cambodia, the face of Communism seems invariably brutal. (Wilson 1991, 1998: 13)

Wilson questions revolutionary socialism, which, in his view, always degenerates into tyranny. He said:

> Is Marxism a sound theory that is betrayed by its practitioners? Would it actually work if human beings were less imperfect? In *The Open Society and Its Enemies*, Karl Popper argued that oppression was inherent in the whole socialist theory from the moment Plato decided that poets were too dangerous to live in his ideal Republic … Others argued that terror is an inevitable consequence of revolutionary socialism, and that all such revolutions are bound to degenerate into tyranny. Marx was wrong about many central issues, and that some of his most important prophecies – like the increasing alienation of the workers, the polarization of the social classes, and the 'withering away of the State' – were simply unrealistic guesses. (Wilson 1991, 1998: 14)

Others see Marxist theory as the political enemy, which should be crushed because it directly challenges the foundation of a market economy and capitalism. This view has been expressed no better than by former British Prime Minister Margaret Thatcher, who said:

> It was not simply Stalin who was an evil man, but that communism, in practice, is an evil system, which gave birth to Stalin …
>
> We must add deterrence and defence to détente, for unless we do, we in the West will find ourselves constantly accommodating ourselves to Marxist values, instead of making the world safe for our own. We must build a world in which freedom is on the offensive. No single Western state not even USA, can stand alone against the power of Russia, nor alone can stem the spread of Communist influence around the world.
>
> For fifty years or more we have been led to believe that decisions made by the State on behalf of the people are in some way both more moral and more efficient than by the individual himself. It is not true. On the contrary, the more you take away from the individual his own powers of decision, the more you increase the risks of tyranny.

> The easy liberal education left the belief that Utopia was soon to be achieved, that with the welfare state, all ills would soon vanish and, with the UN, all tyrannies would soon crumble. That has proved an illusion. (Margaret Thatcher in Wilson 1991, 1998: 270–72)

F. Hayek, on the other hand, claims that socialism has nothing to do with liberalism. He sees that democratic socialism, as the great utopia of the last few generations, is not only unachievable, but even to strive for it would produce something so utterly different that few would be prepared to accept the consequences. In his view, most socialists still believe profoundly in the liberal ideal of freedom but few realize that their programme would mean the destruction of freedom. They are irreconcilable ideals, and yet one still hears such terms as 'individualist socialism'. W.H. Chamberlain, who in 12 years in Russia as an American correspondent, had seen all his ideals shattered, summed up the conclusions of his studies there and in Germany and Italy, thus: 'Socialism is certain to prove, in the beginning at least, the road NOT to freedom, but to dictatorship and counter-dictatorships, to civil war of the fiercest kind. Socialism achieved and maintained by democratic means seems definitely to belong to the world of utopias' (Chamberlain in Love 1998: 49). This criticism was based on a general perception that law as a tool of enforcement ideology in Russia often failed in many areas – such as detention without trial; trials not held in public but before selected onlookers; the refusal to allow the defendant to be represented by a lawyer of his or her choice (particularly in the case of political dissidents). Others observed that so-called socialist law and order often threaten to endanger the strict observance of the rule of law (Lloyd 1982: 996).

In George Orwell's review of Hayek's *The Road to Serfdom* he wrote:

> Professor Hayek's thesis is that Socialism inevitably leads to despotism by bringing the whole of life under the control of the State. Socialism necessarily gives power to an inner ring of bureaucrats, who in almost every case will be men who want power for its own sake and will stick at nothing in order to retain it.
>
> Between them these two books sum up our present predicament. Capitalism leads to dole queues, the scramble for markets, and war. Collectivism leads to concentration camps, leader worship, and war. There is no way out of this unless a planned economy can be somehow combined with freedom of the intellect, which can only happen if the concept of right and wrong is restored to politics. (Orwell in Love 1998: 44)

Yet, as Djilas correctly pointed out, the vision in Marx's original theory was not to destroy what existed in the highly developed countries but to surpass it in terms of the freedom of man. In his words, 'According to Marx's hypothesis and his conclusions on the subject, the revolution would occur first of all in the highly developed capitalist countries. Marx believed that the results of the revolution

– that is, the new socialist society – would lead to a new and higher level of freedom than that prevalent in the existing society, in so-called liberal capitalism (Djilas 1966: 22).

In Marx's vision, not only a higher economic and social form, but also a higher form of human freedom, should replace capitalism. Within it was a yearning for a lost communal spirit and its values, for a unity between man and nature, and for a direct communication between human beings, and also a belief that man's empirical life could and should be reconciled with this true essence. On the other hand, Marx did not favour the dominance of one class over another or the creation of a new privileged elite. He was not in favour of the dominance of one nation, one race, one ideology or religion over others. His was a vision for humanity. In practice, however, this vision has been blurred or even deliberately misused. Stalin's purges and massacres, are often used as a perfect example of Marxist ill intentions, but in reality they are distortions picture of the original Marxist message. State, in Marx's sense, is the intermediary between man and human liberty whereas Stalin abused the state power to maintain his political dominance. He could achieve this only with the structure of power monopoly as a dictator. The public power was abused brutally in this way without any constraints.

Class Struggle – Class Superiority

Marx believed that the leading class, in the process of universal human emancipation, should identify itself with the rest of the society as the general representative of this society. He maintained that the leading party must share the same interests as society itself. However, the privilege that the Party as a particular class has today is contradictory to this general interest.

Universal human emancipation also eliminates the condition of ruling class supremacy. In Marx and Engels' words:

> If, by means of a revolution, it [the proletariat] makes itself the ruling class, and, as such, sweeps away by force the old conditions of production, then it will, along with these conditions, have swept away the conditions for the existence of class antagonisms and of classes generally, and will thereby have abolished its own supremacy as a class. (*The Communist Manifesto*, ME:CW 6:505)

To elaborate this point further, Engels referred back to this passage some 35 years later emphasizing that there was no question of pitting one class against the other; rather, it is the principle that all are the same, regardless of class origin: 'The revolution which modern socialism strives to achieve is, briefly, the victory of the proletariat over the bourgeoisie, and the establishment of a new organization of society by the destruction of all class distinction' (Engels in Marx and Engels 1966: 665).

Class theory is perhaps the most abused area in Marxist theory. The theory arose from the fact that most societies are classed entities. However, to make it a Marxist proposition that each individual has a permanent class label hanging around his or her neck and is to be readily condemned or even executed because of their class is another abuse of Marx's original theory about the struggle between the proletariat and the bourgeoisie. Marx's emphasis was on class conflict as constituting the dynamics of social change and he used this class analysis only when he based his argument on the capitalist means of production, and his view that everyone in society reflects his or her social relations. He shared no common ground with those who wanted to degrade other human beings so that they could feel secure in their own social standing, without any reference to capital or economic analysis. This can only be explained by the power play in the name of class struggle in Marxist terms. In both Russia and China, many innocent people were put in gaol or exiled as 'class enemies' without trial or for no reason, under the despotic systems that arose in those regimes. Marx's class struggle theory was degraded to such a degree that it could be treated almost like a joke, were it not for the tragedies of those people involved. The question is: Who gave those abusers the power to abuse others and where did they get the idea that they had the 'right' to mistreat others in this way? It definitely did not come from Marxist theory. The new state of public ownership obviously did not change people's attitudes or remedy social inequality for that matter.

What Marx did not specify is the fact that power in its arbitrary use is 'classless'. The socialist legality of power concentration opens up opportunities for power careerists in any political system, for power has no class boundaries. It was not Marx's original intention to simply replace one master with another, in the name of class supremacy. On the contrary, it is 'only in the name of general interests that a particular class can claim general supremacy' (Marx 1844 in Tucker 1978: 62).

Dictatorship – Power Monopoly

This concept of class superiority has been used to justify dictatorship theory and social discrimination against all other sectors of the society. As we have seen, class supremacy contradicts the Marxist position on civil society after the revolution. Nowhere in all their writings, did either Marx or Engels ever endorse a regime whereby total power is concentrated in one group or class perpetually without a democratic process or expression of the people, to have a choice or say in the leadership process. The purpose of the revolution is not for a small group of people to seize power and become the new rulers, but to solve the fundamental contradiction of economic relations between the mode of production and the force of production. These are the conditions that Marx specified for the revolution: that the economic conditions must be met, and that the economic relations must be in contradiction with the force of production in the economy. Social relations have to reach a certain stage of development before the revolution can happen. Perhaps Marx's prediction was a rather hasty one, for it seems to have given the green light to a certain group of people in society to seize state power as leaders of the revolution, and to crush not only the bourgeois 'enemy' but the rest of society too. It opened the door for any revolutionaries to seize power in that way under the banner of Marxism. The danger of the theory of proletarian dictatorship lies in its potential to be used to justify dictatorship of all kinds, military or political, for any social group claiming power and dominance in the society. Although Marx warned that the revolution should not be a power game for the political benefit of any particular group, the reality is that it has attracted ideas of all kinds and has become a synonym for any social change by violent and radical means. This is particularly true in developing countries whose economies are weak, and the demand for political change is strong.

The Logic of Dogmatism

Dogmatism is the most important feature in the execution of abuse. It is associated with the notion of truth and, furthermore, the seeming monopoly of the truth. Truth here is an absolute concept: there is only one truth, and only 'I' hold it and no one else. The pressure increases as this logic is followed through: you are either with me or against me, either black or white; because I represent truth, whoever is against me is against the truth. This logic, however absurd it may appear, can nonetheless be very powerful. We have ample examples of this even today, for example in regard to the 'war against terrorism'. Such dogmatism can be found in many ideological schools and is not confined to any particular economic or political conviction. The reason this issue is raised here is that, in the process of mass control and education, this trend often prevails, with a tendency to develop into radical and extremist thought, leading to fundamentalism. The danger of dogmatism should never be overlooked, and it is often found in the practice of turning Marxism into a dogma to fit the political agenda of the time.

Arendt believed that the right to citizenship, the right of a *plurality* of people 'to act together concerning things that are of equal concern to each', is not only denied by totalitarianism, as it is also by every despot, but stands opposed to the principle that guides the acts of destruction that characterize totalitarian systems (Arendt 1973: 478). That principle is an *ideology* explaining the entire course of human affairs by determining every historical event and all past, present and future deeds as functions of a universal process. Looking deeper into the phenomenon of totalitarianism, Arendt saw that the 'idea' – the content of the ideology – matters less than its 'inherent logicality', which was discovered separately and prized by both Hitler and Stalin. In broad outline, ideological logicality operates like a practical syllogism: from the premise of a supposed law of nature that certain races are unfit to live, it follows that those races must be eliminated, and from the premise of a supposed law of history that certain classes are on their way to extinction, it follows that those classes must be liquidated. Arendt's point is that the untruth of this ideological premise is without consequence: the premise will become self-evidently true in the fictitious world created by the murderous acts that flow from them.

In both Russia and China, the law, though unwritten, was painfully clear: the Party had unlimited legal power to do anything to an individual, but the individual could not defy or even disagree with the Party. This obvious violation of the state's role went unchallenged because the individual was either overwhelmed by state power in every sense, or had no other legal access to argue his or her case. The apparatus of the state was such that the notion of protection for the individual was simply nonexistent – as were the legal institutions. The myth was created that man as individual owed the state and the Party everything. In the official rhetoric it is the state that raises the nation, educates the masses, and maintains employment and so on, and yet the Party/state owes the individual nothing. In terms of power relations, the state has the monopoly on power, which meant everything, including the law, while the individual had no power at all. This is another violation of Marxist teaching that power comes from the people who give the Party and the state the authority to represent them.

State Ownership – The Protection of 'the People'

The concept of 'the people' needs further clarification. 'The people' can be everybody and nobody. Often this term is used to mean 'I want it' or the 'Party wants it' and then used as a justification for all sorts of crimes. Russian people were persecuted under the name of 'the people's cause', 'in the interest of the people', or the grounds that 'the Party represents the people'. The Russian experience, however, shows that public ownership did not make all equal and that state-controlled capital does not mean that people own the mode of production at all. We need, therefore, to spell out what people own and how to prove that they are actually benefiting from owning this mode of production, in terms of the factory where they work or the business they participate in. When the state owns the mode of production and is in charge of major national resources and capital, how can profits benefit the people and the workers who directly contributed to the output? These questions are worthy of a separate study.

Djilas links the rise and fall of Marxism to the political and economic progress where the working class could play a greater role in society. He argues that in undeveloped economies the ties with Marx were strong, or at least in outward appearance, whereas in developed economies, the ties were weak. In countries where economic progress was slow and where the working class played an insignificant role in society, there was a tendency to make a system out of Marxist teaching that was unrelated to this economic need, although Marx was always cited as the basis for its ideas:

> In countries where economic forces and social relations were not yet ripe for industrial change, as in Russia and later in China, the adoption and dogmatisation of the revolutionary elements of Marxist teaching was more rapid and complete. A revolutionary trend emerged in the working-class movements; Marxism grew stronger. With the victory of the revolutionary party, it became the dominant

> ideology. In countries such as Germany, where the degree of political and economic progress made revolution unnecessary, the democratic and reformist aspects of Marxist teaching, rather than the revolutionary ones, dominated. The anti-dogmatic ideological and political tendencies generated an emphasis on *reform* by the working-class movement. (Djilas 1966: 23)

The Theory of State Developed by Lenin

Marxist theory of class and the notion of the dictatorship of the proletariat was further developed to justify the power monopoly held by a single political party and its leaders.

Dictatorship Theory

Lenin wrote his famous *The State and Revolution* in August 1917, on the eve of the October Revolution, which established the world's first socialist state. In this treatise he elaborated on Marx and Engel's theory of state and drew his own conclusion that Russia could not wait for evolution to take its own course, and that a violent revolution was necessary to replace the existing bourgeois state in Russia, even though the country did not fit into Marx's capital-based analysis or his prediction that revolutions would take place first in the advanced industrial economies. Lenin affirmed Marx's dictatorship theory and applied it in the context of Russia's own experiences of the revolution. Moreover, he further reaffirmed the necessity of the two-stage proletarian state and of the revolution theory, which he believed could be understood as a whole only as a link in a process – a chain of socialist proletarian revolutions being caused by the imperialist war and a series of civil wars. Similarly in China, Mao seized the chain of social resistances caused by the Imperial Japanese armies, some two decades later.

Lenin's theory on proletarian leadership was first developed in 1902, as a result of the social circumstances that led up to the failure of the 1905 Revolution. In his pamphlet 'What is to be done?' Lenin argued that workers needed political rights, and that the debate conducted by the economists was very restricted and insufficient as a way of finding a fundamental resolution to Russia's social problems. At the time he anticipated that a bourgeois class was too ready to surrender to autocracy on the one hand, and a proletariat class was too disorganized to resist it. The masses, he argued, could not win but only riot. It required therefore a party of professional revolutionaries to lead a genuine revolution to victory. This theory of proletarian leadership of a political organization was later developed as a major feature in Marxist theories of state power and were adopted by many undeveloped nations, including China, This was to have far-reaching implications (Wilson 1991, 1998: 299).

The State as Class Rule

In *The State and Revolution* Lenin saw the state first as a product of irreconcilable class antagonisms: 'The state arises where, when and insofar as class antagonisms objectively *cannot* be reconciled. And, conversely, the existence of the state proves that the class antagonisms are irreconcilable.' Nor was the state an organ for *the reconciliation* of classes. According to Marx, Lenin argued, 'the state could neither have arisen nor maintain itself had it been possible to reconcile classes. The state is an organ of class *rule,* an organ for the oppression of one class by another; it is the creation of "order", which legalizes and perpetuates this oppression by moderating the conflict between classes' (Lenin 1917: 16).

To Lenin, this force, as Engels said, had another role to play in history – that is, the revolutionary role of bringing about a new society. In Lenin's view, the old state as an instrument for the exploitation of the oppressed class would be abolished by such a force. From this basis, Lenin described the basic characteristics of state: the concept of 'public power' that Lenin called 'the state' is a power that arises from society but places itself above it and alienates itself more and more from it. It is an autonomous, armed organization of the population, with many complex, technical levels. It signifies the split of society into antagonistic classes. Lenin argued that such an organization would still be possible in any classed society. By destroying the state apparatus, we not only see the naked class struggle, and how the ruling class strives to restore the special bodies of armed men that serve it, but also how the oppressed class strives to create a new organization of this kind, capable of serving the exploited instead of the exploiters.

The Representative State

Before the state can be put away 'in the museum' or 'wither away', there are certain qualifying conditions. First, Engels wrote, in seizing state power, the proletariat thereby 'abolishes the state as state'. The state was the official representative of society as a whole, but it was this only insofar as it was the state of that class that represented itself for its own time. It is only unwanted when at last it becomes the real representative of the whole of society – it then renders itself unnecessary. Lenin argued, therefore, that the theory of Marx and Engels about the inevitability of a violent revolution refers to the bourgeois state. The latter *cannot* be superseded by the proletarian state through a process of 'withering away' but only through a violent revolution as a general rule. He believed that this was in accordance with Marx's open proclamation in *The Communist Manifesto* of the inevitability of a violent revolution, which he saw as lying at the root of the *entire* theory of Marx and Engels. He concluded that 'the suppression of the bourgeois state by the proletarian state is impossible without a violent revolution' (Lenin 1917: 27).

Furthermore, in response to Marx's ideas, Lenin set out to prove that, first, the existence of classes is bound up only with particular, historical phases in the development of production; secondly, that the class struggle necessarily leads to the *dictatorship of the proletariat*, and thirdly that this dictatorship itself constitutes only the transition to the *abolition of all classes* and to a *classless society*. Lenin drew the conclusion that bourgeois states are inevitably a *dictatorship of the bourgeoisie* and that the transition from capitalism to communism is certainly bound to yield a tremendous abundance and variety of political forms. However, the essence will inevitably be the same: *the dictatorship of the proletariat* (Lenin 1917: 37). This is what he had in mind to replace the 'smashed state machine'. Thus the theory of the proletarian dictatorship was firmly established in practice by Lenin.

Marx did not lay down specifically the political forms of a future stage in which the transition from state to non-state would take place, but Lenin believed that the 'smashed state machine' can and, indeed, must be *replaced*. And the transitional form before the state disappearance would be the 'proletariat organized as the ruling class' in this transition from state to non-state (Lenin 1917: 52). Korsch, for one, believes that the dictatorship of proletariat doctrine was invented independently of the class struggle and was used as an instrument of ideological dictatorship over science and art. He argues that the theory has become a tool for despotism: the view of so-called 'scientific with objective truth' loses its ground when it becomes independent of the workers' movement. In this sense the doctrine became a despotic ideology, enabling the Party apparatus to exercise a dictatorship over the proletariat (Kolakowski 1978: 322).

Socialist Legality in Soviet Law

Pashukanis, a Bolshevik, who was unjustly condemned for sabotage, and who was a leading thinker in the field of legal theory in Russia, saw the state in bourgeois society as a power broker in class conflicts. He maintained that 'class society is not only a market where autonomous owners of commodities meet, but is at the same time the battlefield of a bitter class war, where the machinery of state represents a very powerful weapon.' On this battlefield, relations do not appear to be in the least in the spirit of Kant's definition of law as a minimal limitation on the freedom of the personality indispensable to human coexistence. Using Gumplowicz's words, Pashukanis argued that this kind of law never existed – that the state was a 'power factor' and that the nature of this state power as the organized power of one class over the other was determined by the bourgeoisie and their theory and practice of a 'constitutional state'. He stated: The measure of some people's "freedom" is solely dependent on the measure of their domination by others. The norm is determined, not by the possibility of coexistence, but by the domination of some by others' (Pashukanis 1978: 150).

On the other hand, Vyshinsky, departing from this analysis of economic relations, elaborated the concept of the state further as a new form of organization of the proletariat – the Soviets. This new state targeted the bourgeoisie as its primary enemy, on all grounds, and justified the suppression of this class, ideologically and physically, using a new concept of socialist legality. At least in theory, the new state distinguished the law's dual role: one for the enemy and one for the people. Here Vyshinsky quoted Lenin's words: 'a State which must inevitably be democratic *in a new way* (for the proletarians and the dispossessed generally) and dictatorial *in a new way* (against the bourgeoisie)' (Vyshinsky 1948: 55).

However, Vyshinsky was not so clear on the question of how to achieve this aim without a legal system, which was not only to crush the bourgeois, but also to protect ordinary citizens of the state. Secondly, the Party was appointed as state leader. The Party was 'the highest form of class association of the proletariat' (Lenin) and 'the main guiding force in the system of the dictatorship of the proletariat', among other forms such as the trade unions, Soviets, the cooperatives, the League of Youth and so on (Vyshinsky 1948: 66). 'This was the heart of the matter' (Vyshinsky 1948: 55). Thirdly, the new state had to be democratic, as Lenin saw it, by means of the wider participation of ordinary working people in the state decision-making process, in the name of liberty. In his words:

> The dictatorship of the proletariat means supremacy over the bourgeoisie with the help of force. It is a method of State management combining compulsion and training in discipline. The dictatorship of the proletariat performs this task with the help of Soviet power, which is its own special form of State. The particular feature of Soviet power, as the State form of dictatorship of the proletariat, is that it embraces millions of the masses of working people, drawing them into constant, essential and what is more decisive participation in the management of the State. (Lenin 1947: 61)

Loffe and Shargorodskii, in their study of law (1963) cited in Lloyd (1982), promoted the concept of socialist legality as scientific cognition of the objective laws of development of socialist society. The law, in this sense, is not only punitive but positive as well (Lloyd 1982: 1082). They argued that, in a capitalist society, as in the exploitative socio-economic societies preceding capitalism, the law as a whole is directed toward reinforcing and sanctifying the existing social relationships of dominance and subordination, and its basic task consists of protecting the existing system. Therefore it is the prohibitive (coercive) aspect of law – sanctions, punishment, and their objective properties – that comes to the fore. However, in socialist society, law is directed for the first time not only to changing the existing social relationships but also to transforming them.

In reality, however, Lenin's idea of democracy for the masses, in handing over to the working people all the resources without which it is actually impossible to make real use of liberty and civic rights (freedom of the press, freedom of speech, freedom of assembly, etc.), did not turn out as he predicted. Not only the 'hand over' lacked a concrete mechanism by law to empower the people, but also the individuals in USSR under Stalin lost their basic rights to live, to think, and the right to personal protection by the state.

Product of Power Totality: Dictatorial Purges in Stalin's Regime

Stalin's State Ideology

The Soviet Union became a totalitarian socialist state in the 1930s when Stalin was at the height of his power. At this time he was constantly dissatisfied with unattainable production targets. He closed down almost all economic and statistical journals and began a purge throughout the Soviet regime leading up to the 1932–33 famine in which millions perished. Starving peasants were sentenced to concentration camps for stealing a handful of grain from a collective farm. The resistance of the masses, proletariat, peasantry, and intelligentsia was suppressed by the state leader, and all forms of social life were crushed. Any opposition within the Party was eliminated, with the final purge aimed at the Party itself. The destruction of the Party was achieved during the years between 1935 and 1939 alongside a huge increase in the conflict between the Soviet regime and its own subjects.

Mass executions took place in larger cities throughout the country following 'witch hunts' that were aimed at former oppositionists, as well as Stalin's faithful supporters and servants. The 'Great Purge' started in 1936 following major show trials in which the accused confessed to imaginary crimes and were summarily executed. The legal system was a major casualty. Millions were arrested; hundreds of thousands executed. Torture, which had ceased to be a part of Russian judicial procedure in the eighteenth century, was now widely used and became routine, with cruel methods of extracting false confessions. There was no law to protect ordinary citizens, as investigators were free to inflict any manner of physical and mental suffering to induce people to admit to crimes that the persecutors knew to be false. Such inhumane abuse often reached its peak when those few who had not already succumbed to such measures were told that their wives and children would be killed if they refused to confess.

The whole country lived in fear of the whims of a single ruler. Quotas for arrests and executions were set by the Party authorities and, if the police in a particular area did not fulfil these, they themselves were liable to be executed. Those who performed the task badly might be shot for sabotage and those who did it too well might be suspected of showing zeal to cover up their real disaffection. Not only Russians but foreign communists from Poland, Hungary, Yugoslavia, Bulgaria and Germany were also persecuted. The concentration camps were full. The indefinite imprisonment and death, people knew, had nothing to do with whether a man's work was good or bad, whether he did or did not belong to any kind of opposition, or whether he did or did not love Stalin. The majority of the Party delegates were purged, numerous eminent artists and more than a third of all Soviet writers perished. The climate of atrocity, paranoia and frenzy was so pervasive that one wonders how on earth the state could have acquired such a power over human lives?

The reasons for this, as discussed here, must be attributed to the concentration of power within the Party. Stalin's state, justified by its socialist legality, created a state ideology in which state power was in the hand of a few Party leaders. Based on the dictatorship theory, with the concentration of the power within the Party machine, Stalin was able to make himself a true dictator of the people in a way that contradicted Marx's original claims. The result was a totalitarian regime notorious for its cruelty and abuse of power. This highlighted the shortcomings of Marxist theory: without a mechanism for power check and effective corrective measures, any state, even one that claims to act in the name of working people, is not immune from the abuse of power. There was no real threat to Stalin or his regime, and every possible source of revolt within the Party could easily have been destroyed without bloodshed. Some have suggested that any dictator seeks to acquire total power and abandons the Party as an instrument in the process. Others have argued that Stalin needed to crush any possible rival who might threaten his personal power within the Party (Kolakowski 1978: 84). The role of law in this case was to justify the illegality and suppression of ordinary people. It was a law of state power and personal power, under which no freedom or liberty was tolerated. The perception of the law as an ideological weapon was intensified.

This power relations between Stalin, representing the state, and the Russian people as the state's subjects had the following features. First, it was a distortion of the faith and vision set out by Marx's original idea. It was also a matter of Marxist loyalty that was abused by the Stalin regime. As Kolakowski suggested, it served to destroy any loyalty to any cause other than to the state and its leader, including belief and faith in communist ideology. This helps us to understand how a totalitarian system came to destroy all kinds of communal life not imposed or closely controlled by the state. Under these circumstances individuals became extremely vulnerable because they were now isolated from one another, as well as being totally alienated from the political state,. They thus became mere instruments in the hands of the state (Kolakowski 1978: 86).

Why, though, did no one challenge the violation of the revolution principle and of human rights? The entire population who had previously dedicated their entire lives to the cause and had courageously fought for the nation now offered no resistance to the tyrant. The reason for this may lie in the ideology itself. The citizen belongs to the state and must have no other loyalty. All forms of revolt against the ruling party is against the ideology and labelled as 'deviation', 'revisionism' and so on. On the other hand, it was a personal greed for power that betrayed the common interest envisaged by Lenin. Members of the Party and legal institutions were no longer linked by a common faith and shared values, and the leaders of the government shifted their focus from public to private gains.

The second feature of the state–people power relationship grew out of Party ideology. The Party and its ideology were inseparable – just as in the Middle Ages when no unauthorized person was allowed to comment on the Scriptures, and the Bible itself was the *liber haereticorum*. Marxism thus became an untouchable dogma – the Scripture – used purely as a way of controlling the people and 'believers'. In Kolakowski's words, '[t]he party was essentially an ideological body'. Abuse occurs when ideologies are turned into a party institution, and where faith becomes vague enough to allow corrosive changes.

The third feature was dogmatism, which, as we have already seen, destroys man's capacity to reason. There were those who took the faith in idealism and humanity seriously and who wanted to interpret the doctrine for themselves and to judge whether any change was in accordance with the communist vision of Marxism/Leninism. These potential critics, however, were not allowed under Stalin. The Great Purge was a message to Party members that their loyalty was to the leader and not to communist idealism. The purges served to eradicate any faith other than that in the ruler. Human thought was suppressed and reduced to such a degree that the masses were neither desirous nor capable of independent thought. In Kolakowski's words, 'The paralysis of the individual was complete' (1978: 86).

Fourthly, there was an overall violation of man's liberty, with a plethora of arrests, executions, exiles, false confessions and assassinations. The fact that the police insisted on people signing their own confessions ensured that victims became accessories to the crimes committed against them and participants in the overall falsification. Torture was used not for obtaining truth, but as part of a universal fiction whose nature both the torturers and their victims understood perfectly well. And because everyone participated in this official fiction, the spurious itself became the real.

It seems fair to argue that what made the totalitarian state so powerful was not just its possession of the legal means to legitimize itself, but also the fact that the state was able to control the individual to an extent that went way beyond the law as we see it. Individuals became the victims of class theory and had no legal means or political will to fight for their independence. The law of the state, though unwritten, was painfully clear – the Party had unlimited legal power to do anything to an individual, but the individual could not defy or even disagree with the Party. Arendt once criticized the logic of this kind of total control. In her concept of logicality the original ideal is devoured in a process of ideological politics. She described the process of how an 'idea' is devoured:

> What distinguished these new totalitarian ideologist from their predecessors was that it is no longer primarily the 'idea' of the ideology – the struggle of classes and the exploitation of the workers or the struggle of races and the care for Germanic peoples – which appealed to them, but the logical process which could be developed from it. To Stalin, it was this irresistible force of logic that overpowered the audience. (Arendt 1973: 472)

Arendt noted that it was not the idea or the oratory that moved people but the force of logic that was dangerous. This was a significant shift from the 'idea' of an ideology itself and signifies the danger and power that this logic may bring to believers. In her words, 'The power, which Marx thought was born when the idea seized the masses, was discovered to reside, not in the idea itself, but in its logical process which "like a mighty tentacle seizes you on all sides as in a vice and from whose grip you are powerless to tear yourself away; you must either surrender or make up your mind to utter defeat"' (Stalin's speech of 28 January 1924 in Lenin 1947: 33, vol. 1). In Arendt's words:

> In the process or realization, the original substance upon which the ideologies based themselves as long as they had to appeal to the masses – the exploitation of the workers or the national aspirations of Germany – is gradually lost, devoured as it were by the process itself: in perfect accordance with 'ice cold reasoning' and the 'irresistible force of logic' ... It is in the nature of ideological politics – and is not simply a betrayal committed for the sake of self-interest or lust for power – that the real content of the ideology (the working class or the Germanic peoples) which originally had brought about the 'idea' (the struggle of classes as the law of history or the struggle of races as the law of nature) is devoured by the logic with which the 'idea' is carried out. (Arendt 1973: 472)

The Theory of State Developed by Mao to Strengthen Power Monopoly

Mao was deeply indebted to Engels' and Lenin's teaching on the concept of contradiction, and he further developed his view of law in dealing with social classes primarily based on this concept. The influence of Engels and Lenin on Mao is demonstrated in these words:

> Engels said, 'Motion itself is a contradiction'. Lenin defined the law of the unity of opposites as 'the recognition (discovery) of the contradictory, *mutually exclusive,* opposite tendencies in *all* phenomena and processes of nature (*including* mind and society)'... Contradiction is the basis of the simple forms of motion ... and still more so of the complex forms of motion. (Mao 1957a: 31)

Mao quoted Engels' words on the universality of contradiction and Lenin's example of the class struggle in social science (Mao 1937: 32):

> The law of contradiction is things, that is, the law of the unity of opposites, is the basic law of materialist dialectics. Lenin said, 'Dialectics in the proper sense is the study of contradiction *in the very essence of objects*'. Lenin often called this law the essence of dialectics; he also called it the kernel of dialectics. (Mao 1957a: 23)

> According to materialist dialectics, changes in nature are due chiefly to the development of the internal contradictions in nature. Changes in society are due chiefly to the development of the internal contradictions in society, that is, the contradiction between the productive forces and the relations of production, the

> contradiction between classes, and the contradiction between the old and the new; it is the development of these contradictions that pushes society forward and gives the impetus for the suppression of the old society by the new. (Mao 1957a: 28)

Mao's view of contradiction was a system of many concepts. He divided contradiction into two groups: the universality and particularity of contradiction, and two philosophical outlooks of the matters, which are metaphysical and dialectical conceptions. He then sought out the principal aspect of contradiction and the antagonism in contradiction. Mao used this division of types of contradiction to classify the population of China and dealt with each type accordingly, as if they were legal classifications or codes. This gave legitimacy to the discrimination against certain social sectors or groups according to their political classifications determined by the state and the Party leaders.

Contradiction, for Mao, was a very important and positive concept. In fact, he welcomed the notion and extended its application to the wider society. Mao likened contradiction to war – using martial metaphors such as offence and defence, advance and retreat, victory and defeat – all these being mutually contradictory phenomena. He believed that each cannot exist without the other. The two aspects are in conflict and at the same time in interdependence, and this constitutes the totality of war, pushing its development forward and solving its problems. This, in Mao's view, was also true of the Party. In his words, 'Opposition and struggle between ideas of different kinds constantly occur within the Party; this is a reflection within the Party of contradictions between classes and between the new and the old in society. If there were no contradictions in the Party and no ideological struggles to resolve them, the Party's life would come to an end' (Mao 1957a: 32). The antagonism, for Mao, is the struggle of opposites and is also the class struggle. He said,

> In human history, antagonism between classes exists as a particular manifestation of the struggle of opposites. Consider the contradiction between the exploiting and the exploited classes. Such contradictory classes coexist for a long time in the same society, be it slave society, feudal society or capitalist society, and they struggle with each other; but it is not until the contradiction between the two classes develops to a certain stage that it assumes the form of open antagonism and develops into revolution. The same holds for the transformation of peace into war in class society. (Mao 1957a: 69)

Mao did not refer to law explicitly in dealing with people of different background and attitudes, but he did refer specifically to different types of contradictions. This presumably includes those between Party members, which is referred to as 'ourselves' and the 'enemy'; and those among the people with measures of less severity. The two are totally different in their nature. There is a further division of antagonistic and non-antagonistic contradictions.

However, the definition of 'the people' and 'the enemy', as well as of the non-antagonistic and antagonistic aspects that Mao applied to the same group of 'exploited and the exploiting classes', is not clear. Moreover, the definition of all groups is based on vague political terms rather than their relations of production, such as working class, peasantry, intelligentsia and the national bourgeoisie. Even within the working class, there are working class and other sections of the working people, and contradictions within the national bourgeoisie, and so on (Mao 1957a: 81).

The definition of 'the people', on the other hand, is even more obscure and circumstantial, but was invariably politically phrased. In Mao's words:

> The concept of 'the people' varies in content in different countries and in different periods of history in the same country … For example, during the War of Resistance against Japan, all those classes, strata and social groups opposing Japanese aggression came within the category of the people, while the Japanese imperialists, the Chinese traitors and the pro-Japanese elements were all enemies of the people. During the War of Liberation, the U.S. imperialists and their running dogs – the bureaucrat-capitalists, the landlords and the Kuomintang reactionaries who represented these two classes – were the enemies of the people, while the other classes, strata and social groups, which opposed these enemies, all came within the category of the people. At the present stage, the period of building socialism, the classes, strata and social groups which favour, support and work for the cause of socialist construction all come within the category of the people, while the social forces and groups which resist the socialist revolution and are hostile to or sabotage socialist construction are enemies of the people. (Mao 1957a: 80–81)

In Mao's view, the contradictions between people and the enemy are antagonistic contradictions, whereas, within the ranks of people, the contradictions among the working people are non-antagonistic. Those between the exploited and the exploiting classes have a non-antagonistic aspect in addition to an antagonistic aspect. The contradiction between the national bourgeoisie and the working class is one between the exploiter and the exploited, and is therefore antagonistic in nature, but in China this antagonistic class contradiction can, if properly handled, be transformed into a non-antagonistic one and be resolved by peaceful methods. It can change into a contradiction between ourselves and the enemy if we do not handle it properly. Mao added:

> since they are different in nature, the contradictions between ourselves and the enemy and the contradictions among the people must be resolved by different methods. To put it briefly, the former is a matter of drawing a clear distinction between ourselves and the enemy, and the latter [is] a matter of drawing a clear distinction between right and wrong. (Mao 1957a: 82)

State Power and Dictatorship

Mao made it very clear, as early as 1957, that the dictatorship of the working class was here to stay in China. Its main functions were twofold: to suppress internal class enemies who were hostile towards the new state, and secondly to maintain public order to ensure the nation's unity. Mao even elaborated on his idea of democracy and democratic centralism. He further confirmed the leadership of the working class (the Party) as the state head:

> Our state is a people's democratic dictatorship led by the working class and based on the worker-peasant alliance. What is this dictatorship for? Its first function is to suppress the reactionary classes and elements and those exploiters in our country who range themselves against the socialist revolution, to suppress all those who try to wreck our socialist construction, or in other words, to resolve the internal contradictions between ourselves and the enemy. For instance, to arrest, try and sentence certain counter-revolutionaries, and to deprive landlords and bureaucrat-capitalists of their right to vote and their freedom of speech for a specified period of time – all this comes within the scope of our dictatorship. To maintain public order and safeguard the interests of the people, it is likewise necessary to exercise dictatorship over embezzlers, swindlers, arsonists, murderers, criminal gangs and other scoundrels who seriously disrupt public order. The second function of this dictatorship is to protect our country from subversion and possible aggression by external enemies. In that event, it is the task of this dictatorship to resolve the external contradiction between the enemy and us. The aim of this dictatorship is to protect all our people so that they can devote themselves to peaceful labour and build China into a socialist country with a modern industry, agriculture, science and culture. Who is to exercise this dictatorship? Naturally, it is the working class and the entire people under its leadership. Dictatorship does not apply within the ranks of the people. The people cannot exercise dictatorship over themselves, nor must one section of the people oppress another. Law-breaking elements among the people will be punished according to law, but this is different in principle from the exercise of dictatorship to suppress enemies of the people. What applies among the people is democratic centralism. Our Constitution lays it down that citizens of the People's Republic of China enjoy freedom of speech, of the press, assembly, association, procession, demonstration, religious belief, and so on. Our Constitution also provides that the organs of state must practise democratic centralism, that they must rely on the masses and that their personnel must serve the people. Our socialist democracy is democracy in the broadest sense such as is not to be found in any capitalist country. Our dictatorship is the people's democratic dictatorship led by the working class and based on the worker-peasant alliance. That is to say, democracy operates within the ranks of the people, while the working class, uniting with all others enjoying civil rights, and in the first place with the peasantry, enforces dictatorship over the reactionary classes and elements and

> all those who resist socialist transformation and oppose socialist construction. By civil rights, we mean, politically, the rights of freedom and democracy.
>
> But this freedom is freedom with leadership and this democracy is democracy under centralized guidance, not anarchy. Anarchy does not accord with the interests or wishes of the people. (Mao 1957a: 83–84)

Even in the concept of dictatorship Mao divided it into a two-class-based definition, with two approaches to Marxism, namely dogmatism and revisionism. Written in 1957, one of his most famous speeches continued Mao's 'two lines' style of thinking, distinguishing between the proletariat and the bourgeoisie, in name at least, as no details of his definitions of this terms are found in the same work. In his attack on bourgeois ideology as a response to public criticism, Mao attributed revisionism, as any undesirable notion, to a value notion of bourgeois ideology and once more justified the notion of dictatorship as legitimate. He said:

> Both dogmatism and revisionism run counter to Marxism … It is dogmatism to approach Marxism from a metaphysical point of view and to regard it as something rigid. It is revisionism to negate the basic principles of Marxism and to negate its universal truth. Revisionism is no form of bourgeois ideology. The revisionists deny the differences between socialism and capitalism, between the dictatorship of the proletariat and the dictatorship of the bourgeoisie. What they advocate is in fact not the socialist line but the capitalist line. In present circumstances, revisionism is more pernicious than dogmatism. One of our current important tasks on the ideological front is to unfold criticism of revisionism. (Mao 1957b: 152–3)

It is noted, however, that these definitions of revisionism or dogmatism, like many other such terms, were rarely debated or challenged. They often appeared in the media at the time as authoritative statements rather than subjects open to debate. This two-line style of thinking, simplistic and clear-cut in fashion, later led to a real dogmatism in the treatment of ordinary citizens as bourgeois enemies using Marxist class theory.

This concept of dictatorship was further elaborated by Mao through a Directive of the Party Central Committee (16 May 1966) on the eve of the Great Proletarian Cultural Revolution, published in *The People's Daily* (1966b) of the same period. The news article, named '5.16 Announcement' (*Tong zhi*, in Chinese), was to be read by all in the nation, stated that the struggle between the proletariat and bourgeois classes, and the dictatorship of the proletariat placed upon the bourgeoisie, including those within the Party, had no room for so-called equality or any other relationships between the classes. Therefore the struggle had to be a life and death one, a matter of suppression of one class by the other (Mao 1969: 27). The primary question for the state, and for Mao, was who was the 'Enemy' and who was a 'Friend', an issue, Mao believed, that lay at the heart of both the revolution and the Cultural Revolution as well. This was spelt out in the *Decision on the Proletarian Cultural Revolution by CCP, August 1966* (Mao 1969: 39). The state really had no other function during this period. .

Class Brand

Mao believed that every individual belongs to a particular class and every form of thinking bears an imprint of that class. As the vast population in China took his teaching seriously, this expanded concept of 'class brand' had a profound impact on the minds of the people as a basis for judging each other's character. It also gave a false legitimacy to the discriminatory treatment of certain social groups, in terms of job promotion, work conditions and educational opportunity. All these inequalities were disguised under the banner of class struggle, ignoring its true meaning in Marxist thought. Moreover, in this class nature and all theory of dialectical materialism which is Mao's basic tool for analysis, the purpose is to serve the proletariat. In Mao's words:

> Of these other types of social practice, class struggle in particular, in all its various forms, exerts a profound influence on the development of man's knowledge. In class society everyone lives as a member of a particular class, and every kind of thinking, without exception, is stamped with the brand of a class. (Mao 1957a: 2–3)

> Marxists hold that man's social practice alone is the criterion of the truth of his knowledge of the external world ... The dialectical-materialist theory of knowledge places practice in the primary position, holding that human knowledge can in no way be separated from practice and repudiating all the erroneous theories which deny the importance of practice or separate knowledge from practice. The Marxist philosophy of dialectical materialism has two outstanding characteristics. One is its class nature: it openly avows that dialectical materialism is in the service of the proletariat. The other is its practicality: it emphasizes the dependence of theory on practice, emphasizes that theory is based on practice and in turn serves practice. The truth of any knowledge or theory is determined not by subjective feelings, but by objective results in social practice. (Mao 1957a: 3–4)

The dialectical-materialist movement of cognition has two stages – the perceptual stage of cognition and the stage of conception and rational knowledge, which refers to man's use of concepts to form judgements and inferences. This second stage of conception, judgement and inference is the more important stage in the entire process of knowledge. Mao gave an example of these stages as follows:

> In its knowledge of capitalist society, the proletariat was only in the perceptual stage of cognition in the first period of its practice, the period of machine-

> smashing and spontaneous struggle; it knew only some of the aspects and the external relations of the phenomena of capitalism. The proletariat was then still a 'class-in-itself'. But when it reached the second period of its practice, the period of conscious and organized economic and political struggles, the proletariat was able to comprehend the essence of capitalist society, the relations of exploitation between social classes and its own historical task; and it was able to do so because of its own practice and because of its experience of prolonged struggle, which Marx and Engels scientifically summed up in all its variety to create the theory of Marxism for the education of the proletariat. It was then that the proletariat became a 'class-for-itself'. (Mao 1957a: 9–10)

In a revolutionary period the situation changes very rapidly; if the knowledge of revolutionaries does not change rapidly in accordance with the changed situation, they will be unable to lead the revolution to victory (Mao 1957a: 17).

Mao also argued that the transitional period for China was going to be a long road. As early as the 1950s he openly admitted that 'In China the struggle to consolidate the socialist system, the struggle to decide whether socialism or capitalism will prevail, will still take a long historical period. But we should all realize that the new system of socialism will unquestionably be consolidated' (Mao 1957a: 135). Not only did Mao believe that the class struggle was the central weapon for his theory – one that 'works wonders' in his own words – and that 'the philosophy of the communist party is the philosophy of struggle'; he was also famous for his slogan 'to rebel is legal' (or 'is reasonable'). Based on this logic, the suppressed would defy, rebel and strike for the goal of socialism (Mao 1969: 43). The idea of revolution was based on the absoluteness of the dictatorship, which was expressed in these words: 'our relationship to them is absolutely not one of equal standing, but the suppression of one class by the other, that is, the dictatorship of proletariat class over the bourgeois class. There is not, and cannot be, any other relationship, such as equality, peaceful coexistence, a philanthropic or moral relationship etc. between the exploited and exploiting classes' (Mao 1969: 27).

Deng's Theory of Socialist Principles

As mentioned earlier, Deng was perhaps the first communist leader who talked openly and in great length about the issue of the concentration of power in the hands of the Party leadership in the state apparatus in modern times. In his speech 'On the reform of the system of Party and state leadership' (18 August 1980), Deng recognized the problem and called for change. In his words:

> It is not good to have an over-concentration of power. It hinders the practice of socialist democracy and of the Party's democratic centralism, impedes the progress of socialist construction and prevents us from taking full advantage of collective wisdom. Over-concentration of power is liable to give rise to arbitrary

> rule by individuals at the expense of collective leadership, and it is an important cause of bureaucracy under the present circumstances. (Deng 1984b: 303)

Deng elaborated this idea further and linked this phenomenon of power concentration with the age-old Chinese tradition of officialdom when he said:

> Over-concentration of power means inappropriate and indiscriminate concentration of all power in Party committees in the name of strengthening centralized Party leadership. Moreover, the power of the Party committees themselves is often in the hands of a few secretaries, especially the first secretaries, who direct and decide everything. Thus 'centralized Party Leadership' often turns into leadership by individuals. This problem exists, in varying degrees, in leading bodies at all levels throughout the country. Over-concentration of power in the hands of an individual or of a few people means that most functionaries have no decision-making power at all, while the few who do are overburdened. (Deng 1984b: 311)
>
> This phenomenon is connected to the influence of feudal autocracy in China's own history and also to the tradition of a high degree of power in the hands of individual leaders of the Communist Parties of various countries at the time of the Communist International. Historically, we ourselves have repeatedly placed too much emphasis on ensuring centralism and unification by the Party, and on combating decentralism and any assertion of independence. And we have placed too little emphasis on ensuring the necessary degree of decentralization, delegating necessary decision-making power to the lower organizations and opposing the over-concentration of power in the hands of individuals. (Deng 1984b: 311)
>
> Bureaucracy is an age-old and complex historical phenomenon. In addition to sharing some common characteristics with past types of bureaucracy, Chinese bureaucracy in its present form has characteristics of its own. This is, it differs from both the bureaucracy of old China and that prevailing in the capitalist countries. It is closely connected with our highly centralized management in the economic, political, cultural and social fields, which we have long regarded as essential for the socialist system and for planning. (Deng 1984b: 310)

This issue is still with us today. As I will discuss in Chapter 4, the problem of power concentration has persisted and is embedded within the current Constitution and Chinese legal institutions, which makes the task of reducing this power totality extremely difficult. Deng showed his resolution to deal with this problem. He said: 'The long-standing failure to understand this adequately was one important cause of the "Cultural Revolution", and we paid a heavy price for it. There should be no further delay in finding a solution to this problem' (Deng 1984b: 312). Besides this, Deng argued that China's traditional patriarchalism also contributed to the problem, placing individuals above the organization, which then becomes a tool in their hands. Patriarchalism is an antiquated social phenomenon that has existed from ancient times and 'has had a very damaging influence on the Party' (Deng 1984b: 312). His vision for China's future was, however, not to weaken or relax Party leadership and discipline, but to strengthen them. In his words:

> In a big country like ours, it is inconceivable that unity of thinking could be achieved among our several hundred million people or that their efforts could be pooled to build socialism in the absence of a Party whose members have a spirit of sacrifice and a high level of political awareness and discipline, a Party that truly represents and unites the masses of people and exercises unified leadership. Without such a Party, our country would split up and accomplish nothing … The unity of the people, social stability, the promotion of democracy and the reunification of our country all depend on Party leadership. The core of the four cardinal principles is to uphold leadership by the Party. The point is that the Party must provide good leadership; only through constant improvement can its leadership be strengthened. (Deng 1984b: 324)

According to Deng, the four cardinal principles for the modernization of China are:

1. the upholding of the socialist road;
2. the upholding of the people's democratic dictatorship;
3. the upholding of the leadership of the Communist Party of China; and
4. the upholding of Marxism–Leninism–Mao Zedong thought. (Article 1, Constitution of PRC, 1982)

In practice, however, the June 1989 crackdown negatively tested Deng's vision of promoting democracy as well as the Party's democratic leadership. The incident made it clear that the Party leadership should also face the sanction of the law, and not just make the laws. A democratic leadership must respect people's constitutional rights and be held accountable under the rule of the law, without impunity or privilege. How a ruling party of a socialist state uses power vis-à-vis its people is the ultimate testimony of its true nature. The authority of the Party as state power is not only asserted by law, but is also to be proven by its actions.

I will discuss each of Deng's cardinal principles in more detail below.

The Socialist Road

The socialist principle is, as proclaimed by the Constitution, based on the principle that all power of the state belongs to the people; and that the basic rights of citizens must be protected by law and the state. The Constitution states that 'All power in the People's Republic of China belongs to the people' and that 'The people administers state affairs and manage economic, cultural and social affairs through various channels and in various ways in accordance with the law' (Constitution of PRC, 1982, Article 2).

There are many rights and duties included in the Constitution of the PRC (2004), the most important of which is equality before the law (Article 33). In addition, there are the following rights:

1. the right to vote – regardless of ethnic status, race, sex, occupation, family background, religious belief, education, property status or length of residence (Article 34);
2. the right to supervise (Article 27) and to criticize, complain about, lay charges against and expose any state organ for violation of the law (Article 41);
3. the right to democratic management of enterprises/organizations (Article 17).

The Constitution also safeguards certain freedoms:

1. the freedom of speech, of the press, of assembly, of association, of procession and of demonstration (Article 35);
2. the freedom of religious belief (Article 36);
3. the freedom and privacy of correspondence (Article 40);
4. the freedom of marriage (Article 49);
5. the freedom to research, and to follow literary and artistic and other cultural pursuits (Article 47).

It also safeguards freedoms of the person:

1. to preserve life – no bodily harm or torture;
2. no arrest without approval, no unlawful detention, no deprivation or restriction of freedom of the person (Article 37);
3. residence is inviolable (Article 39);
4. personal dignity is inviolable – no insult, libel, false accusation or incrimination (Article 38). (B. Li and Xu 1986: 50–88)

The importance of these rights is recognized by the Constitution: it states, in the third paragraph of Article 33, that 'The state respects and safeguards human rights.' Chapter 2 of the Constitution deals specifically with the fundamental rights and duties of citizens. For example, in Articles 33–36, it grants all citizens equality before the law, and states that every citizen is entitled to the rights and duties prescribed by the law. Citizens have the right to vote regardless of their ethnic status, race, family background or religious belief. They are granted the freedom of speech, of the press, of assembly, of association, of procession and of demonstration (Article 35) and freedom of religious belief (Article 36).

Under a system of power totality, however, these rights are not protected by the law, because the law is interpreted and administrated by state executives who are answerable only to the ruling party. A socialist state without these basic rights is like an empty shell. At the worst political moments in China when everything was being subsumed by a single political principle, ideology became a convenient tool to reject these rights. In the words of a former Premier of China, Zhou Enlai, commenting on the chanting of Marxist slogans during the Cultural Revolution: 'Principles without humanity are a mere formality' (Phathanothai 1995: 212).

A revolutionary party, once in power, will either renew itself by returning power to whence it originated – the people – or face self-destruction if it rules without the people's will. Some argue that the original intentions of the Party have been lost – that instead of fighting for the betterment of the people as it did in the past, it now demands people shut their mouths and obey Party rules, and all in the name of 'socialism'. In Zhang's words, 'The Chinese Communist Party has long since ceased to be a traditional Communist party. It is now a mélange of factions with diverse goals and differing ideologies'; and 'although the June Fourth democracy movement in Tiananmen Square ended in tragedy, it left an important legacy' (Nathan and Link 1991: xiii).

The People's Democratic Dictatorship

The objective of the revolution is to grant the legality of people's power, which means that power belongs to the people. Without this concept of citizens' civil rights, and the protection of people against abuse of power by the state, any socialist system would be hollow. 'All power in the People's Republic of China belongs to the people … The people administer state affairs and manage economic, cultural and social affairs through various channels and in various ways in accordance with the law' (Article 2, Constitution of PRC 1982).

There has been a suggestion that the word 'dictatorship' should be omitted from the Constitution (*Law Yearbook of China* 1993b: 856) as it reflects the operation of a feudal denotation of absolute power. However, it remains in the Constitution of the PRC (2004) as 'democratic dictatorship'. The issue should be of ongoing interest, as the concept seems both contradictory and confusing. What exactly is the dictatorship and who will be dictated to? In Marx' vision, in a people's state, people cannot be dictated to by the state, but should control the state through their representatives. As some have argued, what is contentious here is that the people have become the *target* of the dictatorship, as happened, for example, in the Tiananmen Incident in 1987, and lose their rightful position as controllers of the state. The relationship between the state and the people is further eroded when the state is able to determine what constitutes a 'thought crime' and who should be punished. For example, the concept of 'counter-revolution' or the 'class enemy' is of a political nature, and is often used in legal cases as a criterion for crimes. It is the state, not the people, that has the power to determine the criteria for this kind of 'thought crime', which is justified in the name of 'public interest'. This contradicts the very meaning of democracy and people's sovereignty. It suggests that people have lost this power of sovereignty and have become the subjects of state power.

Another example of lack of democratic values is the case of Lin Xilin. In the 1950s Lin, a young journalist and a true believer in democracy, openly criticized the party and the leaders, and was persecuted as the most notorious 'Rightist' of the time. She was imprisoned and lost all her personal freedom. Yet, thirty years later, and even after the fall of the Gang of Four, the authorities still refused to exonerate her. In a long and open letter to Deng in 1983 she asked him to clear her name but with no success (X. Lin 1983). She has suffered a great deal, both in and out of prison, and at the time she wrote her letter to Deng she lived in poverty outside China. Although the word 'counter-revolutionary' was later taken out of the Constitution, the underlying power of the state to determine what constitutes a 'thought crime' undeniably persists and remains detrimental to the exercise of Chinese law.

The Party Leadership

Although keeping public power in check is an essential part of law by convention, some Chinese leaders, including Deng, rejected the idea of power separation and refused to share the power of the Party in any form. In a defence of the four cardinal principles, Deng argued that Party leadership would be jeopardized if the law was accepted as a higher authority. In his words:

> These people want to abandon the road of socialism, break away from Party leadership and promote bourgeois liberalization … [S]ome persons are not on the right track ideologically … It is also connected with corrosion by bourgeois ideology from abroad.
>
> The essence of the four cardinal principles is to uphold Communist Party leadership. Without Party leadership there definitely will be nationwide disorder and China would fall apart. History has shown us this. Chiang Kai-shek was never able to unify China. The keystone of bourgeois liberalization is opposition to Party leadership. But without Party leadership there will be no socialist system.
>
> If we don't do a good job in this respect, contradictions may intensify and result in major disruptions. In a word, we must uphold Party leadership and the socialist system. They must be improved, but that doesn't mean we can have bourgeois liberalization or anarchy. (Deng 1981: 369)

We have already discussed what constitutes the Socialist Road and how inadequate it is if we attribute the issue of power abuse to a single analysis of class ideology. To defend the principle of power check, moreover, we need to put state power of all kinds under the rule of law. By this I mean to argue that any form of power can change its nature and betray the people it claims to protect, if it is in total control of all state agencies and is left unchecked. I do not state this as a prediction but as a reality, as something that has already happened in the past. In this sense, no state leadership should be immune from legal sanction if it breaches the regulations that challenge its supremacy in the power structure and restricts its rulings under the rule of law.

Power monopoly is still justified in the name of being anti-bourgeois today. Here the notion of Party Leadership needs further clarification. If this principle is interpreted as meaning a rejection of power checked by law, it will be inconsistent with Article 5 of the Constitution that 'all political parties ... must abide by the Constitution and the law'. This means that the Party is subordinate to the Constitution. The supremacy of the law and the Constitution means that the law has the power to check the Party's operation and sanction any misuse of its power. This also means that leadership status does not grant immunity from the law, or a legal monopoly on power, especially when that power is not elected by any community or people nor subject to removal or objection by the people. To simply reject any call for a check on public power as 'bourgeois' is, therefore, not convincing. The authority of the state mist be subject to the authority of the people under the rule of law, and the authority of the Party transferred to the people through their Congress. In this sense, it is the Party that is subject to the people's will rather than the people being subjected to the rule of the Party. Even in the matter of leadership, this constitutional position on authority and delegation of power should not be altered to justify the structure of power monopoly or power totality. To justify such an alteration is to abandon the people's sovereign rights and the principle of power check as exercised by the people and the law.

Marxist–Leninist–Mao Zedong Thought

To be true to Marxism is to keep Marx's vision in sight about how power should be limited by law. For Marx, the state, after the revolution, is part of the law; but not *above* the law, and no privilege is given to the state executive. Indeed the state is the agent of the people, the executive at the direction of the people. Marx wrote:

> The right of the democratic mass of the people to exert a moral influence on the attitude of the constituent assembly is an old revolutionary right of the people which, since the English and French revolution, could not be dispensed with in any period of stormy action. It is to this right that history owes almost all energetic steps taken by such assemblies. (Marx in Draper 1978: 290)

For Marx, as stated earlier in this study, it was vital to limit executive power and to use the Constitution as a means of curbing abuse of power. One of the major functions of the Constitution was to reduce the state executive's power. Marx advocated every possible means of minimizing the autonomous power of the executive. He believed in a Constitution that restrains the powers of the executive and makes the administration more dependent on the legislature and places it under the control of a supreme court (Marx in Draper 1978: 301).

What restrains this executive is nothing less than the law. Marx wrote: ‘The Courts of law, empowered to decide definitively upon all the acts of the Executive, were rendered omnipotent.’ The courts also have the final say ‘in all equations of bureaucratic discipline’. Courts can remove any minister declared guilty of misinterpreting its resolutions; the Prince’s ‘right of grace’ is shorn, and so is his control over members of the administration. Marx continued:

> The Representative Chamber selects out of its members a permanent committee, forming a sort of Areopagus, watching and controlling the Government, and impeaching the officials for violation of the Constitution, no exception being granted on behalf of orders received by subalterns from their superiors in rank. In this way, the members of the bureaucracy were emancipated from the Crown. (Marx in Draper 1978: 302)

Marx saw the people as the legislative body. He defined ‘the voters’ as ’the people who make the legislative body’ (Marx in Draper 1978: 294). Later, Marx pointed to the Paris Commune’s system as a triumph of democracy because it minimized and thoroughly subordinated executive power, placing, for example, the control of the courts as well as the army in the hands of the people (Draper 1978: 316).

As discussed earlier, Marx and Engels never endorsed power totality in the post-revolutionary government. On the contrary, they promoted a people’s assembly that would keep power in check by means of the rule of law under the Constitution. Marx, in particular, rejected the total structure of power as found in the feudal system where civil life was politicized in every aspect and which subjected people to its tyranny. The theory of proletarian dictatorship was never meant to justify a dictatorship of a few individuals over the majority of the people, but was meant to act on behalf of the people to reject the privileged few. It could hardly apply, therefore, to a society where the bourgeoisie was not yet fully identified or developed as a social or political class on an economic basis. The subjective determination and condemnation of people’s thoughts, according to ‘political classifications’ made and ordained by the power-holders, is therefore a gross abuse of Marxist class theory and of Lenin’s theory of dictatorship. It is nothing more than a revival of the feudal relationship between the lord and his servants, who had no freedom to select or determine their ruler – only the freedom to obey or praise the master. To be true to Marx’s vision of the workers’ state, this feudal style of power structure must give way to the will of the people as channelled through their representatives and delegates in the government. In this respect, even bourgeois society has its merits, since it gives people greater control over how power is used and limited by the platform of law. To deny that this is a significant achievement in modern legal philosophy and representative government is to deny the developmental nature of Marxist historical materialism.

It would be a futile effort to turn the wheels of history back to a previous stage when power was left in the hands of a few, unconstrained by the society.

Another position put forward by Marxist state leaders is a concept of law that derives its validity from its perception of its own cultural uniqueness. Tumanov, for example, writing in 1969, stressed that Soviet jurisprudence had a unique character that had nothing in common with Western legal philosophy. From this Curzon concluded that 'Marxism rejected peaceful coexistence in the area of philosophy and ideology' (Curzon 1979: 179). This 'uniqueness' is later echoed by Chinese leaders who have termed the current reforms in China as 'socialism with Chinese characteristics', by which they mean the maintenance of the Party's power monopoly alongside an expansion of the state's market economy. If the concept of power is based on the traditional conception of a 'fallen' human nature, then there is nothing unique about justifying its use as a weapon to defeat 'class' enemies. If, however, it is derived from a human nature rooted in reason, then power is only a means to serve humanity, never an end in itself. This is, in Kant's terms, a *practical imperative*: ' to treat humanity, whether in your own person or in that of any other, in every case as an end withal, never as a means only' (Curzon 1979: 75). Therefore, to keep a party in power is never an end in itself, but only a means of serving humanity, to be judged and altered by humanity as it sees fit. In this sense, power totality can never be made perpetual, as it cannot serve 'the end' in its best interests.

On Stability

Stability, or public order, is an abiding concern of the Chinese government and the Party for the obvious reason that social disorder and regional or factional conflicts in such a vast land like China, with more than 50 different ethnic minorities and various religions and cultures, is a very real possibility. Moreover, there are numerous areas where hundreds of millions of people still live below the poverty line – in spite of the fact that China has enjoyed unprecedented economic growth and accumulated great wealth by both the state and private citizens (CCTV News on SBS May Association 2007). Both geographic size and disparity of wealth threaten social and regional unrest. Stability is thus of vital political importance, as expressed in 2000 by the former President of the PRC, Jiang Zemin:

> Doing a good job in public order is a major social issue, and a major political issue as well. It has a bearing on the fundamental interests of the masses of the people, the prolonged political stability of the state, the governing status of our party, and the implementation of our party's basic line. If our public order is poor, the people's lives and property cannot be guaranteed. This will affect not only the image of the party and the government in the people's eyes but also the overall interests of reform, development and stability. (Keith and Li 2006: 184)

Unfortunately, under the system of power totality, stability and public order have also been used as justifications for more draconian state punishments, in several political campaigns as well as through revised codes of Chinese criminal law. This is an area where the government prefers severe measures to crack down both on criminal activities as well as political dissidents in the name of 'anti-subversion', at the cost of free expression. This is also a question of criminal justice and human rights, under the rule of law. The criminal law has a direct bearing on both the legitimacy of the state and the well-being of the people, and is a basic law that safeguards millions of households.

Given China's rapidly changing social and economic environment, and the marked influence of the West, China's jurists and legislators have undertaken unprecedented studies of international standards of criminal justice, and engaged in a selective and conscious adaptation of international norms to local conditions. At the time of the newly revised criminal law (hence CL97), there was optimism that judicial justice and the protection of rights would be enhanced by its comprehensive stipulations. In the deepening of market reform, the CL97 dropped the special provision on counter-revolutionary crime and added 'new economic crime' as more important than the Cultural Revolutionary issues of class enemy and class struggle. The new law also provided the state with a new front for public order and social stability. During the late 1980s and 1990s, there was a growing interest in the legal definition and the protection of what were the newly emerged concepts of 'rights and interests'. At the same time there was a new national debate about the need to establish 'the rule of law' to protect human rights. In 1996 Party and jurist debate resulted in a new formulation of constitutional law as 'ruling the country relying on law and establishing a socialist legal system country', a formulation that was subsequently included in the 1999 Constitution.

At the same time, procedural justice grew in importance. Under the 1996–97 reforms, the revised procedural law was supposed to balance judicial justice and the protection of human rights and enjoyed a status equal to that of the criminal law, so as to facilitate social stability. This served to reject the exclusive emphasis on the punitive function of criminal law. As Keith noted, 'The substantive importance of procedural protection in criminal justice was highlighted for the first time in a self-conscious challenge to a criminal law tradition that had so rigorously supported severe criminal punishment as the means by which to achieve social control' (Keith and Li 2006: 15).

The primary purpose of criminal law is seen as providing social control, although the prevention of 'social harm' caused by 'criminal action' is often the reason given by the state authorities for 'cracking down' on criminals. This is a political decision and has resulted in constant so-called 'cracking down' and 'striking hard' campaigns. The state's arbitrary power vis-à-vis punishment has been subjected to much jurist debate in recent years. A senior criminal law expert, Gao, for example, calls for the CL97 to adopt the notion that punishment should fit the crime and upbraids the neo-traditionalist system of 'heavy penalties' as 'feudal criminal law' (Keith and Li 2006: 21).

The 'heavy penalties' have resulted in heavy casualties. The 2001 'strike hard' campaign in Jinan City, for example, produced an instance of 'sort things out' – a public gathering in which 20 suspects involved in 112 cases were 'tried'; ten were dealt with sternly, 'while the other ten were dealt with leniently and not held accountable because they had turned themselves in and made a clean breast of things' (Keith and Li 2006: 148). The 'scientific' treatment of facts, accuracy and legality gave away to mass psychology. According to a State Council report for the year 2003, public security agencies handled 2.341 million criminal cases; of this total, 57,505 cases related to activity jeopardizing public security; 184,018 cases involved the violation of the personal and democratic rights of citizens; and 278,969 cases involved property crime. In the newly recognized area of 'extended detention', the cases involved 25,736 people, with 259 cases of illegal detention, 29 cases involving illegal search, 52 cases concerning confession under torture, and 32 relating to the abuse of prisoners or detainees (Keith and Li 2006: 143). But why such heavy penalties? It is all in the name of social order and stability – for social control. The 1999 national plan, for example, called for a 'comprehensive management of public order' directed to pre-empt and fight crime. It was organized by an extensive network connecting families, public security agencies, educational institutions, street committees and so on, to form a social force as a public security 'system' to manage public order (Keith and Li 2006: 14).

Criminal law is, in fact, not so much for dealing with the criminals as such, but rather is rather concerned with how to categorize criminals and their crimes and who has the power to do so. As mentioned earlier, the policy of 'strike hard' has been a persistent feature of the criminal justice system since 1983 (Deng 1984a: 238–9). For the present authorities, the question now is not whether to continue this policy or not, but whom to strike, and how to limit the 'strike' to the most heinous and serious crimes. It is estimated that the number of executions in China could drop by 30 per cent as a result of a recent review of all death sentences by the Supreme Peoples' Court (SPC) (Trevaskes 2007: 2). Based on Trevaskes' study, since early 2007 a fascinating debate about the death penalty has been unfolding at the highest levels of politics in China and is currently being played out in the state print media and on the Internet. It is a debate instigated by Chief Justice Xiao Yang, president of the SPC, aimed at limiting the death penalty to all but the most heinous criminals by emphasizing the principle of leniency as an alternative to the more politically popular principle of severity. In 1983 provincial courts were delegated the responsibility for reviewing and approving death sentences handed down by interior courts. This decision, coupled with the overzealous use of the policy of a 'severity and swiftness' against serious crime, is the key reason for the persistently high number of executions in China.

The decision to return the authority to review and approve all death sentences to the SPC from 1 January 2007 has given human rights and China law specialists reason for optimism and the number of executions should drop as a consequence. The National People's Congress (NPC) called the decision the most important reform of capital punishment in China in more than two decades. However, this decision has not changed the official 'strike hard' policy, as manifested by the Communist Party's leading politico-legal bureaucrat, Luo Gan, who made it clear in December 2006 and again in February 2007, that the CCP would continue to maintain the policy.

Unchecked Power as a Source of Instability

Stability has been used to justify the structure of power totality. However, it is clear that real stability lies in an independent power check mechanism and that, to the contrary, power totality threatens the long-term interests of the people and the nation. This is because the real instability lies in the fundamental contradiction inherent in a concentration of power in the system. State officials at every level should abandon their supralegal power; otherwise there can be no real reform or long-term stability in China.

Today, in the name of stability, people have been unfairly punished on the one hand, and state power strengthened on the other. However, it is the legal privilege and power structure, not the people, which present the greatest threat to the country's long-term interest and development. It would be unfortunate if the stability debate were to become yet another excuse to preserve the old power structure. The lesson learnt from the Cultural Revolution is that it was the concentration of power that was the biggest cause of instability. In short, the more total the political control is, the more unpredictable the state of affairs becomes. For example, when a new category of 'economic crime' emerged following social unrest in 1984–85, vice rings began to develop in the cities of the eastern seaboard, and the murder and crime rates rose sharply between 1982 and 1985. This crime surge invariably involved Party and state officials who abused their positions of authority to profit from the economic crimes. These and other developments suggested that Chinese society was becoming increasingly corrupt and amoral, importing many of the evils traditionally associated with the capitalist West (Derbyshire 1987: 56).

Must people sacrifice their basic rights for stability? This study has argued that the real instability lies in the fundamental contradiction that lies at heart of the system when under power totality and that we should subject state officials at every level to democratic scrutiny and the rule of law, otherwise there can be no real reform or long-term stability in the country. Our focus must be on the abuse of power by officials, and not on a 'witch hunt' against the people, as happened during the Cultural Revolution.

Furthermore, it is important that people must have a claim on the ruling party as their sovereign through the authority of law. The Constitution of the PRC grants the Chinese people this authority of sovereign power. This means that people should have the legal protection to choose their leaders and representatives in the government. They should have the legal right to criticize the ruling organization as they see fit, not as the rulers see fit; and have the authority to grant or take away the legitimacy of state administrators and the ruling individuals or parties. However, in reality, this concept of legitimacy, if used under a system of power totality, would mean stripping the people of this authority and even making it illegal for the people to exercise this authority.

Power Needs Check outside Its Own Authority

It is clear that a ruler's own authority is insufficient to curb the problem of power abuse, for the reason that any power needs regulation by separate authorities. This view can be supported by the fact that one is limited in one's own capacity for self-rectification of power abuse. Here are some examples of this limitation.

Top Leaders Cannot Rectify Power Abuse

It is apparent that even Mao could not stop the abuse of power by the Gang of Four – a product of the system of total power concentration. It was recorded that six months after the trial of the Gang of Four:

> [O]n 29 July 1981, the CPC Central Committee published an authoritative official verdict on Mao Zedong and the last twenty years of his life – the 'Resolution on Certain Questions in the History of Our Party since the Founding of the People's Republic'. In this document, Mao's contribution to the building of the CPC and PLA, to victory in the liberation war and the consequent creation of the People's Republic, and the safeguarding of the nation's independence, unity and security was recognized and praised. He was, however, criticized for becoming tyrannical and obsessed with a misguided leftist line during the last twenty years of his life, culminating in the disastrous 'Cultural Revolution'. Mao was thus 'de-deified' and slavish worship of his thought and writings was now frowned upon. Instead Mao's was seen to be just one of the many contributions to the creation and development of Chinese communist thinking, in what became a new vogue for eclecticism and collectivism. (Derbyshire 1987: 48)

Deng, too, proved unable to rectify his own abuse of power. Although Deng resolved to create a new collective form of Party leadership; to impose a greater separation between the Party, state and military spheres, following their convergence during the Cultural Revolution, and to provide the series of checks and balances that would prevent the concentration of power in the hands of any single body or person, his own departure from 'democratic centralism' was complete when he forced the CPC's General-Secretary Hu Yaobang to resign for his liberal views, together with a number of other freethinkers in the Party. In his words, 'If you are a member of the Chinese Communist Party, you have to accept Party orders.' Deng's role in the Tiananmen Incident is indisputable. It is therefore evident that the concentration of power in the hands of any single body or person cannot be rectified by the very same entity, and that series of checks and balances independent of the power and the Party are needed to prevent the power abuse.

Party Corruption

In the campaign against 'economic crime' it was found that corruption among Party and government officials was widespread:

> [B]y December 1985 a government investigation had found that more than 67,000 party and government officials had been involved in illegal businesses and corrupt practices. The most spectacular included a £53,000,000 smuggling operation in Fujian province and a $1.5 billion import-export embezzlement racket set up by party officials in the free-trade zone of Hainan Island between January 1984 and May 1985. (Derbyshire 1987: 56, footnote)
>
> […]
>
> Particularly notorious in this respect were the families of the veteran Politburo members Marshal Ye Jianying and Peng Zhen, whose daughter was under suspicion for 'economic crimes'. However, even Deng Xiaoping and Prime Minister Zhao Ziyang have been known to have used their influence to advance the careers of their children and close relatives, arranging scholarships abroad and supporting their rapid promotion to high academic and State administration posts. Such favouritism towards family or clan members formed an essential part of the Chinese mandarin tradition. (Derbyshire 1987: 60)

This involved Party and state personnel who became involved in vast black-marketeering, fraud and embezzlement rings as they began to use authority and their ability to grant or withhold licences to line their own pockets and to keep ahead of artisan and peasant farming neighbours in China's great new economic race (Derbyshire 1987: 56, footnote).

There are no grounds for a Marxist state to contradict democratic values and oppose its people. However, a supralegal power with the power of veto over elections, with control of the media and the ability to carry out arbitrary dismissals and arrests, has positioned itself beyond the law and thus loses its mandate and legitimacy to rule. The four cardinal principles become meaningless if this problem is not rectified. The power to veto the result of an election is an example of arbitrary conduct violating democratic values and the constitutional rights of the Party members and the masses. In a study, it was found that:

> Although the new party members, with a slow shift to more democratic and secret balloting systems for leadership posts, served to break up old patronage networks, the party retains the power to veto the elections … Shaanxi province pioneered the switch to more open party electoral systems when, in November

> 1984, the new provincial first Party Secretary was chosen from a list of thirteen and elected by a secret ballot of three hundred county and provincial party officials. The CPC Central Committee retained, however, the power of veto during this election. In Jiangxi, the first ever female provincial first Party Secretary, Wan Shaofen (53), was also appointed during this period. (Derbyshire 1987: 55, footnote)

Determining Power Abuse

How can we determine if the power is being abused or monopolized? There are some clear indicators, that show that a 'change of colour' has taken place, where power intended to be exerted 'for' the people has become power exerted 'against' the people:

1. where opinions and criticism are systematically suppressed;
2. where the idea of democratic values is feared and not accepted;
3. where people's grievances are unresolved and their complaints ignored;
4. where people are have no role in decision-making;
5. where the 'two faces' of the law reveal inequality before the law;
6. where equality before the law fails in practice, i.e. where harsh penalties are meted out to the people, but state officials found guilty of corruption are given only light punishment;
7. where the rhetoric of legal protection for all fails to match the reality;
8. where there are 'two bosses' in law, and 'the rule of men' prevails;
9. where the legal system is financially and politically controlled by the ruling interest;
10. where the rulers have supralegal privileges.

In many cases, the word 'democracy' is perceived to be as bad as 'bourgeois liberalism' (Deng 1981: 55). 'Black and white' judgments persists, especially, among the middle ranks of local state officials. Xue explains: 'They have hardly been educated or have not seen any overseas or developed countries. … They are very black and white.' (SBS interview with Xue, 2007). There are also those 'who are hostile to democracy and regard it as a great scourge that must be fiercely suppressed' (W. He 2004, May). This happened as a result of a campaign against Western 'spiritual pollution', equating democratic values with decadent bourgeois ideologies. This only confirms that, without power check, state power under a single authority can easily deny the people's right to select, criticize and oppose the state officials who are supposed to represent the people's interest for the common good.

It is clear that corruption is both the end-product of the structure of power totality that shelters the corrupt officials from legal sanctions and the main source of the state's instability and public discontent. Surveys suggested that people see corruption as the nation's top priority. According to a survey on one of China's largest news websites, asking, 'What issues in the upcoming NPC and CPPCC sessions attract you most?' the overwhelming concern of the public was the issue of anti-corruption. 'Anti-corruption is the top concern for some 83 per cent of those who took part in the survey' (*The Beijing Times* in Gerard 2004).

Corrupt Public Officials Erode Public Ownership

The greatest challenge in combating corruption comes from the local Chinese state officials and government who typically resist the laws established by the Constitution for their own benefit (Peerenboom 2002: 280–342). Often it is such government officials who determine who should be charged with criminal offences, who is undermining state security and who is engaged in terrorist activity (Peerenboom 2002: 280–342). It is the authority of such state officials not the authority of the law that is the final judge. These state officials who violate the law must be challenged expeditiously; otherwise their power will inevitably erode the very foundation of the socialist state. The laws themselves are important as legal norms, but the legal authority and binding measures to remove these corrupt officials are still more important, for as long as these careerists are in power, the law can only be toothless or become even more inimical to the interests of the very people it claims to protect. It is the matter of whose hands the law falls into that ultimately decides the final verdict.

Article 12 of the PRC Constitution (2004), under the heading 'Protection of Socialist Public Property', states that:

1. Socialist public property is sacred and inviolable;
2. The state protects socialist public property. Appropriation or damage of state or collective property by any organization or individual by whatever means is prohibited.

However, the evidence of people suing the state shows the danger of state officials, by virtue of their public office, who control and profit from the sale of public property, thus violating the principle of public ownership in the Constitution. They act as if the land were their private property, and are able to make commercial transactions as the owner of the property, without the community's consent, which no individuals or state officials in any capitalist state could do so freely. This happens in a socialist system because the decision-making power is concentrated in the state officials' hands, not in the law itself. Under such circumstances the concept of public ownership ceases to have any relevance.

Djilas once warned us that the New Class of socialist regime emerging from state executives who possess 'legally' both public and private properties is more powerful than the private ownership in the capitalist society, for their control over state assets is boundless and total, with the maximum benefit accruing to the 'elite' class under such a system. He observed that the ruling party elite enjoyed privileges over the masses in the former communist countries – alienating the worker and peasant classes from the owning 'privilegentsia in the press of the country' (Djilas 1966: 9).

Political privilege spilled over into the economic field as well. As Marx had written, 'the bureaucracy possesses the state as private property' and this was extended to the state-owned production. In this way, public ownership is eroded by the 'rule of man'. The new class, with its power over public property, is more dangerous than if it were placed in a free market economy, for the benefit this official position can bring, in the name of 'the people', is limitless. It can access and possess commodities that one would not be able to obtain normally in the market economy.

Jones and Mill once noted that 'in Oriental society the officials enjoyed advantages of income which in the West accrued to the private owners of land and capital' (Draper 1978: 636, vol. 1). If a ruling class is classified as the main beneficiary of economic privilege, as a result of the corresponding political privilege of one's official office, this ruling class must be challenged by the rule of law.

Legitimacy Cannot Justify Power Totality

Potter argues that a monopoly on power means that a regime can both use the law to legitimize itself and yet at the same time is not limited by adherence to that law. He argues that, by relying on the socialist legal system as a source of legitimacy, the Chinese regime strengthens its ability to justify specific actions by reference to law. However, the use of law as legal symbolism alone has also challenged the Party's monopoly on political power, as illustrated during the 1989 Tiananmen Incident, and has presented dangers to the regime. In Potter's words:

> In order to avoid having its authority challenged by means of the very principles from which it seeks to derive legitimacy, the regime has attempted to ensure that the legal system remains subservient to the political needs of the Party … It has tried to make certain that popular notion about law do not overreach its own view that law should be merely an instrument of rule rather than a set of generally applicable principles that regulate the state as well as the people it governs … the regime can claim legitimacy based on its adherence to the rule of law without its power being limited by such adherence. (Potter 1991, 1994: 325)

Potter sees that there is no law at all if there is no equality before the law. He compares the official and popular ideas about legal relationships, as part of Chinese legal culture, and found that the regime's claim on legal formalism 'ignores substantive aspects of justice in the context of political conflict', and that the prosecutions of former Red Guards demonstrated the injustice of these proceedings despite their reliance on formal criminal procedure, 'because often the circumstances of the accused differ from those of the accuser by little more than serendipity'. He uses the well-known case of Wei Jingsheng, a dissident jailed for his criticism of the regime, to illustrate how injustices can be perpetrated even though cases rely on formal criminal procedures; in this instance because Wei was denied an effective opportunity to defend himself. 'Similarly, the declaration of martial law in Beijing in 1989 was widely criticized as unjust because the procedure used precluded opposition either to the declaration or to its enforcement' (Potter 1991, 1994: 357).

Potter's article highlights the continuing contradiction between the doctrine of legal equality and the regime's political inequality, and the continuing monopoly of political authority that this entails. This has become a major concern in the legal reforms. Potter's argument calls for a substantive fairness in the law, between the accuser and accused, and between state doctrines on legal reform and substantive legal equality.

Conclusion

In this chapter I have examined some basic concepts of Marxism and demonstrated how these concepts have been abused by various legality theories to justify the power totality. However, I have also shown that this abuse of Marxist theory has been carried out for the purpose of abusing power. Marx never endorsed any kind of power totality at the expense of people's liberty and democratic values. It is in fact a betrayal of the original intent of the Marxist revolution, and an unbroken continuation of the old feudal power structure. Evidence shows that people are still unprotected and that power totality within the ruling party has brought about widespread corruption.

The rule of law in recent years has not seriously challenged this power totality, owing to lack of independence or a legally binding authority. This must change, and such change must be brought about by means of the law. But why, exactly, should we consider law as the solution? In Chapter 4 I will address this question and provide rationales for using law and legal philosophy to tackle the problem of power totality.

Chapter 4
Law as Part of the Solution

Introduction

In the previous chapters, we have established that a power totality is problematic and undesirable, and that it is a serious abuse of Marx's original vision for a workers' state. It is therefore necessary to reject this form of power, and reconfirm some of the basic principles in the use of state power as a public property, rather than an exclusive right of a few who stand outside and above the law. In this chapter, I will argue that there are several grounds on which to argue why law can be part of a remedy for curbing power abuse. First, the law should recognize that power should be checked as a principle. Secondly, the law has an instrumental role in power check. Thirdly, as legal history shows, the law has provided a vital forum for rejecting power totality and bringing the monarch under the law (as with the Magna Carta). I go on to stress, once more, the importance of the authority of law as well as of an independent judiciary. This discussion leads on to a discussion of the prospects of separating the judiciary from the government, and separating the government from the Party. This change will no doubt require the commitment and the willingness of the ruling party to the principle of power check on one hand, and the legal protection of people's rights on the other. The limit of law will depend on this commitment to the power check principles, and also on the changing concept of authority as the power is to be transferred from one exclusive group to the people through their representatives. The law should facilitate this transition of power through the Constitution.

This chapter will establish power check as a principle, and show how, in legal history, law has rejected power totality. It will discuss the importance of the authority of law by means of an independent judiciary, and explain the necessity to gain this independence of jurisdiction by separating it from the state power and government. It argues that law is desirable and how it can function in different state models.

Progress and Problems

China has made remarkable progress in recent years. In terms of economic growth, China is meeting or exceeding expectations on most measures – given the high correlation between wealth and income as an indicator of human well-being. 'China outperforms the average country in its income class on most major indicators of human right and well-being, with the exception of civil and political rights'

(Peerenboom 2006: 192). China has also made impressive progress in improving its legal system in a short time, having restarted from scratch in 1978. 'As of 2002, China's legal system ranked in the 51st percentile on the World Bank's rule of law index, having risen from the 32nd percentile in 1996' (Peerenboom 2006: 195). Progress is being made on other fronts as well. On the anti-corruption front, for example, it was recorded in *The Beijing Times*, that

> The central government's determination to fight against corruption can be seen in the punishment of thirteen ministerial-level officials for corruption, including the former Vice-Governor of Anhui Province, Wang Huaizhong, and the former Minister of Land and Resources, Tian Fengshan, throughout 2003. Professor Wu Jiang from the National School of Administration said the central authorities have done 'efficient and effective' work over the past year, for example, in fighting SARS, making efforts to curb unemployment, increasing farmers' income and realizing an annual economic growth rate of 9.1 per cent. (*The Beijing Times* in Gerard 2004)

There are problems, however, which put the legal reforms in serious jeopardy. The problems cover the three elements discussed in Chapter 1 of this study, namely: the protection of people; the persistence of total power structure (as a feudal legacy); and limited power checks on state officials. There are relevant laws with regard to these issues in the Chinese legislature, such as the Law of the PRC on Public Security Administration Punishments (2005); Land Administration Law of the PRC (2004); The Organic Law of the People's Courts of the PRC (2006); and Decision of the Standing Committee of the NPC on ratifying the UN Convention against Corruption (2005). However, these laws do not reflect the reality in many ways. The contradiction between the proclaimed principles and the reality has been obvious. The problems are also interrelated. The failure to protect people is a result of the existing total power structure, in which corrupt officials have a firm control over all legal matters. In this situation, law has no authority over the power holders, and the corrupt state officials remain outside the law. Furthermore, these officials, mostly belonging to the lower-middle ranks of the local government offices, are still in a position to manipulate the law to their own advantage, as they did during the Cultural Revolution, but in a different form. So the old power structure has persisted and, in most instances, flourishes. It should also be noted that the police and procurators, as part of the law-keeping force, have played an arbitrary role in many cases. The use of threats, thugs and torture to abuse vulnerable targets were all too familiar in the old feudal society as part of its legal culture. Such tactics have changed. Instead of dismissing the law, as in the 1960s, the power holders and lawbreakers are now *behind* the law, using law against law and against innocent people. Even those lawyers who are advocates for people's legal rights cannot escape unlawful prosecution.

Power Check as a Principle

Power check as a principle is based on two basic concepts: one is the doctrine of the separation of powers under public scrutiny, and the other is the mutual and systematic constraint of all public power by law. These two concepts will be explained below.

Doctrine of the Separation of Powers

The concept of Separation of Powers dates back as far as ancient Greece. The concepts were refined by contemporaries of the original framers, and those refinements influenced the establishment of the three branches in the Constitution. Aristotle favoured a mixed government composed of monarchy, aristocracy and democracy, seeing none as ideal, but arguing that a mix of the three would combine the best aspects of each. In his *Oceana* (1656), James Harrington brought these ideas up to date and proposed systems based on the separation of power. John Locke, in the second treatise of his *Civil Government* (1690, 1924), separated the powers into an executive and a legislature. Montesquieu's *Spirit of the Laws* (1748) expanded on Locke, adding a judiciary.

The French Revolution was a response of the populous to the extreme case of an absolute monarch who combined unlimited power in all three domains, namely: the power to make laws; the authority to exercise them at his pleasure; and a state constitution that granted him this unlimited power. In such a case, the power holder is not legally answerable for the legality or morality of his decrees, nor is he bound by procedures, or any other kinds of limitations or requirements in exercising his powers. In this sense, whatever he decrees is constitutionally valid. The Constitution aims to rule out this extreme case of power monopoly, by adopting not only a separation of those powers but making rules that impose limits on those powers. Often these limitations are in the form of individual and group rights against government – rights such as free expression, free association, equality and due process of law. Based on the principle of power separation, the law can check power by determining the scope of authority, the mechanisms used in exercising the relevant power (such as procedural requirements governing the manner or form of legislation) and civil rights. In the feudalist model, where power is concentrated in one entity, there is no 'legality' because the rules defining the ruler's authority impose no such limits. By limiting the authority to legislate, to implement, or to adjudicate, on the basis of law, which exceeds the scope of his legislative power, the law thus limits the total power or power monopoly in one entity. Locke sees that a political power is:

> a right of making laws, with penalties of death, and consequently all less penalties for the regulating and preserving of property, and of employing the force of the community in the execution of such laws, and in the defence of the

> commonwealth from foreign injury, and all this only for the public good. (Locke 1690 in Carpenter 1999: 118)

Clearly, if such a political power is concentrated in one authority, with the right of making laws and execution of such laws, and with the control of all penalties at the expense of preserving private properties and civil rights, the power will not be checked effectively by the rule of law.

Locke (1632–1704) noted the temptations to corruption that exist where 'the same persons who have the powers of making laws to have also in their hands the power to execute them'. Locke's views were part of a growing English radical tradition, but it was the French philosopher Baron de Montesquieu (1689–1755) who articulated the fundamentals of the separation doctrine as a result of visiting England in 1729–31.

Mutual and Institutional Power Check

Montesquieu, whose influence with the American founders was great, believed that state power must be checked by a separate judiciary as principle. In his words,

> When the legislative and executive powers are united in the same person, or in the same body of magistrates, there can be no liberty because apprehensions may arise, lest the same monarch or senate should enact tyrannical laws, to execute them in a tyrannical manner.
>
> Again, there is no liberty, if the judiciary power be not separated from the legislative and executive. Were it joined with the legislative, the life and liberty of the subject would be exposed to arbitrary control; for the judge would be then the legislator. Were it joined to the executive power, the judge might behave with violence and oppression. (Montesquieu 1748 in Rosen and Wolff 1999: 117)

In his *The Spirit of Laws* (1748) Montesquieu considered that English liberty was preserved by the country's institutional arrangements. He saw not only the separation of power between the three main branches of English government, but within them also – the decision-sharing power of judges with juries, or the separation of the monarch and Parliament within the legislative process.

Locke's and Montesquieu's ideas found a practical expression in the American Revolution in the 1780s. Motivated by a desire to make impossible the abuses of power they saw as emerging from the England of George III, the framers of the Constitution of the United States adopted and expanded the separation of powers doctrine. To help ensure the preservation of liberty, the three branches of government were both separated and balanced. Each had separate personnel and there were separate elections for the executive and legislature. Each had specific powers and some form of veto over the other. The power of one branch to intervene in another through veto, ratification of appointments, impeachment, judicial review of legislation by the Supreme Court (its ability to strike down legislation or regulations deemed unconstitutional) and so forth, strengthened the separation of powers concept, even though this inevitably involved each branch in the affairs of another and to some extent actually gave some of the powers of one branch to another (Spindler 2000).

Instrumental Role of Law

Law, many argue, is an instrument of domination, rather than an instrument to challenge power domination. In this instrumentalist view, the Critical Legal scholars (CLS) argue that law in capitalist societies is neither as neutral nor as autonomous as it appears to be. This is because the interests of the dominant classes are better protected and supported by the legal system, which puts the powerless in a disadvantaged position in legal disputes (Hunter, Ingleby and Johnstone 1995: 47). Furthermore, the definition of the 'rule of law' entails many concepts. The standard comparison is 'between the rule of law and the rule of men, between the supposedly stable, impartial, general, measured and ordered nature of the former, and the idiosyncratic, arbitrary or capricious nature of the latter' (Hunter et al. 1995: 46).

CLS offers three interpretations of the 'rule of law': law and order, the 'inner morality' of law, and formal equality before the law. It also compared this definition with an American one. The US legal philosopher Lon Fuller's view of the rule of law, for example, is in terms of the *obligations* of lawmakers and law enforcers, rather than their *powers* to ensure social order.

Others see law as an instrument of justification, for example, in the case of the Negro slaves, where legal documentation was used in the court to justify the legitimacy of the slave trade. As Genovese argues, without denying an ethical dimension to state power in all its normal managerial functions, state power represents an attempt to monopolize and legitimize this domination in its quest to maintain its power. In this process, law has itself become a social force, with its undeniable influence in shaping the class relations of which it is an instrument of domination. The legal order, ideas and institutions influence the wider social order and system of state rule. Moreover, law is used to present the state as the expression of the people, that 'the fashionable relegation of law to the rank of a super-structural and derivative phenomenon obscures the degree of autonomy it creates for itself' and 'for no class in the modern Western world could rule for long without some ability to present itself as the guardian of the interests and sentiments of those being ruled' (Genovese in Beirne and Quinney 1982: 279).

Foucault, on the other hand, sees law from a different perspective, as the exercise of power within modern societies, thus equating law with violence. His view may be summarized thus:

1. Law will always go together with the exercise of violence and physical repression, so to say that law is against terror is false.
2. In modern societies, the exercise of power is based much less on overt violence and repression than on subtler mechanisms with violence implicit.
3. The new methods of power rest not on right but on technique; not on law but on normalization; not on punishment but on control.

Following Foucault, power is defined by Castel in these words: 'the exercise of power involves a passage from authority-coercion to manipulation-persuasion'. The role of the state is seen as a repressive apparatus (army, police, judicial system, etc.) as the means of exercising physical violence. This negative view of state and law, elaborated by Poulantzas, suggests that there is ideological–symbolic manipulation, the organization of consent, and the internalization of repression (Genovese in Beirne and Quinney 1982: 189).

Power Check and the Role of Law

The state can transgress law-rules of its own making by acting without reference to the law, but also by acting directly against it. Poulantzas argues that each juridical system allows the 'Power-State' to disregard its own laws, in the name of the higher interests of the state – that 'state illegality is always inscribed in the legality which it institutes'. 'Thus, Stalinism,' he goes on to state, 'and the totalitarian aspects of power in the East are not principally due to violations of socialist legality' and that 'it is a question here not merely of oversights or blind-spots arising out of the ideological operation of concealment underlying the legal order, but of express devices that allow the law to be breached.' He is correct in pointing out the fact that a state that violates its own law is no less part of the structural functioning of the state, because the state-institutional structure is always organized in such a way that both the state and the dominant classes operate at once in accordance with the law and against the law. However, law is not all purely negative because law is something other than law. And even in its repressive role, law involves a positive aspect: it dictates positive obligations (Poulantzas 1978: 76–92). It is this positive obligation that we shall focus on when discussing the need for power check by law later in this study.

E.P. Thompson has greater faith in the rule of law. He once hailed governance by law as a human great achievement, beside court cases and legal rules. In his words, 'what is remarkable is not that the laws were bent but the fact that there was, anywhere in the eighteenth century, a rule of law at all' (Thompson 1975: 258–69). He even concedes that the origin of rights and wrongs of law may have coexisted between the rule of law and Marxism, through different perspectives. To him, law is an instrument of both the ruling class and the ruled. His acknowledges this in these words:

> The same conclusion may be reached through a different adjustment of perspective, which may coexist with some of the same arguments. This flourishes in the form of a sophisticated, but (ultimately) highly schematic Marxism, which, to our surprise, seems to spring up in the footsteps of those of us in an older Marxist tradition. From his [Marx's] standpoint the law is, perhaps more clearly than any other cultural or institutional artifact, by definition a part of a 'superstructure' adopting itself to the necessities of an infrastructure of productive forces and productive relations. As such, it is clearly an instrument of the de facto ruling class: it both defines and defends these rulers' claims upon resources and labour-power … Hence the rule of law is only another mask of the rule of a class. The revolutionary can have no interest in law, unless as a phenomenon of ruling-class power and hypocrisy. (Thompson in Beirne and Quinney 1982: 130)

However, while Thompson confirms the class-bound nature and function of the law, he rejects Marxist ulterior reductionism and tries to modify its typology of superior and base structures. He argues that the law when considered as institution (the courts, procedures, etc.) and as personnel (the judges, the lawyers, etc.) may easily be assimilated to those of the ruling class. Institutions and personnel are not all that the law is about, however. The law may also be seen as ideology, or human relationships, or sanctioning actions to social norms. Law is a necessity: 'it is not possible to conceive of any complex society without law', and has its own logic, rules and procedures (Thompson in Beirne and Quinney 1982: 258–69).

What law provides, Thompson argues, is a forum where the ruled can actually fight for their rights by means of law. In his view, law is diverse enough to impose class power, and does not subordinate itself to the functional requirements of socio-economic interest groups. Law is more substantial than that. To extend Thompson's view, it may lead us to perceive that law is not only necessary in any complex society, but may also be used for human relationships and rights. It may sanction power abuse and limit the extent of monopoly of power by individuals or organizations. This concept of law as a forum is an important one, for without it, for instance, the monarch's concessions would not have been formalized in the case of Magna Carta (discussed below).

How, then, does class power fit into the law? The answer is a complex and contradictory one. Thompson sees that on the one hand, law does mediate class relations to the advantage of the rulers and can become an instrument by which rulers impose new laws to their even greater economical advantage. On the other hand, the law can inhibit the actions of the rulers and their arbitrary and extralegal power (such as direct unmediated force, arbitrary imprisonment, the use of troops against the crowd, torture, etc.). Law can be mystifying to the people, and may disguise the true realities of power, but, at the same time, it may curb that power and check its intrusions (Thompson in Beirne and Quinney 1982: 258–69).

Law Rejects Power Totality – English Legal History

As already indicated, the importance of the law as a platform for the rejection of power totality can be seen, for example, in the legal history of England. Certain historical factors facilitated this development, principally the opposition to the monarch's total power led by those at the middle level of society between the King and the commoners who had both the economic and military means for the challenge, and the tradition of an independent judiciary tradition which was able to provide a legal forum to achieve this.

The Magna Carta of 1215 signifies the end of power totality headed by the King of England. Although most of the document's clauses deal with specific grievances rather than with general principles of law, its crucial significance lies in its subjection of the monarch to the law, as a result of the growing opposition of barons through their representatives in the Parliament. Scope for abuse in the feudal system at the time was great and had been the subject of complaint long before King John came to the throne. Abuses were aggravated by the difficulty of obtaining redress for them. Not surprisingly in the Magna Carta, about two-thirds of the clauses are concerned with matters such as these and with the misuse of power by royal officials. The provision of the means for obtaining a fair hearing of complaints achieved corresponding importance, not only against the King and his agents but also against lesser feudal lords. (By contrast, it is worth reminding ourselves, the Chinese emperors were not subjected to such laws and there was no sizable opposition or legal forum from which to challenge the power totalized in the ruler.)

The English judiciary tradition also saw the Parliament responding to public pressure to adopt new laws, as in the case the Habeas Corpus Act (1679). The significance of Habeas Corpus may be seen to reconfirm the authority of law in the governance of the country. Although the key issue the Act dealt with was specific (on detention), the general concept of a critical right was established as a legal consequence of this Act, which was later written into the Constitution for the United States (Habeas Corpus Act 1679).

The legal history of England during the early seventeenth century was a good example of the Parliament challenging the total power of the King. In 1628 the Third Parliament met and presented a petition to King Charles I, which he accepted. The terms included that no person should be compelled to pay a loan or tax levied without the consent of Parliament; that no subject should be imprisoned without shown cause; and no person should be tried by martial law. When Charles exercised his arbitrary power to raise money illegally, and refused to surrender to the Commons the command of the militia, the Civil War (1642–48) broke out. The Parliamentary forces defeated the Royalist forces. Because Charles refused to recognize the authority of the court by which he was brought to trial, he was executed. 'The absolutist rule of James and Charles had bred militant opposition which passed over into civil war. There was to follow a unique interregnum in which a new type of government committed itself to an intensive programme of constitutional and legal reform' (Curzon 1979: 41). This challenge was made possible by the fact that those who opposed the King's total power – the propertied classes – had both economic and military means, just as their representatives in Parliament had considerable bargaining power and skills.

In the eighteenth century the law and the rhetoric of law enjoyed unusual pre-eminence in England. Royal absolutism was placed behind the norms of law, and immense efforts were made to project the image of a ruling class which was itself subject to the rule of law, and whose legitimacy rested upon the equity and universality of legal forms. The rulers played the games of power according to rules which suited them, but which they could not break or the whole game would be thrown away. Thompson argues that not only were the rulers inhibited by their own rules of law, but they also believed sufficiently in these rules and in the accompanying legal rhetoric to allow the law itself to be a genuine forum within which certain kinds of conflict could be decided. The ruled also accepted the rule of law as their right (Thompson in Beirne and Quinney 1982: 258–69).

Total Power and Power Check in China Today – Case Studies

Although the law can be a forum for power check, leading to an end of the total power structure, in reality in China the traditions of the old power structure still prevail, unchallenged by an independent judiciary or other independent authority. Evidence shows that the problem, identified in Chapter 1 of this study, has persisted, even after the end of the Cultural Revolution and after the official confirmation of the rule of law as state policy. This shows, first, that people's basic rights are not protected; and, secondly, that we need structural changes to limit the executives' power. The following cases are cited from studies undertaken by others. In each case, I present the relevant facts and then comment on the issues raised.

Case 1

In 2005 a migrant worker named Wang Binyu was quickly executed for the murder of his boss (as well of three of the latter's relatives who came to his aid). His motive was the unpaid wages that his boss had withheld for two years at a time when Wang's father urgently needed surgery for a leg fracture. Wang was also barred from entering his dormitory to sleep. (The factory boss relented and paid the 2004 salary but only after making large deductions for fees and boarding expenses. However, he refused to pay the 2005 wages until next year.) Some time after his death, when the story of his trial and execution, finally trickled out, there was a media and public outcry. For three weeks, accounts of the brutal treatment Wang had endured as a migrant worker, of his anguish and wasted life, rippled across China on the Internet and in the Chinese newspapers. But all this was suddenly silenced when online discussion was censored and news media coverage banned. (Yardley 2005b)[1]

Comment Here a lack of protection of citizens' basic rights coincided with the law's lack of authority and a low standard of conduct on the part of the court official. This can be demonstrated as follows:

- *Legal procedures eroded*: Wang's final appeal was rushed to court, his father was never notified, and his lawyer was forbidden from participating. 'All of you are on the same side!' the 28-year-old Wang shouted during the hearing, 'If you want to kill me, just kill me.'
- *Court officials lied*: Before the appeal, the Wang family gave a power of attorney to Mr Wu. But Wu said court officials had initially lied, telling him that the appeal was already over and then later refused to let him take the case. Instead, a lawyer approved by the court represented Wang. Meanwhile, the same judges who were hearing the appeal also concurrently handled a mandatory final review of the case. It meant that judges were reviewing their own ruling – a practice that legal experts say is not uncommon, and provides little real check on the use of the death penalty. 'An unjust procedure will undoubtedly lead to unjust results,' said Mr Wu.

The courts and the police took a tough line in the execution process, and hardliners in the Party and the governments are loath to restrict the power of the police and the courts in this matter. In October 2005, 'The People's Supreme Court announced that it would reverse a decision from the early 1980s that ceded the final review on many death penalty cases to provincial high courts … This shift meant that provincial courts could often operate without any oversight.' It was said that Deng Xiaoping ordered this move as he considered that courts were moving too slowly to crack down on crime. Under the new policy, however, the PSC will reclaim responsibility for reviewing all capital cases. As a result the execution rate could drop by as much as 30 per cent, according to the state news media, a reduction that could save thousands of lives. One solution Professor Y at Tsinghua University Law School offered is to require 'Unanimous consent among judicial panels making final reviews.' Professor He, on the other hand, argued that 'only deeper constitutional reform to establish a more independent judiciary, could remove the political pressures that can seep into many high-profile death cases' (Yardley 2005b).

1 All quotes taken from Yardley 2005a, 2005b and 2005c are courtesy of *The New York Times*, © [12 November and 21 December 2005] *The New York Times* all rights reserved. Used by permission and protected by the Copyright Laws of the United States. The printing, redistribution, or retransmission of the Material without express written permission is prohibited.

- *Officials' motive/role in the case*: The factory boss violated the law by refusing to pay wages that were years overdue, withholding them for another year, and deducting large sums from the wage as fees, without any legal penalty. The local officials were eager to execute Wang because a reversal of the death penalty could have harmed their careers.

The court officials in Ninxia lied to Wang's father in a crucial point. They told him to come and collect his son's unpaid salary, and after a long journey across two provinces he found that it was a lie. The lure of wages to get him there was to sign his son's death warrant. Illiterate, 'the father could only smudge the paper with his thumb' (Yardley 2005b).

- *Excessive rate of execution and no protection for defendants*: Wang's case indicated 'how a system built for convictions has few safeguards or protections for a defendant facing death'. In Wang's father's words, 'It was wrong of him to kill people, but there was a cause.' Wang's anger reflected a deep public disgust with and resentment of corruption and inequality in the exercise of criminal law. People perceive the legal system as favouring the wealthy and well-connected. One person wrote at a Chinese website: 'Wang was forced to fight against those who exploit and tread on the poor. Why is the law always tough on the poor?' (Yardley 2005b)

The number of executions is a state secret due to the sensitivity of the issue globally. But a high-level delegate to the National People's Congress in 2004 publicly estimated that it was 'nearly 10,000' per annum. In 2004 Amnesty International documented at least 3,400 executions in China – of the 3,797 documented worldwide that year; the real number was probably much higher. 'Outside scholars have put the annual number as high as 15,000 [...] There is widespread suspicion, even within the government, that too many innocent people are sentenced to death' (Yardley 2005b).

Case 2

A desperate father wanted to sell his eyes in order to pay for his son's legal defence (there is flourishing black market in human organs in China). The son was wrongly accused and sentenced to life in prison. During the space of a year Xie had two trials and two appeals. The Anhui Province High Court overruled the guilty verdict, citing 'insufficient evidence' and 'certain unclear facts'. Nonetheless, the case was returned to Chaohu Intermediate Court for a new trial, which lasted only a few hours and resulted in another guilty verdict, regardless of the new discovery of flaws in the evidence. The High Court upheld the conviction. Xie petitioned the High Court officials, but without success (Yardley 2005a).

Comment Again a deficit in the authority of the law failed to protect people under a power structure where the judiciary has no independent standing to challenge corrupt officials and agents such as police and procurators, who, in the eye of the ordinary people, are traditionally the tool of powerful and repressive regimes. Also remarkable was the callous indifference of the Chaohu judge, who is reported as having joked: 'There's no hurry, after all, it's a life sentence.' He advised Xie to visit his son in prison regularly to 'really get to know him, make sure you are convinced he is innocent' (Yardley 2005a).

Once again the case demonstrates the insidious effects of the total power structure:

- *Legal procedures eroded*: The ruling in the Anhui court did not mean the case was over. Appellate courts in China rarely release defendants, even if ruling in their favour' (Yardley 2005a). Instead, the case was returned to Chaohu Intermediate Court for a new trial.
- *Flawed evidence*: The flawed evidence included a dubious shoe print and the fact that the victims never identified their attacker. Xie's lawyer discovered that the digital photo of the shoe print from the crime scene was dated a month after the attack.
- *Court's limited power*: 'Chinese law,' Yardley (2005a) writes, 'does not allow judges to throw out evidence or overturn convictions on the basis of police misconduct. More significantly, the High Court was reluctant to overturn any conviction because that might damage its relationships with the prosecutors and police, as well as with Communist Party leaders eager to be seen as cracking down on crime. One of the provincial officials listed on the ruling said, 'In China, the rules sometimes do not matter … If you go after legal justice, it might cause more harm to social stability' (Yardley 2005a).
- *Lawyers' limited power*: The court placed restrictions on Xie's lawyer. 'The judge intervened every time the lawyer was trying to say something important, he would just say, "hurry up and make it simple" […] They didn't put in rules of evidence. They didn't put in requirements that witnesses appear at trial. Lawyers weren't given the ability to really prepare a case. They kind of created the shell of an adversarial process, but they didn't create the guts of it,' says J. Hecht, deputy director of the China Law Centre at Yale University (Yardley 2005a).
- *Blatant police misconduct*: Two days after the attack, the police approached Xie, the father, and told him he was a suspect, and then demanded that Xie 'prove that he is innocent'. At the police station, investigators took Xie's fingerprints and pushed him into a bare cell, and later did the same to his son. In the interrogation room, a detective slammed a pistol on a table and threatened the son: 'If you don't confess, we will skin you alive.' The police had coerced the witnesses to give a false confession, and Xie recorded their testimony and handed the tape to the judge. The police

also coerced a confession from the son, by beating him 'with sticks and [keeping] him awake for seven days'. He confessed to end the torment. Xie tried to hire a private firm in Shanghai for an independent analysis of the evidence, but was told that this only works for the government. No witnesses were called and the judge did not give Xie's lawyer a chance to question the testimony. 'Chinese law requires that evidence be subjected to cross-examination, but legal analysts say this requirement is regularly overlooked' (Yardley 2005a).

- *Court in fear of police and prosecutors*: The case occurred at a time of widespread unease about crime in China. A murder spree by a university student in western China had sparked a nationwide manhunt and stoked public fears about crime. In Xie's town, investigators had to 'devote all their energy to solving the case, easing people's worries and maintaining social security and stability,' said the head of the public security bureau, on the local *Chaohu Daily* newspaper (Yardley 2005a).

Under circumstances such as these, it is very difficult for a defendant to get a fair trial. The Law has been unable to replace a system that guarantees convictions with one that guarantees the rights of the accused. Power holders believe that the law erodes power, not enhances it. In Xie's case, no one helped him. 'There must be one person in the Communist Party who is honest and who believes in justice,' Mr Xie said, 'If I can't even find one, then the Party is not going to last long.' Law reforms in 1996 extended a criminal defendant's right to counsel and sought to create a more impartial judiciary. And yet, still, the vast majority of cases adjudicated end with convictions (99.7 per cent of cases 770,947 adjudicated in 2004 ended in a conviction) (Yardley 2005a).

The following cases show how, under China's total power structure, the judge and the court are powerless to implement laws that are detrimental to the interests of government officials. In this way, written laws often serve the government and the police but not the people.

Case 3

In 2003 in a mundane case about seed prices, Judge Li, faced with a conflict between national and provincial law, ruled the provincial law invalid. Despite the fact that Judge Li had submitted a draft of her ruling to the court director, who in turn had forwarded it to a trial committee, and despite everyone having signed it off, Li was put under great pressure by the Provincial People's Congress to undertake self-criticism and her job was thrown into jeopardy. In 2004 Henan's High Court reheard the case and ruled exactly as Judge Li had, but with one difference: it criticized her for invalidating the provincial law (Yardley 2005c).

The case indicated the rising influence of legal reformers. Scholars and lawyers rallied to Judge Li's defence and saw her ruling as a test case in the battle for a more autonomous court system. A member of the Beijing Lawyers Association,

Xiao Taifu, for example, who petitioned the central government on Judge Li's behalf, said that: 'For the first time, a judge announced a local law or regulation was void. It was historic. For the legal process in China, it was a first, and it carried deep meaning.' The reaction to the ruling on the seed case proves how political influence remains deeply embedded in the legal system (Yardley 2005c).

Comment The interference of the Provincial Congress was not only unreasonable but also constituted a serious compromise of the court's integrity and independence, which should be granted unequivocally by the Constitution in such a way that this kind of obstacle cannot happen again. Mr He, the constitutional scholar, rose to Judge Li's defence in an open article. He argued that the seed case was one of the most important in the legal evolution of China because of the attention it focused on judicial independence: 'It may not be *Marbury v. Madison*,' Mr He said, 'but it is a very important case.' Without this independence, any legal reform will not achieve the task it is set. Judge Li had, as it turned out, stumbled upon the fundamental issue of the rule of law over the rule of man. If judges were supposed to refer conflicts in law for review by the Standing Committee of the National People's Congress, or by the various political-legal committees, local governments, and the police and procurators, what legal power would be left for the law? If judges are expected to follow the decisions made by all these sub-political and legal bureaucracies and their agencies and networks, why do we bother to have the thing called the rule of law at all (Yardley 2005c)?

This case is all about whether judicial independence can or cannot curb government power under the existing system. Often, it seems, the courts are simply used as tools to reinforce the state power. In the legal reforms, there are often unresolved issues of judicial independence, particularly the willingness of the governing party to permit an independent judiciary to administer the rule of law.

In many countries, a judge overruling a lower-level law would scarcely attract attention. But in China, 'the government, not a court, is the final arbiter of law'. The provincial legislators considered the ruling a judicial revolt and tried to crush it. 'An order by those in power has forced local leaders, none of whom dared to stand on principle, to sacrifice me,' wrote Judge Li. This is not just about Judge Li, but is about state resistance to any rule of law that does not endorse local interests or serve the power of local 'lords'. The position of the judges and the court in China are peculiar, in the sense that political considerations are deeply entrenched within the legal system and legal decision are open to various levels of political scrutiny (Yardley 2005c).

Other indicators in the case also show how the rule of law is obstructed owing to the structure of total power:

- *Inseparable power at work*: The case shows how political pressure infuses the legal process. A city official sent a letter from one company engaged in the seed dispute to Li's supervisor, with a warning instruction for the court: 'Please pay attention.' 'I felt they were making assumptions that I was already taking sides,' said Judge Li. A representative from one of the companies also approached the office of the director of the Luoyang court, and the director invited Li to meet him. 'I considered this very inappropriate, but I couldn't say so because of the director.' So she told the man to come to her office, but pretended to be stuck on a long telephone call until the man left.

The Provincial People's Congress also applied pressure, clearly seeing Judge Li's ruling 'as a naked challenge to the lawmaking authority of the People's Congress'. Provincial officials publicly described the ruling as 'a serious breach of law'. In an interview, the head of the legal office, Mr Mao, said that 'The authority of the National People's Congress system is not to be challenged.' 'Courts have no right in a verdict to say which law is invalid.' This reaction really stunned Judge Li, for she had studied Chinese law and top leaders' speeches. It is clearly stated in China's Law on Legislation that local laws that conflict with national laws should be abolished. She thought that including this point in her opinion was within her judicial purview. Neither her director or anyone on the trial committee seem to have realized the significance of her ruling at the time either; neither did they have any intention to challenge the political system (Yardley 2005c).

But it was Judge Li alone, not the court officials or the director who had also approved the decision, who faced the possibility of serious punishment. 'I felt persecuted. Everyone I talked to told me what I had done was wrong,' she recalled. She had to fight to restore her reputation, so she left for Beijing to seek help. She wrote a long letter in which she promised to 'undergo criticism and education' if she had erred. 'But if I'm right, I will protect my integrity and defend the integrity of the law, even if it means being like a moth that flies into a flame.' News of the affair reached the Supreme Court and then attracted the attention of the Chinese media and of scholars and lawyers pushing for legal reform.

Scholars organized a legal conference at an elite university in Beijing to debate the seed case and other issues about judicial autonomy. Perhaps this public attention, and the possible intervention on her behalf by the People's Supreme Court, saved Judge Li's job. In the summer of 2004 the Standing Committee of the central government announced a new review panel to mediate on the matter of conflicting laws. Some hailed the panel as the equivalent of a constitutional court, while others believe that the responsibility should be left to the courts. Nonetheless the inseparable structure of the power system has remained largely intact. The local bureaucratic network, as shown in this case, involving the legal office, the director, the Congress, and government officials, has remained the same – ready to bite its next victim (Yardley 2005c).

- *The status of the court*: Political pressure on judges is routine, as part of the state bureaucracy. This subservient status of the court system is apparent in this case. By comparison, the police under the Ministry of Public Security enjoy much higher status in the state structure. For example, nationally, the chief judge of the People's Supreme Court is not even a member of the central decision-making entity of the Party – the Politburo – whereas the head of the Ministry of Public Security is.

- *Judge under pressure*: 'I'm just an ordinary person, a female judge who tried to protect the law. Who is going to protect my rights?' wrote Judge Li. Yardley (2005c) notes: 'Judges often must answer to government officials as much as to the law. Political pressure is common, and private trial committees often dictate rulings.' The dispute over the seed case indicated that 'being a judge involved far more than simply interpreting laws'. Any judge who acts on conscience does so at a risk, as Judge Li reflected: 'When I look back on the cases I dealt with, I have no regrets.' She also learned that reality is quite different from what her legal education taught her; this is 'more like legal theory' – how things should be – 'but it did not teach us how it really worked in China.' Her idealistic belief that judges ruled independently was quickly dispelled. She still believes in the rule of law, but is more realistic about the confusing position judges are often put in. 'It is not that they do not know how to do cases professionally. It is just all these relationships to coordinate. And they also have to weigh consequences,' said Judge Li (Yardley 2005c).

The reality is that cases are heard by panels of judges, whose rulings are often reviewed by supervisors and, in major cases, by private trial committees of court officials. Although judges are responsible for rulings that carry their names, the decisions are actually made by others in the court. Where government officials or influential citizens complain about a ruling, a judge can nonetheless be punished, fined or even fired. As a result, some judges try to reduce the potential mistakes by taking on fewer cases (Yardley 2005c).

- *Pressure from behind the scenes*: Judges are appointed by the local people's congresses and the courts receive their budget from local governments. Moreover, the Party branches 'operate committees that can apply pressure and exert influence on a court behind the scenes'. For example, a presiding judge in the north-eastern city of Harbin told *The Workers' Daily* that government officials had overruled three different innocent verdicts and ordered the courts to convict a local businessman of fraud. The judge was later censured for publicizing the case (Yardley 2005c). On the other hand, the system also makes it easy for corrupt court officials to exploit their positions. For example, 'in April 2004, two vice directors of the Middle Court in Wuhan were sentenced to prison for selling verdicts in exchange for $500,000 in bribes. The directors paid judges to participate in the scheme' (Yardley 2005c).

Understandably the public are sceptical about judicial independence, given the poor quality of judges and judgments, and the perception that too many judges are corrupt or unqualified. Many believe that the court system must become more autonomous to eliminate corruption in the legal system. The point here is that it should be transparent who has made a decision and where to draw the line of accountability. The current system of inseparable power makes any demarcation of responsibility impossible. As Professor He argues: '[Y]ou can only have accountability if you have independence. Otherwise, it is never clear who made a decision' (Yardley 2005c).

Training, too, has a role to play. The National Judges College – the primary educational arm of the Supreme Court – receives roughly 10,000 judges every year for a month's professional training. Already the emphasis has shifted from political to impartial rulings. In the past, judges were taught to serve the interests of the Communist Party, but now 'we train them with a modern theory of law: that the courts are impartial; on the need for legal justice and of innocence until proven guilty,' said the president of the college, Huai Xiaofeng, 'We stress that during a trial, you cannot favour the government or the National People's Congress. In the past, they told them to emphasize the political qualities. Now, we tell them to emphasize the law and the facts' (Yardley 2005c).

The following two cases are further examples of how the law lacks authority to protect people's interests, and serves only the interests of the state and the police – that is, where the power resides.

Case 4

In this case peasants in Shiqiao, Hebei Province, badgered the court clerk to accept their application to sue the officials who had seized their prime farmland. For two years they tried everything under the law to have their case brought before the court. Even a written rejection would have been a positive thing, enabling them to appeal to a higher court. But their request was quickly returned in a plain envelope, unmarked, unprocessed and officially ignored. They met obstacles at every turn. 'The only party that used the courts successfully was the state-linked construction company. It won an injunction in March declaring the peasants' protests illegal.' This is despite the fact that the right to demonstrate and protest is part of the Constitution (Kahn 2005a).[2]

Courts often refuse to issue any verdict at all when people sue the government; or even fail to acknowledge that the legal complaints exist at ll. The procedure of 'registering a case' (*li-an* in Chinese) is 'so fraught with official meddling that for

2 All quotes taken from Kahn 2005a and 2005b are courtesy of *The New York Times*, © [21 September and 28 December 2005] *The New York Times* all rights reserved. Used by permission and protected by the Copyright Laws of the United States. The printing, redistribution, or retransmission of the Material without express written permission is prohibited.

many with complaints against the government, the judicial system is closed for business' (Kahn 2005a).

In 2004 the National People's Congress (NPC), the state's highest legislative body, passed China's first property rights law, which was heralded as the government's commitment to the rule of law. This gave some encouragement to the peasants in Shiqiao. They filmed a short documentary declaring their ancient right to the soil and recited those government policies that prevented the loss of farmland. Later, however, the peasants discovered that the court and law were working in favour of the powerful construction company and the government, which benefited from the company. The villagers were outraged that the court had acted so quickly to protect the company, after suppressing their own suit. Mr Li, the defendant, said, 'I discovered that the law is what they say, what they practise is power' – that there was a contradiction between the written law and reality (Kahn 2005a).

'The number of people wanting to sue the government is large and growing, but the number of people who succeed in filing cases against the government is miniscule. So you could say there is a gap between theory and practice,' comments Xiao Jianguo, a legal scholar at the People's University in Beijing who has studied the issue. Protests around the country over land seizures, pollution, corruption and abuse of power, are erupting, with 74,000 officially recorded incidents of mass unrest in 2004. This is the very core of the democratic nature of the rule of law, which faces its greatest challenge in the court procedures and, more importantly, in the independence of the court (Kahn 2005a).

Meanwhile, it was an uphill struggle all the way to court for the people from Shiqiao:

- *The heavy fee charge*: The court clerk, after consulting with his boss behind the scene, said that the court would take the case only if they paid a filing fee of $2,300, several times a farmer's annual per capita income. Nonetheless, eleven families contributed and the case was established (Kahn 2005a).
- *The deliberate delay*: Months passed with no trial date. The plaintiffs demanded explanations and were finally granted a meeting with the top local court official, Ms Chen.
- *The court has no power*: Ms Chen indicated that 'the court would like to see the case go to trial, but the matter was unfortunately too sensitive'. In the peasants' words, 'She told us *the court did not have the power to challenge the government.* It might be better for everyone if we withdrew the case. She said if we did, she would refund the fee' (Kahn 2005a). Mr Li, one of the leaders of the peasants, declined to withdraw and told her that 'the law is either a tool that can be used by the people, or it isn't. You can't offer it and then take it away.' Ms Chen quickly left the meeting room without notice. Meanwhile the new road was laid over farmers' vegetable plots, and high-rise buildings sprouted. The construction company did not wait on the court's decision (Kahn 2005a).

- *Physical confrontation*: The peasants' leaders were so frustrated by this setback that they 'planted themselves in front of bulldozers, harassed workers and generally disrupted construction'. This protest later developed into a tense standoff and a riot, whereupon the local authority dispatched the local police and paramilitary troops to stop the protest. The police confiscated cameras and an elderly man was trampled. Villagers turned unruly and began smashing windows and trying to overturn police cars. Fifteen local residents went to jail; three were still behind bars nine months later (Kahn 2005a).
- *Court on the powerful side*: The Binhai Construction Company filed its own civil lawsuit seeking an injunction against the leader Li's interference. This time the court acted promptly. 'Four days later, the court issued a peremptory ruling without trial. Li Yonglu's actions were declared illegal.' The local officials distributed copies of the ruling to everyone in the district, and the local Party boss read the text of the ruling over the village's loudspeakers. The court clearly acted in the interests of the local government.
- *The peasant leaders gave the law another try*: This time the peasants found a prominent lawyer named Zhou who often pursues difficult cases against the authorities. Zhou was of the view that the Binhai protest violated national land laws, which require State Council approval for any development of prime farmland, and that the peasants could sue Hebei Province for allowing the project to proceed. However, he did not expect this to happen: 'China's administrative law stipulates that cases against a local government must be filed first in its jurisdiction, where local party bosses hold sway. It can be appealed, but only after the local court rules or rejects the case.' It is the Party bosses, therefore, not the law, who make the ruling (Kahn 2005a).
- *Finally*: The procedural flaw and delay is obviously a strategy the court uses to avoid appeals. 'Courts legally must issue written rejection notices if they choose not to take the case. But to avoid appeals, court clerks often decline to take possession of legal papers. No rejection notice is needed if the case does not, in China's political-legal cosmos, formally exist.' So after all these struggles, in the Shiqiao land case, the disregarded and returned application was the only verdict the court could offer to the people of Shiqiao. It is no wonder that people have no faith in the judicial process when the law is susceptible to such manipulation (Kahn 2005a).

Comment It is evident that legal procedures play a crucial role in implementing the legal rights proclaimed in the laws. The court procedures, for example, are the necessary forum for unsettled disputes, an area where the court has often failed to protect people's rights, but has protected the government instead. 'It is not clear how many protests follow failed attempts to settle disputes in court. But lawyers say the judicial system bars its doors to so many contentious cases that it effectively forces people to take to the streets' (Kahn 2005a). Other conclusions that one might draw from this case include:

- *Inseparable power corruption network*: The District Government Construction Bureau is linked to the Binhai Construction Company, which was to build a road and housing on the farmland and instructed peasants to stay off their land. 'The controls actually provide a perverse incentive for local officials to seize and develop as much farmland as possible. Farmers need only be compensated for lost farm income, generally far below soaring real estate market values. Government-linked middlemen can make a fortune.' The district government offered a pitiful compensation, between $2,500 and $5,000 a *mu* (a sixth of an acre) even though the market value exceeded $35,000 a *mu*. 'Government agents were pocketing the difference' – a magnitude of seven times in profit for the corrupt public officials (Kahn 2005a).
  The unwarranted contradiction between the state and the people thus becomes a reality. State officials desperately hold on to their posts and privileges by limited elections, control over the court and lawyers, suppression of free speech, and denying public participation in law making – but at the same time, granting extensive discretional power to state officials.
- *Authority hired the thugs*: A government effort to quell a land protest in a nearby city, Dingzhou, captured attention all over China, shortly after the Shiqiao protest. 'Hundreds of hired thugs armed with hunting rifles and clubs forced villagers to give up land for a power station. Six farmers died and dozens were injured in a bloody crackdown captured by a farmer's video camera.' The result: 'The Communist Party boss in Dingzhou and 26 others went on trial for the killings in early December.' The use of such strong-arm methods by the local authorities and the police is a serious criminal offence but they remain untouched by law. This is a common practice in many parts of China (Kahn 2005a).

When China's top judge, Xiao Yang, inspected Hebei's courts following the Dinzhou incident, he told the state newspaper that 'the courts too often treated important cases as "hot potatoes" better left untouched, marginalizing the judicial system. "If the courts bow to the government every time, the people will have no faith in the judicial process," he warned' (Kahn 2005a).

Case 5

A steel mill worker in Henan Province, Mr Qin, falsely confessed to a rape and murder under torture and was sentenced to death. His life was only spared because the real killer turned himself in.

In this instance the police themselves clearly acted like thugs, without any concept of law or basic human rights. How can the state clear up such disgraceful behaviour in the police force? How can anyone trust the police as an agent of the law when they act like criminals? They 'wrenched Qin's arms high above his back, jammed his knees into a sharp metal frame, and kicked his gut whenever he fell asleep' (Kahn 2005b). They took Qin away for questioning at midnight from the steel plant where he worked. The police would not tell him why he was being detained. (They relied only on some children who recalled seeing him on the day of the murder.) After initial questioning, Qin was handcuffed and shackled, still unaware what he was being accused of. 'I kept asking them what this was all about, no one would tell me.' Then the detective, Shen, lied to Qin that they were investigating the theft of an alarm clock and Qin's fingerprints matched those found on the clock. Qin insisted he had not stolen it and the pressure intensified. The senior detective, Shen, organized 'four teams of two policemen each'. to interrogate Mr Qin in consecutive six-hour shifts, day and night, for three days. The questioning quickly turned to torture. 'It would take a superman to resist,' Qin recalled. Shen told Qin that the theft of the alarm clock proved that Qin had killed Ms Jia. And in the end Qin had to confess to a story whose every detail was fabricated by the police (Kahn 2005b).

In the eight months between his arrest and his trial Qin urged his family to disregard his so-called confession. 'Every word … is a joke. To this day, I have no idea what the victim looks like, and I certainly didn't know the colour of her pants' (Kahn 2005). 'In prison, Mr Qin tutored himself in criminal law. His letters cited passages that he felt would aid his defence. Article 38 of the Chinese Constitution forbids extracting confessions by torture and 'set-ups'. Article 46 of the 1996 Revised Criminal Procedure Law declares that 'oral confessions' are not sufficient grounds for conviction. Article 12 mandates that 'suspects must be presumed innocent until proven guilty' (Kahn 2005b).

But in this instance Detective Shen had the power to decide on Qin's guilt: 'I stake my 20 years of leadership experience as a guarantee,' Shen said to Qin's brother, 'If your brother did not commit this crime, then I will accept punishment' (he still remains free till this day) (Kahn 2005b).

When the trial opened in April 1999, 50 relatives and villagers went to Anyang to testify on Qin's behalf. But the three-judge panel ordered the trial to be closed to the public and excluded them from the courtroom. The prosecution brought no witnesses and the judges prevented Qin from contesting his coerced confession, Qin's lawyer argued that the prosecution's case, which depended wholly on the confession, was invalid. However, the trial was over before lunch, though the verdict came only six months later. Qin was guilty of rape and murder and would be executed. During two years on death row, among the 15 people in his cell, he saw a dozen cellmates escorted away in the early-morning hours and executed with a bullet to the back of the head. He was spared that fate not by his appeals, or by new DNA evidence, but simply by chance. A retired soldier named Yuan walked into another police station and told the officer on duty that he had raped, robbed and strangled 18 women, including Ms Jia, from whom he had stolen the clock (Kahn 2005b).

Comment There are several aspects of this case that cry out for a greater protection of people's basic rights and, most importantly, to a legal forum that can grant such rights by the authority of the law. This authority is not possible under the current structure. Change, therefore, is not only indispensable but also inevitable to keep the state power in check. Without this change, the nation will sink further into an arbitrary and corrupt rule of man, and will not follow the rule of law as set down in the Constitution. Case 5 raises several points that are important to the argument for a check on state power:

- *Nature of corruption*: Under the current inseparable structure of power, and also a top-down political system, the police, prosecutors and judges respond mostly to the sentiments and policies issued from above; as Mr Li said, 'they pay a much higher price for failing to maintain the appearance of social order than for torturing suspects'. 'The judicial system is set up to protect the authority of the government, it is not set up to protect the rights of suspects.' On death row Qin wrote to his family claiming, 'Our public security system is the product of a dictatorship. Police use dictatorial measures on anyone who resists them. Ordinary people have no way to defend themselves' (Kahn 2005b).
- *Inseparable power structure and motive make law a terror to people*: Qin's case showed how political motives and collusion among police, prosecutors and the courts could make the law a source of terror for people who lack the power or money to defend themselves. After the coerced confession, the court then handed down a death sentence. 'A panel of judges then convicted him and sentenced him to death' – without due legal processes (Kahn 2005b).
- *Proven innocent but not free to save face*: Qin's life is nothing compared with the career and reputation of the officials, police detective and the court, once the wrongful arrest, prosecution and conviction were made public. So the officials' response was to continue their arbitrary conduct, suppress the new information, and keep Qin on death row!
- *The power 'haven' must be exposed*: the power holders, the authorities in Linzhou, who were handling the case of the criminal Yuan, and those in Anyang, responsible for Qin's incarceration, had a secret deal among themselves; agreeing to keep the crucial part of Yuan's confession secret. Yuan would be prosecuted for 17 of the 18 murders, leaving Qin's conviction intact. 'Their attitude was that if my brother was released, 20 officials would suffer,' said Qin's elder brother, 'but if he was executed, only one person would suffer' (Kahn 2005b). This agreement held for more than a year while Qin continued to be held on death row. 'It came to light only after an official in Linzhou joked about the matter to a reporter for a national legal affairs publication. Although the reporter did not publish an article on the subject, he did alert authorities in the capital, who ordered an inquiry.' Even so, the result of Qin's case was disheartening and yet predictable: Mr Qin

has never been declared innocent of murder, because the authorities have refused to exonerate him fully. He was barred from talking about the matter with the news media or to petition higher authorities, while Shen has been promoted to a higher position in the police. 'They hope they can just make this disappear with no hard feelings and no problems for anyone involved,' Qin said. The police, it seems, have become a 'haven' for the criminal-minded like Shen who are able to exert their tyranny at will, without ever being caught by law because they are part of that law. Clearly, we must correct this situation with tougher mechanisms that target those, like Shen, who are unworthy of the position and trust people place in them (Kahn 2005b).

- *Criminals made the Chinese way*: 'The police and courts still rely mainly on pre-trial confessions and perfunctory court proceedings to solve criminal cases instead of the Western tradition of analysing forensic evidence and determining guilt through contentious court trials.' Court documents do not make clear whether physical evidence – fingerprints, blood, semen, traces of clothing – could have identified the killer. 'If there were such forensic leads, they were not followed' (Kahn 2005b).
- *Contradiction between law and reality*: In 1996 the government overhauled criminal law procedures. It toughened an existing ban on forced confessions, while declaring that suspects were entitled to a presumption of innocence. However, in reality, as in China's long history, 'a confession amounted to a submission to authority, while a plea of innocence was viewed as a form of rebellion'. The idea of law is not an objective code that everyone follows; it is the extension of the power of the authority, which determines if one is to live, or to die. The thugs in the police force fulfil this task cruelly, in the name of public 'stability', at the cost of human lives. Obviously this idea of law is not the rule of law, but the rule of man – rule of power (Kahn 2005b). 'Justice in China is swift but not sure. Criminal investigations nearly always end in guilty pleas. Prosecutors almost never lose cases brought to trial. But recent disclosures of wrongful convictions like Mr Qin's have exposed deep flaws in a judicial system that often answers more to political leaders than the law' (Kahn 2005b).
- *Torture is widespread*: 'China's criminal laws forbid torture and require judges to weigh evidence beyond a suspect's confession. But lawyers and legal scholars say forced confessions remain endemic in a judicial system that faces pressure to maintain "social stability" at all costs.' This includes taking human lives (Kahn 2005b).
- *Legal privilege and protected class*: 'Beijing draws the line at legal challenges to senior officials or important government agencies. The courts rarely, if ever, rule in favour of political protesters. Even in business cases, political influence often proves decisive' (Kahn 2005b).

The cases discussed above show that, under the current system of power structure, people are not protected and the power has become arbitrary and abused without legal constraints. These cases indicate the seriousness of the problem and its undesirable consequences; they also indicate a continuation of some feudal practices such as the use of thugs and torture. These cases also indicate the excessive power wielded by the police over civilians, and how law often serves to protect the police rather than the people. The officials do not serve the law; the law serves the officials.

All this argues for a check on the power by the higher authority of law that expresses the concerns and interests of the people. The source of this higher authority, as will be argued in the next chapter, comes from the belief that any state power must be checked and limited; and that we must subject such a power to the will of people, not vice versa. This is a principle that is yet to be realized or accepted in China today.

Nature and Objective of the Check

The Nature of Power Check

The nature of power check is to subject power holders, be they Party officials or state executives, to the people's right to recall them from their public posts, by the virtue of the authority of law and not their own authority. This is to establish the authority of law as a remedy for abuse of power in the past. It is also a rejection of the structure of total power in a single authority, and of the legal privilege and immunity that are both causal and consequential within this power culture.

The media is another area that can keep the state power and Party officials in check via public scrutiny. Not surprisingly, this is the area that has been closely monitored and censored for a long time. There are topics forbidden by the state on radio and TV media and a recent media law has extended this restriction to non-Chinese companies as well. A new draft law concerning the media covers not only Chinese media but all foreign media in China as well, with heavy penalties if one reports the 'wrong' thing. The law calls for fines of up to $12,500 if news media produce 'unauthorized reports' on outbreaks of disease, natural disasters, social disturbance or other so-called sudden incidents that officials determine to be false or harmful to China's social order. Wang Yongqing, vice minister of the legislative affairs office of China's State Council, or cabinet, said at a news conference that the law should apply to all news organizations, including foreign newspapers, magazines and broadcast outlets that usually operate under different rules from the local Chinese media. Wang's briefing was aimed at reassuring the news media that the proposed law aims mainly to punish government officials who do a poor job of managing sudden incidents, like health emergencies or coal mine accidents. The clause pertaining to the media, Wang said, is intended only to prevent malicious behaviour by news media that wilfully mislead the public (Kahn 2005b).

Freedom of speech is one of the most important values in a civil society. Banning a writer like David Irving from entering Australia, for example, was seen as a threat to freedom of speech by the Queensland Civil Liberties Council. This is because, while one may disagree with the views of others, it is necessary that their views be heard. Yet, the press freedom and the right of the community to have access to information is not a problem faced by China alone. Professor David Flint, the chairman of the Australian Press Council, once warned that the freedom to inform was 'more under threat than ever' with journalists regularly being jailed for contempt of court through withholding sources, and that there was a need to instil the value of 'our fundamental liberties', such as press freedom (Anonymous 1993a). Up to 1997, in China, for example, there were four kinds of human needs the state authority never allowed people to talk about on radio stations, namely: 'religion, independent legal system, sexual topics, and freedom of the press' (Interview with Xue 2007).

The Objective of the Check

The objective of the power check is to establish a mechanism for the check of state power that must be independent and binding. This mechanism would entail a structural change in the current Constitution; and allow an independent legal authority for the task of power check under the Constitution. To achieve these goals, however, the authority of law must first be established. The realities of present-day China often indicate that such an authority of law is not yet in place, and that state officials are not subject to any penalties when they violate the law. The chief struggle, then, must be to break down the legal privileges and political dominance of the state officials who are often in control of legal outcomes. It is this that will determine how law is applied and whether the state power abides by law or law serves those in power. A requirement for economic growth is legal and political stability. Under a 'rule of men' system of government, legal and political stability are not present and the law is applied to support the vested interest of the ruling hierachy. Such a legal system is the opposite to a system of 'rule of law' where the nation operates by a set of stable guidelines usually supported by a constitution and where the law is fairly and equitably applied to all levels of society.

Source and Model of Power Check

There are three sources to keep state power in check, namely:

1. a constitution, which sets up the principle and the legal framework for power check;
2. an independent judiciary to interpret the Constitution; and

3. a legal philosophy derived from the common law and the people's sovereign power over state leaders and leading organizations.

These three sources are explained below, as well as the desirability of having such authority of law as a power check device.

The Constitution

The source of the power check should, first, come from the Constitution. John Rawls' concept of a constitution has two properties: the principle of majority rule and the ideal procedure that forms a part of his theory of justice. In his words, 'A just constitution is defined as a constitution that would be agreed upon by rational delegates in a constitutional convention who are guided by the two principles of justice … When we criticize laws and policies we try to show that they would not be chosen under this ideal procedure' (Rawls 1972: 356). This coincides with Mill's idea of a sovereign state and a perfect government that has a full participation of the people. In his words:

> The only government which can fully satisfy all the exigencies of the social state is one in which the whole people participate … and that nothing less can be ultimately desirable than the admission of all to a share in the sovereign power of the state … It follows that the ideal type of a perfect government must be representative. (Mills 1861 in Acton 1972: 216)

Mill's idea of people's representative government is, however, incorporated within the rule of law. As Aristotle once warned us, a demagogue arises where the laws are not sovereign. This is because several individual rulers, not ruled by law, seek to act like the sole ruler and thus they become despotic. Aristotle argues against this kind of constitution in these words:

> When Homer says that to have many chiefs is not good, it is obscure whether he means this kind of constitution, or that where there are several individual rules. Anyhow, this kind of demos, not being ruled by law, seeks to act like the sole ruler that it is. It becomes despotic; and flatterers are held in honour. Such a demos is the analogue of tyranny among the monarchies. They both have the same character. They are both despotic towards the better persons. The demagogue and the flatterer are the same and analogous. Each attains their greatest power with each, the flatterers with the tyrants and the demagogues with this kind of demos. (Aristotle in Rosen and Wolff 1999: 106)

A constitution can act as a monitor to constrain the power of government agencies. A constitutional system of separated powers and checks and balances is designed to achieve this end. It can create a system of mutual regulation in which each agency depends on one or more of the others to accomplish anything. This system assumes that certain other legal rules will not be transgressed – namely those rules that define the relative competences of the various departments. As Kay noted: 'Checks and balances assume the agencies will observe those definitional rules that deprive them of the powers for lack of which they must depend on the other agencies' (Kay in Alexander 1998: 41). Thus the foundation of constitutionalism is based on the idea that public power should be controlled by a superior law. The formal promulgation of rules by legitimate authorities will result in texts that exert a normative force on the state officials to whom the rules are addressed. In this sense, to understand the concept of constitutionalism is to understand the operation of that force.

Independent Judiciary

The source of the power check should, secondly, come from the authority to interpret the Constitution by an independent jurisdiction. Joseph Raz (1998: 153) argued that 'legal interpretation is much more than a method of establishing what the law is', taking for granted that the courts have the authority to interpret the laws including the Constitution. Moreover, 'it is part of the practice of legal interpretation as it is in many countries that courts are not bound to follow past interpretive techniques … This is the case, for example, in all common-law jurisdictions' (Raz 1998: 177).

Obviously, the authority to interpret the Constitution as an independent legal entity is a prerequisite in this interpretation exercise. Moreover, this authority to interpret the Constitution is important because it is a challenge for the courts to decide how to achieve the value embodied as the heart of the legal norm. As Perry noted:

> A specification of a principle for a specific class or case is not a deduction from it, nor a discovery of some implicit meaning; it is the act of setting a more concrete and categorical requirement in the spirit of the principle, and guided both by a sense of what is practically realizable (or enforceable), and by a recognition of the risk of conflict with other principles or values … The challenge of specifying an indeterminate constitutional norm, then, is the challenge of deciding how best to achieve, how best to 'instantiate' in the context of a particular conflict, the political-moral value (or values) at the heart of the norm, it is the challenge of discerning what way of achieving that value, what way of embodying it … (Perry in Alexander 1998: 113; Perry 1998)

Alexander (1998) discusses the function of authorities and authoritative decisions as they relate to ultimate political/moral principles that justify particular actions in more detail, on the premise that such an authority to interpret the constitutional norms is granted to the courts and the judges. In China, however, this authority to interpret the Constitution needs to be established first, as an independent legal entity, without political interference.

Legal Process and Public Scrutiny

The source of the power check should come from the legal process in law and public scrutiny. Power check is a historic process, as seen in the development of common law. The law works against tyrants, for tyrants can work only in a centralized system, where the rules issue from a single authority. In the case of Magna Carta (1215), for example, the singular authority of the King was successfully challenged by the due process of the law and was a product of legal bargaining and the work of many hands. Moreover, some argue that common law would work only if participants in the law-making process are working on behalf of all people in the community, rather than following rules issued by a single authority. This process of public participation is the basis of the system of common law. It requires a structural change in the due process and is well expressed by Landry:

> Tyrants can only get a hold of a central system where the rules issue from a single authority (*government*); tyrants cannot get a hold of a system which depends on a spontaneous participation in the law-making process on the part of each and all of the inhabitants of a country, viz., a system of common law. (Landry 2004: 2)

The Desirability of Law

There is a strong argument to suggest that public power should be regulated by mutual checks, and that there are grounds for the preference of law as a higher authority. This has been done without jeopardizing the central role of government under the rule of law in many countries. These grounds are examined in terms of the desirability of law as follows:

- *It is vital for economic growth*: It is often argued that legal reform factors are vital for China's current economic development. 'Without sound legal institutions, positive social and economic development cannot be achieved … Without common law and law of equity, there would have been no effective legal framework for the growth of the market economy … Without sound laws and regulations, there is no way of establishing a market system' (W. He 2004, May).The legal system has played a great role in economic growth and is likely to play an even greater role in the future, which is consistent with the experiences of other countries in Asia and elsewhere (Peerenboom 2002: 450–512).
- *It is vital for public confidence*: State leaders capture public support by responding to 'public feelings', which is an important rationale for political decisions. Jaing Zemin, the former CCP leader, for example, acknowledged that the survival of the Party is linked with 'public feeling'. He said:

> Whether the people are for or against is the basic factor deciding the rise and fall of a political party and a political power. An honest style of government has always been an important factor for popular support, good government, and the stability and prosperity of the society. This is an important lesson of the law of the rise and fall. The collapse of every dynasty in Chinese history and … the loss of power in contemporary world of the political parties which had been in power for a long time were all closely connected with the trend of public feeling. (Keith and Li 2006: 7)

- *It is vital for political predictability*: As demonstrated earlier in this study, the fate of a state was extremely unpredictable when power fell into the hands of political careerists; their right over an individual's life and death was limitless and the effect of any written laws was determined by the will power of a few individuals. Law was easily transcended and there was no legal certainty for anyone. Deng, the leader of the Chinese Communist Party, recognized this issue of political unpredictability in the leadership and danger of power concentration in the early 1980s. In his words, 'As far as the leadership and cadre systems of our Party and state are concerned, the major problems are bureaucracy, over-concentration of power, patriarchal methods, life tenure in leading posts and privileges of various kinds' (Deng 1981: 309). As a consequence, the nation was at the mercy of the internal struggles within the powerful Party machine, and no one was spared in this power struggle, not even at the very top level of the state leadership. The trial of the Gang of Four is one example of this kind. (For details of the trial see Derbyshire 1987: 47.)
- *It is vital for the government's credibility*: It can be argued that people place more trust in the government if it deals with their affairs on a solid legal basis (W. He 2004). When people can lodge their concerns and grievances through legal channels, on a rational basis with evidence-based procedures, instead of with dogmatic and political threats, they will be more willing to place trust in the government's authority. The summary of cases of media litigation discussed in this book, for example, illustrates that people have begun to use the media and litigation for the first time under the new laws and regulations, in order to test the government's credibility. It is important that such grievances and complaints from the masses are resolved satisfactorily by means of law.

Other State Models and Debates on Power Check

Models of state suggested by legal scholars vary to a great degree, but the consensus is that law must check the state power, and make both the Party and the government accountable to the people.

In the Australian model of power separation, executive power is sometimes viewed as raw power. It exists in its purest form in the case of the absolute ruler or tyrant. It is central to the idea of the rule of law that executive power should exist only if it has a firm legal basis in a constitution, legislation, judicial decisions, or some combination of these. An alternative and more limited view of executive power sees it as the administrative and bureaucratic power to apply and enforce rules, instead of the legislative power to make rules.

The separation of executive and legislative power requires an institutional separation between the executive and the legislature. It is the power of the executive that pre-eminently needs to be checked and balanced. The checks and balances on the power of the legislature may be:

- constraints to maintain the representative nature of the legislature by elections;
- call of rights restraints to protect the infringement of individual and minority rights;
- federal restraints to protect the legislative power of legislatures at one level from encroachment by other levels of government.

The checks and balances are imposed on the executive by the doctrine of responsible government. The boundary between the executive and legislative is often blurred and problematic. Judicial power is usually described as the power to adjudicate disputes according to the pre-existing legal rights of the parties concerned. It is inevitable that courts are required to interpret legal rules.

This is the model of responsible government under the Westminster-based system in Australia. The executive is responsible to the legislature, which in turn is responsible to the electorate. It is based on a two-house parliamentary system, with elections to elect both houses. The government is formed from the party having a majority of seats in the lower house. Government ministers are responsible to Parliament for their portfolios. The Members of Parliament have the right to question ministers. The government is collectively responsible to Parliament and is required to have the confidence of the lower house. Otherwise it is obliged to resign. The legislature functions to control the executive (Hunter, Ingleby and Johnstone 1995: 53–5).

There are other theories and debates on the nature of law, and the aim of legal reform in China. Some argue that the law should not be used for the ruling class to retain its arbitrary power; that law has a duty to challenge this power by upholding the principle of basic democratic rights and greater equity before the law. But most importantly, the law must have authority over the state executives and the ruling party, as the rule of law and Constitution claims. Otherwise it will be just another tool for the rulers. The debate on this point is summarized below.

Rule by Law or Rule of Law?

It is clear, based on Potter's (1994) article, that under the structure of power totality in a socialist system, where all power agencies are under a single authority, for the rule of law to have legitimacy, it will need to be a rule by law for that authority. Some Chinese scholars argue this with more emphasis on moral grounds. Pan Wei, for example, believes that the law should be based on 'generally accepted moral principles of the time', accepted as just by the public. Similarly others believe that rule of law must entail justice for all, and should not just be norms to be followed. Some go even further to distinguish rule of law from ruling with law. Deng, for example, argued for a well-structured legal and political system adopting the principles of the rule of law (Peerenboom 2002: 70). The two phrases look similar and yet there is a fundamental difference in the meaning they entail, based on the power they represent.

The main difference between the two is that rule by law refers to law as a form of instrumentalism where law is a tool to be used by the state to control others without conferring restraints on itself. In such a way, law is not supreme, and there is little separation between law and politics. In essence, it is the will of the state – the dictates and policies of the rulers dominate laws. On the other hand, rule of law requires that law imposes meaningful restraints on the state and its rulers, as well as on the populace. Clearly the difference is whether law can hold the state officials accountable for their actions, and they are dealt with in due course without privileges before the law. It is equally clear that the central ingredient in this debate is about the power of the state and its leaders, versus the power of law to constrain the state. In other words, the rule by law means to use law to rule and hence implies a more instrumental rule by law. By contrast, rule of law means to rule in accordance with law, and implies that the law also binds the government. Naturally the latter is more closely related to the original purpose of the rule of law.

There are so-called 'thick' and 'thin' theories currently under debate among the jurists working in China. The 'thin' theories are in general agreement that the rule of law should impose meaningful limits on state actors, and recognize the supremacy of the law and the equality of all before the law. Moreover, for there to be a rule of law, there are certain standards to be met as a minimum requirement. These elements of a 'thin' theory are in addition to meaningful restraints on state actors, and are basic legal safeguards. They reflect Hart's (1961) concept of secondary law and criteria of law as norms. These elements, as Peerenboom listed here, in fact, highlight the areas in which much improvement is needed in China. In summary they are:

- There must be procedural rules for law-making and, to be valid, laws must be made by an entity with the authority to make laws in accordance with such rules;
- Transparency: laws must be made public and readily accessible;

- Laws must be generally applicable: that is, law must not be aimed at a particular person and must treat similarly situated people equally;
- Laws must be relatively clear;
- Laws must generally be prospective rather than retroactive;
- Laws must be consistent;
- Laws must be relatively stable;
- Laws must be fairly applied;
- Laws must be enforced: the gap between the law as presented in the statute books and the law as exercised in practice should be narrow;
- Laws must be reasonably acceptable to a majority of the populace or people affected (or at least the key groups affected) by those laws (Peerenboom 2002: 65).

The 'thick' theory is a broad concept of social and political philosophy that addresses a range of issues beyond legal norms and the legal system. This broader social and political notion presents a more comprehensive general philosophy or worldview including religious beliefs, metaphysics, aesthetics and so on. My argument here supports both 'thick' and 'thin' theories, in the sense that it is 'thin' because it recognizes the enforceability and openness in the rules of law in order to protect individual civil rights, but also 'thick' because law is taken as the symbol of power that is designed to challenge and curb another power – the power of the state – which is in theory subordinate to the will of the people but is in reality the dominant force.

Which Kind of State Best Suits China?

There are discussions about the type of state preferable in a developing economy like China's. Four types of models have emerged during the debate. as a result of a wide variety of beliefs and conceptions of what constitutes a just socio-political state. The Chinese views on this can be divided into four groups:

Liberal Democratic

- The independence and autonomy of the law are valued highly.
- There is a freely elected legislature (not appointed by the Party).
- The judiciary and judges are independent as in the West.
- Judges can be removed only for limited reasons and by strict procedures.
- The appointment process of judges is non-politicized.
- There are various mechanisms to control administrative discretion.
- The legal system is capable of holding even top-level government officials to account.
- The legal profession is independent and often self-governing.

Communitarians

- There is a moderate to high degree of separation between law and politics.
- There is a freely elected legislature.
- There is strong public participation in the making, interpretation and implementation of the law.
- A corrupt government can be thrown out.
- The legal system is strong enough to hold even top-level officials to account.
- Individual rights and efficient government are protected.
- There is an autonomous judiciary: life tenure for judges and apolitical processes for appointing and removing judges.
- The liberal notion of a neutral state is rejected in favour of a moral agenda set by the ruling elite.
- Court and judges focus on harmony, stability and community interests over individual interests and economic interests (whereas neo-authoritarians and statist socialists place more emphasis on economic development and on upholding the authority of the state).

Neo-authoritarians

- There is a moderate separation between law and politics.
- The legislature is not elected.
- There is greater judicial independence.
- The independence of the courts and individual judges is limited in various ways by the National People's Congress's supremacy and supervision over the courts.
- There is a professional and honest civil service.
- The legal system is capable of combating government officials' corruption.
- There is greater public participation.
- There is more expansive yet still limited freedom of association, speech and the press so that the public can play a greater role in the monitoring of government officials.
- The purpose of administrative law is rational and efficient governance, not the protection of individual rights.
- The elite corps of civil servants are to be given great flexibility in formulating policy and implementing rules, the main form of legislation in day-to-day governance.
- The legal profession is granted limited independence but is subject to supervision by the Ministry of Justice, albeit a cleaner and more professional one.

Statist Socialists

- There is a moderate to low level of separation between law and politics.
- Party policies that were once substituted for or trumped up as laws are now transformed into laws.
- Laws are made according to stipulated procedures for law-making.
- The legislature is not freely elected.
- The Party ensures its policy become law when it is united and willing to spend the political capital to do so.
- There is more limited judicial independence.
- Courts have a functional independence, and government branches are not to interfere in specific cases. Courts may decide cases without Party approval of the judgment. But the courts may still be subject to macro supervision by the NPC, the procuracy and Party organs. The court upholds the four cardinal principles (a position not supported by either neo-authoritarians or communitarians).
- Individual judges' autonomy and independence is more restricted. Accordingly, most cases are decided by a panel of judges, and a special adjudicative supervision committee within the court has the right to review particular decisions in case of manifest error.
- The legal profession is granted a similar partial independence: lawyers must meet political correctness standards to practise law and pass the annual inspection test.
- The Ministry of Justice retains most of the authority in supervising the legal profession, including the power to punish lawyers. In part because of such political reasons, but mainly due to corruption and rent seeking by the Ministry and its local affiliates, lawyers try to forge close clientele relations with the Ministry.
- In the area of administrative law, government officials are granted considerable discretion, in part so that they may be more responsive to shifts in Party policy, but mainly for other reasons, including the need to respond quickly and flexibly to a rapidly changing economic environment.
- There are limits on civil society, freedom of the press, and public participation in the making, interpretation and implementation of the law, making it difficult for the public to monitor government officials.
- The lack of elections eliminates whatever leverage the public might have over officials resulting from the possibility of voting the current government out of office (Peerenboom 2002: 84).

These four viewpoints are the product of the present realities of China from one end of the spectrum to the other. From these models we can draw the following implications:

- The law has a positive role to play in restricting state power;
- The law should be given a greater degree of power and authority in checking public powers;
- The independence of the judiciary should be strengthened as a separate entity for power check.

The central contention among these four groups, however, is over the power of state officials vis-à-vis the independence of the legal system and, in particular, the judiciary. The unwarranted contradiction between the state and the people thus becomes a reality. State officials desperately hold on to their posts and privileges by limited elections, control over the court and lawyers, suppression of free speech, and denying public participation in law making – but at the same time, granting extensive discretional power to state officials.

The line is thus clearly drawn between the state officials' power, and the power of the legal entity. Care must be taken, or legal reform, in the name of the rule of law, may easily be substituted by rule by law, and the whole purpose of limiting the state executive's power would be lost. The role that the Constitution will play will depend, to a certain extent, on which version of rule of law prevails. It is predicted that the Constitution will play an important role if a neo-authoritarian or communitarian form of rule of law is adopted. 'Although the tension between strengthening and limiting the state would still be manifest in constitutional law, at minimum there would be greater emphasis on individual rights.' As a result, 'the Constitution would probably become directly justifiable. It might also be subject to less change' (Peerenboom 2002: 89).

Conclusion

This chapter has answered the question of why the law has a crucial role to play in the power check. It gives several reasons why we need the power check in principle and why law is important in the implementation of this principle to challenge power totality. I have argued that, in order to take up this challenge, the law must have its own authority and independence without interference from those in power. The law is desirable for reasons of stability, predictability and continuity, but, more importantly, it can also provide a forum where people are free to exercise their right to check power. It can also provide a structure where public power can be checked mutually by several agencies within a single system.

Chapter 5
How Law Checks Power

Introduction

In the previous chapters, we have established that law is part of the solution in the battle against power totality. In this final section, we will discuss some of the legal measures in the process of power check and how law can help remedy the abuses of the past. I will argue that the Constitution has an important role to play in the power check and that there are several steps to take to reach the goal of power check. We need first of all to establish the principle of power check in the Constitution and to grant the independence to China's legal institutions. Furthermore, we need a structural change that will put in place a mechanism for the supervision of power. Based on other models, I will propose a model for a Constitutional Office and an Administrative Court that will be able to sanction corrupt state officials and power agencies (including law enforcement agencies). Finally, I will discuss the implications of this study in the light of the ongoing struggle between ideology and humanity and the repositioning of Marx's original vision.

Power Check as a Principle in the Constitution

The debates about what constitutes constitutionality have been continuing among Chinese constitutional law scholars since 1981. The controversy over China's constitutional supervision mechanism, and supervision over the National People's Congress (NPC) and its Standing Committee (NPCSC) is also generating heated debates and deep concern (see F. Lin 2000: 287–96). Under both the 1954 and 1978 Constitutions, the NPC and NPCSC had the authority to conduct constitutional supervision. When the 1982 Constitution was drafted, different views were put forward on the subject of what form of constitutional supervision mechanism China should have. The drafting committee of the 1982 Constitution was in favour of the establishment of a Constitutional Committee (Chen 1988: 257). The idea was abandoned due to the fact that it was difficult to define the legal status and the authority of such a committee; and also due to a lack of experience required in this respect (J. Hu 1998; Liu 1981). In my opinion such a committee must be established soon. The reason for this has been stated earlier – that is, the expediency and importance of this matter is beyond any doubt. China needs power check by a separate and independent entity, to be placed directly under the Constitution – and China needs it now.

The Three Aspects of Power Check in the New Structure

There are three aspects of power concentration, which should be addressed, namely: the Party and the government; the government and the law; and the independence of the judiciary. As part of the power check mechanism, these aspects are important as preconditions for any proposed model.

1 Separation of the Party and Government

The need to separate the Party from the state was highlighted by the Chinese leader Deng in his objectives for reform. Derbyshire (1987: 45) sums up Deng's intentions thus:

> firstly, to create a new collective form of party leadership which would share the workload and provide continuity after his death; secondly, to effect a greater separation between the party, state and military spheres of government, following their convergence during the 'Cultural Revolution'; thirdly, to provide the series of checks and balances which would prevent the concentration of power in the hands of any single body or person; and lastly, to define more clearly areas of responsibility and establish proper lines of accountability within a political system which would still be dominated from above by the CPC. [Communist Party of China]

Many scholars acknowledge the necessity to separate the CPC organs from state organs. For example, the decisions on the five-year national plan and so on should be made by the NPC or the NPCSC (Cai 1998: 338, n. 15). This has been argued by the scholars such as Liao Guangsheng, in his article titled 'The Constitution of the Party, the Constitution of the state and the relationship between the Party and the government' (Songran 1987: 67–70), and He Huahui, in his study of the People's Congress system in China (H. He 1992: 158–60, 262–75).

There are three major differences in law-making capacity between the Party and the NPC, which should be taken into consideration in this process:

1. The CPC has a guiding role and the NPC follows it in its decision-making.
2. For the CPC, the lower Party organ should abide by the decision of the higher; the NPC, however, should follow legal procedure to exercise its power of decision-making, which is democratic. (Procedure)
3. The CPC's decision is only binding on its members, but the NPC's decision has legal effect binding upon all the people within the jurisdiction of the Congress and can be enforced by state force. (Consequences and legal effects) (H. He 1992: 159, n. 8).

2 Government under the Law instead of under the Party

The nature of the People's Procuratorate[1] is defined as the state organ for legal supervision (Article, 129 of the 1982 Constitution; also Article 1 of the 1983 Organic Law of the People's Procuratorate). This shows a different legal status from that of other state enforcement organs, such as the public security and the courts. The People's Procuratorate has the authority to ensure the implementation of the Constitution and the law. Its supervision is conducted by judicial functions over other state organs, such as the public security organs, state security organs, people's courts, prisons, detention centres, labour reform organs and labour re-education organs. Its function is limited to certain administrative activities by the relevant judicial organs, and does not extend to other areas. Unlike the people's congresses, the People's Procuratorate has no power to repeal any inappropriate administrative rules and regulations. Its supervision over personnel or ordinary citizens is limited to where they have committed crimes leading to criminal liability.

From the cases cited in Chapter 4 of this study, it is clear that actions of the people's procuratorates can be draconian, acting as arms of the police and increasing the burden of law and order on ordinary citizens. It is also clear that the procuratorates can be extremely powerful, and can even overpower the courts and influence the judiciary process. It has acted vigorously during the anti-crime campaigns for the state government and the Party, imposing heavy death penalties. It seems unconvincing that such an organ in reality really protects people's basic rights. A more appropriate concern of the procuratorates would be the investigation of corrupt state or party officials.

But this is not the case. The people's procuratorates in fact leave the Party and state executives untouched: 'The people's procuratorates do not have jurisdiction over the ordinary violation of discipline of the Communist Party of China or administrative rules that are not classed as violations of criminal law' (F. Lin 2000: 235). In a sense, these organs have functions similar to those of the police in criminal cases. They are responsible for the People's Congresses, as well as for other governmental bodies. In origin, they derive from Lenin who believed that the procuratorates should not only conduct public prosecutions but also comprehensive supervision of the implementation of law by governmental organs

1 The people's procuratorates in the PRC China are law supervision organs of the state. The state has the Supreme People's Procuratorate as well as local people's procuratorates and military procuratorates. The people's procuratorates have four levels, namely: the grassroots, intermediate, higher and supreme people's procuratorates. The Supreme People's Procuratorate (SPP) is the highest procuratorial organ of the state and represents the state in independently implementing the right of prosecution. It is responsible to the Standing Committee of the National People's Congress. Its major tasks are to exercise leadership over local people's procuratorates at all levels and special people's procuratorates in implementing their supervision functions and ensure the unity and correct implementation of state laws (see www.china.org.cn/english/features/state_structure/64414.htm).

and their personnel. However, in present-day China their function seems to serve to protect, rather than to curb, the abuse of power.

This fact seems to have been acknowledged by the state legislature. The 1979 Organic Law of the People's Procuratorates limited its functions to the investigation, prosecution and supervision of other judicial organs. With the amendment of the Criminal Procedural Law in 1996, the scope of cases that may be directly investigated by the people's procuratorates has been further clarified and limited. Article 18 of the amended Criminal Procedural Law provides that

> Crimes of embezzlement and bribery, crimes of dereliction of duty committed by State functionaries, and crimes involving violations of a citizen's personal rights such as illegal detention, extortion of confessions by torture, retaliation, frame-up and illegal search and crimes involving infringement of a citizen's democratic rights – committed by State functionaries by taking advantage of their functions and powers – shall be placed on file for investigation by the people's procuratorates. (F. Lin 2000: 241)

Lin's article locates three main areas for legal investigation, namely:

1. crimes of embezzlement and bribery;
2. crimes of dereliction of duty; and
3. crimes of citizens' personal and democratic rights.

For cases involving serious crimes where state functionaries have taken advantage of their functions and power, the people's procuratorates may also conduct direct investigation. Such a decision has to be made by the Procuratorates at the provincial level or above (Article 18 (2) of the 1979 Criminal Procedural Law amended in 1996).

3 An Independent Judiciary with Binding Power

It is recommended that the Judicial Committee and the Politics and Law Committees be abandoned, and that the structure of the courts be simplified. There are redundant functions within the court system, as well as redundant hierarchical structures and personnel, such as the heads of the divisions and bureaucrats within the court system, whose numbers should be reduced. A single vertical line of supervision by the courts and for the courts should be established, without other interference. The basic courts deserve most support and funding, as 'over 90% of cases in China are tried by the basic courts, so the proper operation of the basic people's courts is crucial to the implementation of the rule of law principle in China' (F. Lin 2000: 219). This may be explained in terms of courts and judges:

Courts One proposal put by the Chinese legal scholars is that judicial authority should be subject not only to supervision but direct order. It is suggested that the people's courts should be subject to vertical leadership from the courts at higher levels and that the horizontal leadership of the courts by the people's congress at the corresponding level be abolished. Nor should the court be subject to the leadership of the Party organ or the executive branch of the government at the same level. Many such recommendations have been made for judicial reform in China (F. Lin 2000: 234). In fact, the courts should not be subject to the government executives, people's congresses, and the Party organs at *any* level, for that matter. Otherwise there is no rule of law in any real sense. Moreover, such a situation contravenes Article 125 of the 1982 Constitution, that judicial power should be exercised independently, 'in accordance with the provisions of the law'.

Judges Scholars have proposed that the judiciary should be neutral and impartial. Two conditions for this have been put forward. One is the independence of judges, so that judges will no longer be accountable to any other governmental organ, only to law (L. Wang 1998: 9). 'This is consistent with Marxism as Marx once said that "judges have no other bosses except law"' (F. Lin 2000: 233). The other condition is that judges must ensure that all parties can exercise equally and fully their procedural as well as substantive rights.

Lawyers Lawyers, as a part of this change, should gain a considerable degree of independence. At the same time they are expected to obtain a high level of proficiency. They need to be equipped with not only the techniques and knowledge of the law, but also the philosophy and the moral obligation for the protection of the public against the power abuse. They are the vanguard for the principle of keeping state power in check by defending the constitutional rights of the citizens. They have a mission, which was expressed thus by one Chinese legal scholar, making an instructive comparison with the US legal profession:

> Jurists also need to be aware of their own mission. In *The Last Lawyer*, Tony Kronman, the former dean of Yale Law School, argues that today's lawyers resemble less and less their predecessors from the early years of the American republic. In those days, a lawyer was also a politician. Today, on the other hand, lawyers show less concern for politics, because all they care about is making money. Lawyers no longer aim to reform politics and improve society.
>
> Historically, lawyers are very influential in politics. 'Most of the American Founding Fathers were either lawyers or had a legal background, and as a result, the American political class came to be led by people with legal backgrounds. More than half of America's presidents have had a legal background.' It's good for a country to be governed by people with a legal background.
>
> Law is a discipline that is particularly concerned with society. Society is the laboratory where all our theories are put to the test. I believe that if your theory has no connection to society, and if you fail to criticize and expose corrupt social

practices and violations of the law, you lack social concern. Such scholars fall short (W. He 2004, May).

The Current Constitution of the PRC

The most significant achievement of the Constitution of the PRC (amended in 2004) is its confirmation of citizens' Basic Rights, and its commitment to the rule of law. There are two crucial principles in the Constitution: first, the basic rights of citizens and the acknowledgement that all the powers belong to the people; and second, the authority of the Constitution and the authority of the law.

As discussed previously, the protection of people's basic rights should be the priority of any new structure. This protection should be legally binding as it is endorsed by the Constitution of PRC. I repeat these principles here as the objective of power check.

Constitutional Principle 1: Basic Rights Protection

In 2004 the Constitution underwent further revisions which offer the potential for future legal development and human rights protection:

- The right to vote – regardless of ethnic status, race, sex, occupation, family background, religious belief, education, property status or length of residence (Article 34);
- The right to supervise (Article 27) to criticize, complain, lay charges against and expose any state organ for violation of the law (Article 41);
- The right to democratic management of enterprises/organizations (Article 17).

The Constitution also safeguards certain freedoms, including:

- The freedom of speech, of the press, of assembly, of association of procession and of demonstration (Article 35);
- The freedom of religious belief (Article 36);
- The freedom and privacy of correspondence (Article 40);
- The freedom of marriage (Article 49);
- The freedom to research literary and artistic and other cultural pursuits (Article 47);

as well as freedoms of the person:

- The preservation of life, and freedom from bodily harm or torture;
- The prohibition of unlawful detention, deprivation or restriction of freedom of the person (Article 37);
- The inviolability of residence (Article 39);

- The inviolability of personal dignity; freedom from insult, libel, false accusation or incrimination (Article 38) (B. Li and Xu 1986: 50–88).

The Constitution moreover enshrines the dictum that 'All power in the People's Republic of China belongs to the people': 'The people administer state affairs and manage economic, cultural and social affairs through various channels and in various ways in accordance with the law' (Article 2).

Constitutional Principle 2: The Authority of the Constitution and the Rule of Law

The Constitution is paramount in legal hierarchy The 1982 Constitution has been widely regarded as the best China has ever had (F. Lin 2000: 17). It formally confirms that the Constitution is at the pinnacle of the legal hierarchy and is the foundation on which other legislation is enacted. No laws or administrative rules and regulations may contravene the Constitution. Such a hierarchy of primary and subordinate legislation is essential for the integrity of the Chinese legal system (Wen 1994: 215–16).

The commitment of the CPC to the adoption of the rule of law principle in the PRC was formally confirmed by the 1999 amendments to the Constitution. In addition, the term 'counter-revolutionary crime' was replaced by the term 'offence against national security', in alignment with the latest amendment to the Criminal Law.

No legal privileges for state executives The 2004 Constitution states that the Constitution 'is the fundamental law of the state and has supreme legal authority' (Preamble, p. 7) and that

> No laws or administrative or local rules and regulations may contravene the Constitution. All state organs, the armed forces, all political parties and public organizations and all enterprises and institutions must abide by the Constitution and the law. All acts in violation of the Constitution and the law must be investigated. No organization or individual is privileged to be beyond the Constitution or the law. (Constitution, Art. 5, p. 10)

Problems with the current Constitution There are, however, several areas in the Constitution that make the law less effective as a tool for power check, namely: the lack of independence of the courts and judges; lack of a separate power check entity; lack of procedures (against state officials and against violation of basic rights); and leadership as it relates to the law. I discuss each of these in turn below.

Lack of Independence of the Courts and Judges

Owing to the lack of independence of the judiciary, it is suggested that the judicial committees be abandoned. The judicial committees were established by people's courts at all levels (Article 11 of the 1979 Organic Law of the People's Court as amended in 1983 – hereafter, the Organic Law). The task of the committees is to sum up judicial experience and discuss important or difficult cases and other issues relating to adjudicative work (Organic Law, Art. 11 para. 1). The structure of the courts of the PRC consists of a president, vice-presidents, chief judges of divisions, associate chief judges of divisions and judges. The president of a court has the authority to nominate candidates for the judicial committee of the court, and presides over meetings of the committee. Under the democratic centralism rule, the committee discusses all issues within its jurisdiction, but the president of the people's court has the final decision-making authority concerning all issues submitted to the committee (Organic Law, Art. 11 para. 1).

The need for judicial committees has long been controversial. Those in favour of them argue that they improve the quality of the judgment and reduce the pressure on the judges. Those against them believe that judges should be able to rule a specific case without any interference; and, if his or her judgment is deemed unfit, it may in any case be overruled by the court with appellate jurisdiction. Moreover, opponents note that the decisions of the committees are made in a short period of time, usually about 10 minutes, so it is impossible for them to take into account the full complexity of a specific case. The bias of the presiding judge may also undermine the fairness of the case (F. Lin 2000: 216).

Even so, some constitutional scholars in China believe in 'the authority of the courts in exercising adjudicative power independently'. The concept of this independence, however, differs among different legal theorists. To some, independent adjudicative authority means the exercise of the authority by the courts and not by individual judges (C. Wang and Zhang 1993: 17). The judicial committees and their supervision of the judges, in this view, are consistent with the concept of judicial independence.

'In China, the concept of judicial independence is not a favoured term. Instead, officials prefer to use the term "the authority to exercise adjudicative power independently"' (F. Lin 2000: 216 n.). The Constitution states that 'The People's courts exercise judicial power independently, in accordance with the provisions of the law, and are not subject to interference by any administrative organ, public organization or individual' (Constitution 1982, Art. 126). However, it is undeniable that the court as a legal institution is not independent. And individual judges do not enjoy independence in adjudication – for their decisions must be approved by the divisional head and the president of the court – and yet this approval of cases has no statutory justification. Under the Organic Law and the relevant procedural laws, only individual judges and collegial panels within a court may try a case and make a judgment (F. Lin 2000: 231). The original purpose of approval is to prevent individual judges from making improper judgments, and this is not achieved by the approval procedure. The existing internal structure of the court, moreover, gives too much power to the heads of divisions to approve certain cases, thus weakening the integrity of both individual judges and collegial panels.

It is clear that judges bear the title but no power. Although the ruling is exercised collectively, the judges as individuals give out the ruling in their names and therefore bear the responsibility for any errors of the ruling, which seems unfair on the judges. The president and the divisional heads who have the power of veto in legal cases should instead share the responsibility and be accountable for their actions.

The lack of judicial independence is also seen in a lack of statutory interpretation authority in the courts, except the NPCSC, confirmed in the latest Law on Legislation. Article 2 of the Resolution of the NPCSC on Strengthening the Interpretation of Law (adopted on 10 June 1981) states that 'The SPC [Supreme People's Court] is the only court that has authority to give judicial interpretation'. Thus it limits other courts' power to give judicial interpretation. The Supreme People's Court may only interpret a national law in actual adjudication. In theory it is a limited authority, but in practice it has issued opinions regarding the interpretation of various national laws (F. Lin 2000: 231). In addition, higher-level courts often give directions and orders to lower-level courts, thus undermining the independence of adjudication by the lower-level courts.

More importantly, the judiciary as a whole is subject to interference from local governments. This was acknowledged by the President of the Supreme People's Court in his 1997 *Annual Report to the NPC* (Wang and Yao in F. Lin 2000: 231 n. 135). The courts also face supervision by the People's Congresses and their standing committees over specific cases, which is another improper restriction over the independence of the judiciary. Some scholars argue that the supervision by the People's Congresses over the courts should be of a general and abstract nature, rather than taking the form of direct supervision of individual cases (Wang and Yao in F. Lin 2000: 232).

Other external obstacles the judiciary face include:

1. It is subject to executive interference, although in theory judicial authority is separate from executive authority. 'Executive branches at all government levels actually control the funding and personnel arrangement of the people's court at the corresponding level.'
2. It is subject to interference by Party organisations at corresponding levels. The local Party branches issue direct instructions or make decisions, which interfere with the independent adjudication of the local courts.
3. It is subject to improper interference by People's Congresses. On one occasion, deputies to the Sichuan Provincial People's Congress strongly criticized the President of its Higher People's Court for accepting a specific case and refused to give him an opportunity to explain his reasoning (Dai Dingjian in F. Lin 2000: 232 n. 141).

The case of Judge Li discussed in Chapter 4 of this study showed this kind of external interference from the local government as well as from the local People's Congress. Such 'supervision' by the congress has undermined the independent adjudication authority of the People's Court.

To sum up, the restrictions the current judiciary and court systems face are:

- The emphasis is on the court as a collective, not on independent judges.
- A judge's ruling must be approved by the divisional head and president of the court.
- The final statutory interpretation authority resides in the NPCSC, not the courts.
- Higher courts often direct lower courts.
- The judiciary as a whole is subject to interference from local government.
- The judiciary is subject to congresses and their standing committees.
- Local government has control over the personnel, funding facilities and administration of the courts.

The Lack of a Separate Power Check Entity

These are the structural problems in the Constitution, which affect judicial independence and also indicate an inseparable power concentration. The purpose of power check, as we have discussed in Chapter 3, has not been fulfilled by the current power check structure in the Constitution. There are no clear restraints or power demarcations between the three most powerful elements of the state, namely the executive branch, the CPC and the People's Congress. Interference with the judiciary is a result of power combined in controlling the law, rather than being controlled by law. This has made the argument for a separate power check mechanism even more pressing. It must be the role of the Constitution to overcome this structural problem.

That said, the people's courts themselves need to be checked. Lin argues that 'While acknowledging the importance of judicial independence, it should also be noted that an appropriate mechanism must be established to ensure that the exercise of independent adjudication authority will not lead to the corruption of the people's courts' (F. Lin 2000: 233). This is because the corruption within judicial organs including the courts is also serious. According to Professor Guo Daohui, in the Ninxia autonomous region there were 60 wrongly judged cases in 1997, and many of them involved corruption of judges. In Liaoning province, during an investigation which lasted for 15 months, 563 cases were found to involve judicial corruption and personal relationships (Guo 1999: 85; F. Lin 2000: 233). To combat this, it is acknowledged that 'external supervision is essential to the control of judicial corruption. Social supervision, especially supervision by the media, has also been strongly advocated' (Guo 1999; F. Lin 2000).

The people's courts, the people's procuratorates, and many government organs are all subject to the leadership of the Committee of Politics and Law within the

Party organization. In many places, the head of the Committee of Politics and Law is the director of the public security bureau at the same level. This means that the head of Public Security can order the courts at the same level. Such a committee structure concentrates power and can lead to prosecutions and criminal defence being overseen by the same group of people.

Lack of Procedures

Another problem is a lack of procedures in the Constitution to deal with government officials. Article 41 of the 1982 Constitution has also provided a constitutional supervision over governmental officials in cases of unlawful (including unconstitutional) and derelict acts. But, as Lin points out, various procedural administrative laws (e.g. the Review Law, Litigation Law and State Compensation Law and so on) are not open to ordinary individuals or legal professionals, because they

> do not have a formal legal channel through which they can challenge the constitutionality of the acts of governmental officials. Strictly speaking, only the NPCSC or the NPC have the authority to decide the constitutionality of the acts undertaken by governmental officials under the existing constitutional setting. The NPC and NPCSC have the authority to remove senior governmental officials from their positions if they commit unconstitutional acts (Article 63 of the 1982 Constitution). Article 41 of the Constitution may well be regarded as the constitutional grounds for either the NPC or NPCSC to exercise their supervision authority over the constitutionality of the acts undertaken by governmental officials. However, procedural law is still required for either the NPC or the NPCSC to exercise such authority (F. Lin 2000: 325).

Others see law as the most important authority of constitutional supervision: 'Many countries grant such authority to the judiciary (F. Lin 2000: 315).

The procedure to review and to impose penalties if legal procedure is not followed is also important. The cases cited in Chapter 4 show that a lack of review of such procedure left the cases unsolved and the law ineffective. The normal procedure for criminal cases is that, if the president of the court commences a case, the case must be submitted to the judicial committee for discussion and decision (Art. 177(1) of the 1991 Civil Procedural Law). If the SPC or the higher level people's court discovers the existence of error, it can either ask for the case to be transferred to its body for retrial or designate a court to try the case (Art. 177(2) of the 1991 Civil Procedural Law). If the retrial process is initiated by the parties concerned, the procedure depends on which judicial organ they brought their claim to. The people's courts at all levels must be accountable for handling a petition lodged by a party to a case against a legally effective judgment or order. Many courts have also set up an appeal adjudication division to receive petitions for the parties concerned (F. Lin 2000: 230). In the Administrative Litigation Law

(1990), violation of legal procedure is separated from violation of substantial legal provisions and both of them are grounds for judicial review in China (see Art. 54). However, as shown in the cases discussed in Chapter 4 of this study, procedural justice is completely disregarded in criminal justice. As for the court or judges, as Lin rightly pointed out, certain internal administrative penalties should be imposed if they do not follow the legal procedures (F. Lin 2000: 230).

Leadership and the Law

This lack of legal independence is also evident in relation to the leadership. The court is subject to the Committee of Politics and Law within the Party organization, which consists of, among others, the president of the court, the chief-procurator, the director of the Public Security Bureau and the director of the Justice Bureau at the corresponding level. This Committee of Politics and Law 'ensures that all judicial organs, including the people's court, are subject to the leadership of the CPC. This often turns out to be the dictatorship of the secretary-general of the Committee of Politics and Law' (F. Lin 2000: 232).

On the other hand, the court is unable to constrain the legal privileges enjoyed by Party officials. In the discussion of the authority enjoyed by the people's procuratorates according to the Constitution and relevant laws, it is clear that there are limits to this authority, in particular in relation to the privilege of the Party. The exercise of procuratorial authority when a member of the CPC is involved 'is subject to external interference. … Only when that investigation is complete will the case be transferred to the people's procuratorate at the corresponding level for public prosecution' (Lin 2000: 244). For example, the case involving the former Mayor of Beijing Municipality has been held up in the Central Commission for Disciplinary Inspection of the CPC for several years (Liu 1999: 46 n. 136). A political decision must be made by the CPC Central Commission for Disciplinary Inspection, as to whether or not the Mayor should be subject to criminal punishment, before the Supreme People's Procuratorate can become involved. This is an example which seems to suggest that the actual status of the Party is higher than the Supreme People's Procuratorate. The leadership of the CPC seems to remain above the law in many accounts, and this can be rectified only by a separate legal mechanism outside the party itself.

The Supreme People's Procuratorate is also subject to the leadership of the Committee of Politics and Law within the Party organization as with the courts. In many places, the head of the Committee of Politics and Law is the director of the Public Security Bureau at the same level. This means that the Director of the Public Security Bureau can hand down orders to courts at the same level. Such a leadership structure 'can lead to interference by an organ with the executive branch of a local people's government with the exercise of independent prosecuratorial authority … Such a practice does not have any legal ground to support it and is purely a practice of the CPC' (F. Lin 2000: 245).

The People's Congress

As the assembly of people's representatives, the People's Congress is perceived negatively as a 'rubber-stamp' for the Party by many. In theory, the Peoples' Congress is the governmental organ that exercises state power. Lenin once stated that 'All other governmental organs are created by and responsible to the People's Congress and the People's Congress is superior to all other governmental organs' (Lenin 1971: vol. 3, 133–4). This statement is consistent with Marx's concept of the new state, in which the congress is elected by voters as legislative authority. On the other hand, the People's Congress should never be placed under the dictatorship of the ruling party, for Marx and Engel's never endorsed a party supremacy above the will of the people and unconstrained by law. In principle, the people's representative organ should have the authority to appoint government officials. The voters have the authority to remove representatives from their positions at any time if the latter do not execute their jobs properly. Engels, at a later stage, further clarified the concept of decision-making authority as 'all political authorities, including the executive authority, should be concentrated in the hands of the people's representative organ' (Cai 1998: 3).

This democratic form of government is far superior to a totalitarian one. In order to prevent representatives from abusing their power and becoming masters rather than servants of the people, 'Engels proposed two specific measures: one, to make the representatives subject to direct election and supervision of the voters, and two, to deprive them of any financial privileges by paying the representatives the same wages as the workers' (Cai 1998: 6). Cai argues that Lenin endorsed this idea of the representative organ as the highest power comprising all powers in order to realize the dictatorship of the people, that all powers should be concentrated in the hands of the people's representative organ, that is, the People's Congress. All representatives of the congress are subject to the people who can remove their representatives at any time. 'Lenin believed that only if such authority to remove representatives was acknowledged and implemented could the system be treated as a genuine democracy' (Cai 1998: 14).

This state organ of congress was later translated to the Party and became a concentrated power that cannot be removed or appealed against by the people at all. In other words, the status of the Party has divorced itself from the original criteria of the people's representatives. Every state's ruling party enjoys decision-making authority; which can make its leadership a dictatorship, as seen in recent history. The Party used to exercise direct leadership over all national affairs and issue orders to all governmental organs and the people directly. The decision-making authority of the CPC virtually replaced the decision-making authority of the People's Congress: 'In practice, the decision-making authority of the People's Congress became useless' (Cai 1998: 335).

This problem was acknowledged by the CPC itself. In 1987, in its Thirtieth Plenary Meeting Report, the CPC stated that the leadership of the CPC should only be *political* leadership (PRC 1990: 433). Thus the exercise of such leadership is to convert the CPC's policies through legitimate channels into legislation of the state. It also acknowledges the necessity to separate the CPC organs from state organs. Lin, however, argues that any decisions adopted by the CPC should not have any direct effect at all, because in order for them to become legally effective, the decision made by the CPC must go through the People's Congress and be adopted by the Congress (F. Lin 2000: 100).

The NPC is the decision-making authority. It is designed to be 'the balance imposed by legislature over the executive branch of the government and the supervision by the legislature over the executive branch' (Zhu Guanglai 1987 in Lin 2000: 97). It is particularly important for the local congresses to have this decision-making authority as a means for people to express their interests and to make decisions through the relevant people's congress. This authority should be extended. One view is that this decision-making authority should be used to amend, supplement and interpret legislation. Such authority is available only to those with legislative authority (NPC) and their standing committees (Zhu Guanglai 1987 in Lin 2000: 99).[2]

In theory, the NPC has the authority to decide major issues, and the government is responsible for their implementation. In practice, the CPC has more authority through the executive branch than the decision-making authority of the people's congresses (Cai Dingjian 1998b: 340). The consequence is that officials from the executive branch of the government have a higher status than those from the Congress in the relevant party organ. The executive branch thus has more authority than the NPC, which is a fundamental violation of the principle of power check. Of concern is that 'the CPC often makes decisions jointly with the executive branch of the government' (Lin 2000: 101). Thus, the demarcation of authorities between the Congress (decision-making) on one hand and the government (the administrative power of the executives) on the other is obscured. The lack of real power of the NPC in asserting its proper role of decision-making, by the control of the Party and governmental executives, has resulted in the lack of respect for the body and given it the reputation as a 'rubber stamp' (H. He 1992: 156–8; F. Lin 2000: 201). This is an issue of leadership crossing the legal demarcations of law-making and law implementations, jointly with the state executives, at the expense of the people's representative organ, the Congress. This issue has to be rectified if China is serious about the rule of law and the power check by law. Success in this area requires a separate and independent mechanism to limit the power of the executives and Party bosses, outside the existing system of the CPC and the government.

It is fair to say that there still are various structural problems within China's constitutional structure, and that these have seriously undermined the effectiveness

2 In China, only the NPC, NPCSC, provincial congresses, these autonomous regions and municipalities directly under the central government, or major cities, have legislative authority. Other people's congresses and their standing committees do not have this legislative power (see Article 63 of the Law on Legislation).

of the power check. The main reason for this is the lack of a framework for an independent legal entity equipped for the task. The legitimacy of the Party leadership, granted by the Constitution, seems to provide a legal immunity from fair legal procedures and equality in law. Furthermore, government executives enjoy the benefit of being protected by a total power structure in which they are also immune from legal sanctions because there is no demarcation of legal responsibility and public accountability between the government, the Party, and the judiciary institutions. When the need arises, it is only the Party power that seems to work from above, through various politburo-legal committees top-down, subjecting everything in its way to its power. Meanwhile, basic human rights remain unprotected by the law.

China has adopted an instrumentalist approach towards its Constitution. It has been used as an instrument for political struggle in the past, such as the Constitution of the Soviet in 1934 and the 1975 Constitution during the Cultural Revolution, and for economic development from the 1980s onwards. The Constitution has evolved from an instrument for so-called class struggle to an indispensable tool for economic development, evident in its frequent amendments in recent years. It is hoped that the Constitution will develop beyond its economic instrumentalist functions, and will become indispensable in its role of power check, by providing a comprehensive framework for limiting the power of the state executives and denouncing any legal privilege in the implementation of the law.

Models of Power Check: Supervision

The Mechanism under the 1982 Constitution

The 1982 Constitution grants the authority of constitutional supervision to the NPC and NPCSC. In its Preamble (Arts 5, 62 and 67) it lays down the constitutional basis for the constitutional supervision mechanism. It states in Article 5 that 'All acts in violation of the Constitution or the law must be investigated' and 'No organization or individual is privileged to be beyond the Constitution or the law'. Many have interpreted this as giving the NPC and the NPCSC the constitutional supervisory authority (J. Hu 1998: 200). The Constitution also makes provision for the NPC to establish various special committees, which will examine and draw up bills and resolutions. These special committees have been assigned the task of assisting the NPC and NPCSC in conducting constitutional supervision stated in other relevant legislation, such as the Organic Law of the NPC.

The 1982 Constitution has expanded the authority of the NPCSC in its legislative power and constitutional supervisory power. The NPCSC has been granted the authority to make laws and to interpret the Constitution and national laws. In cases of inappropriate use of power by the NPCSC, however, the 1982 Constitution has also added another check and balance. It gives the NPC the authority to alter or annul any inappropriate decision of the NPCSC (Art. 62(11)).

The Problems of the Existing Mechanism

The Constitution and laws are believed to be the manifestation of the will of the CPC that represents the people, and the NPC has the authority to amend the Constitution (1982 Constitution, Art. 62(1)). The NPC and NPCSC also have the authority to enact and amend laws. It can be argued that, in this respect, the NPC and NPCSC are two authorities controlled by the same state organ, the only difference being in procedural arrangements. Most people in China are not aware of such a difference, and it is not easy to make such a differentiation in China because the CPC dominates both politics and the legislature (F. Lin 2000: 314). Some further argue that either the NPC or the NPCSC has performed unconstitutional acts. For example, the Criminal Law and Criminal Procedural Law are laws whose basic principles cannot be amended by the NPCSC (Art. 67(3)) and yet the NPCSC has in fact partially amended certain basic principles of those two laws (Guo 1999; F. Lin 2000: 319).

The constitutional supervision mechanism laid down in the 1982 Constitution is both more detailed and more structured than those of the 1954 and 1978 Constitutions, yet the actual implementation of it by the NPC has not been satisfactory: 'Neither the NPC nor the NPCSC has formally annulled or repealed any laws, administrative regulations, local legislation and local rules' (F. Lin 2000: 299).

There are problems in the existing mechanism in the role of constitutional supervision. These problems suggest reluctance on the part of the NPC and its standing committee to allow constitutional supervision to be conducted independently by legal experts, similar to the function of the court. This suggests a lack of confidence in the existing legal system, the court, and the lower level of legislature, in their capacity to give rulings in accordance with the law. The constitutional supervision cannot be conducted satisfactorily in the existing structure because:

1. the NPSCSC has both a shorter meeting season and has many other functions (21 in all), the main one being to legislate (Art. 67);
2. the members of the NPCSC have other full-time positions and it is therefore difficult to concentrate on constitutional supervisory activities;
3. the special committees of NPC, though assigned to assist the NPC and NPCSC in constitutional supervision, rarely provide such assistance in reality. This is due to the fact that none of these committees are allowed to make decisions in their own name – they must report their opinions or proposals to the NPC. This means that any decision on the unconstitutional acts still needs to be made by the NPC or the NPCSC. Moreover, these special committees already have heavy workloads in legislation and other duties;

4. while the special committees employ specialists as advisors, they allow them only the right to give their opinions without voting power. Nonetheless these specialists are expected to play a key role in constitutional supervision;
5. since every such special committee is obliged to assist the NPC, their authority or duties are very diversified and widespread, with the increasing possibility of diminished responsibility and expertise.

Many unconstitutional activities exist, as illustrated in this study, which have not been property handled in the past. This has highlighted the need for a specialized organ dealing with constitutional supervision. (For a detailed discussion of such unconstitutional activities, see Guo 1999, vol. 5.)

Models of Constitutional Supervision

The Chinese constitutional expert Lin Feng has summarized six main models of constitutional supervision:

1. *Supervision by ordinary courts (e.g. Japan)*: The Japanese Constitution provides that the Supreme Court has the final adjudicative power to decide whether any legislation, order or regulation is consistent with the Constitution. It does not limit such authority to the Supreme Court alone, so theoretically the ordinary courts may also conduct constitutional supervision (Art. 81 of the Japanese Constitution).
2. *Supervision by the supreme organ of state power (e.g. Sweden, Vietnam and China)*: In the case of Sweden, a legislative committee is established within the Parliament under the 1974 Act of Parliament (the Reksdag Act). It is one of 16 standing committees and is responsible for constitutional supervision.
3. *Supervision by a special institution (e.g. Iran, Egypt, Austria, German and France)*: This may be a constitutional court or committee supervising the implementation of the Constitution. Germany, for example, has a constitutional court, and France has a constitutional committee to conduct constitutional supervision.
4. *Supervision by the President (e.g. Afghanistan and Iraq)*: When being sworn in, the President must promise to comply with and supervise the implementation of the Constitution.
5. *Supervision by the Parliament, executive and judiciary jointly (Switzerland)*: The federal Parliament, federal central government and federal courts have the task of supervising the implementation of the Constitution.
6. *Supervision by the supreme organ of state power and procuratorate (e.g. North Korea)*: Under the North Korean Constitution, the Central People's Committee, which is the highest organ of state power, has the obligation to supervise the implementation of the Constitution. The procuratorate also has the obligation to supervise the consistency of resolutions or orders

of state organs with the Constitution (Arts 103(5) and 144(2) of the 1972 North Korean Constitution) (Lin 2000: 301–2).

The Objects of Constitutional Supervision

The objects of constitutional supervision differs in degree and scope from model to model:

1. To examine the constitutionality of certain legislation. In Sweden, for example, the parliamentary legislative committee can only examine the consistency between legislation and other documents adopted by Parliament and constitutional documents.
2. To examine the constitutionality of legislative documents, the activities of state organs and their personnel in the exercise of their powers.
3. To determine the constitutionality of any law, order, regulation or official act, as in Japan.
4. To examine the constitutionality of legislative documents, the activities of state organs and their personnel and various other organizations in the exercise of their powers.

Procedures for Constitutional Supervision

In terms of the procedure by which constitutional supervision is actually conducted. There are four main practices, as follows:

1. *No provisions for the procedure of constitutional supervision*: Taking Japan as an example, its Constitution provides the basic contents of constitutional supervision for the supervisory organ, but no details as to how the supervisory power should be exercised.
2. *The procedure of constitutional supervision is stipulated by other legislation*: This is the case under the Constitution of Kuwait.
3. *The basic principles governing the procedure of constitutional supervision is provided by the Constitution*: Thus Italy's Constitution provides that the examination of the constitutionality of legislation and of the exercise of state power by central covenantal organs and local governments will only be conducted when actual disputes or conflicts arise. The examination of the constitutionality of the actions by the President or ministers is conducted only when they have been accused. Italy's Constitution also provides that other relevant rules will be provided for by other legislation.
4. *The Constitution directly provides for detailed supervisory procedures*: Austria is an example of this kind. Upon the request of the Supreme Administrative Court or other court, reviews may be conducted of the constitutionality of state legislation (F. Lin 2000: 319).

Based on these models and the hierarchic status of the NPC and other legislation, it is suggested that relevant provisions in the Constitution on constitutional supervision and interpretation should be amended (Cai 1998: 147).

The Proposal

Structural Overview

Based on the existing models both in China and in other countries, and taking into account the problems discussed in this study, a model with three components is proposed here as a remedy. The discussion on constitutional supervision provided in Lin Feng's study is both comprehensive and complex. By comparison, the remedy model advocated in this study will focus on limiting the state executive's power only, rather than providing a review mechanism of constitutionality in general. The three components of this proposed model are: a constitutional office, an administrative court and a judiciary system directly under the Constitution. Although the following explanation is a much-simplified version for the purpose of theoretical debates by both the public and specialized legal scholars alike, the remedy is directed at the power abuse in its current forms.

Figure 5.1 Relationship between People's Congress, the State Council and the governments

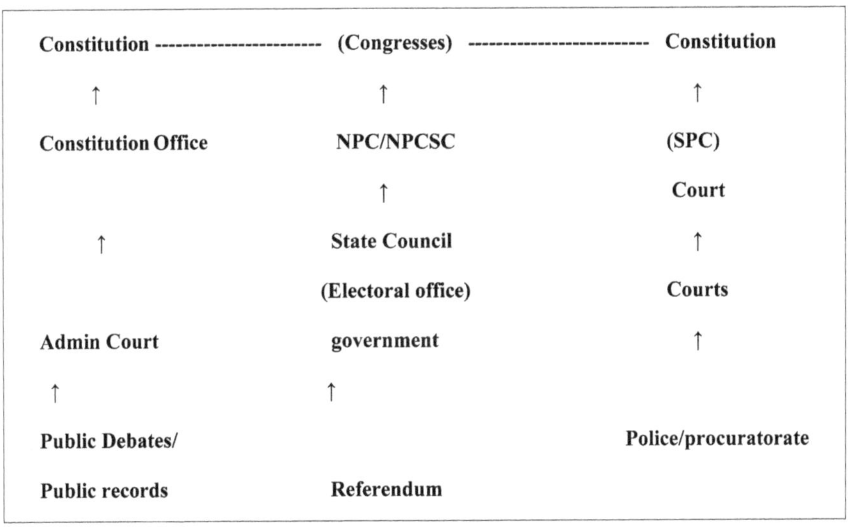

I would propose that the Constitution provides for the basic principles concerning the power check supervision. The Constitution should also grant, in all necessary terms, the establishment of a power check framework, which includes a constitutional office, an administrative court, and a court system that is independent of other state organs in all aspects – financial, administrative and political. The relationships between these establishments and the People's Congress, the State Council and the governments can be explained in diagrammatic form (See Figure 5.1).

The Constitution should provide the basic principles of constitutional supervision.

Principle: This model is based on the supervision principle that all power needs a counterpart – all power check needs to be open to public scrutiny (and the media).

Explanation:

- Congresses checked by Constitution and Electoral Office/public (mid vertical line)
- Government checked by Administrative Court and Congress (mid vertical line)
- Court checked by Constitution Office and Congresses (right vertical line)
- Police and Procuratorate checked by the courts (right vertical line)
- Constitution by majority of Congresses and referendum (not NPCSC)
- Constitutional Office checked by Constitution, NPC and public
- Administrative Court checked by Constitution and its Office
- Public has direct access to Constitution Office and election of Government/ Congress

I discuss the three main components of this proposed 'remedial model' below.

Component 1: The Constitutional Office

The first component of the remedial model is a constitutional office whose authority and procedures are granted by the Constitution. The Constitutional Office will be responsible to the Constitution and the people directly and must be located outside the legislature of the NPC.

The objective of the Office is to examine the constitutionality of legislative documents and amendments make by the NPC and NPCSC, and the activities of state organs and their personnel and various other organizations in the exercise of their powers. It also examines the consistency of the conduct of public office executives of state organs, political parties and social organizations at any level, including that of the NPC, within the Constitution.

The Constitutional Office's authority is granted by the Constitution, which enables the Office to declare an unconstitutional Act void or even to repeal it, and to order the relevant organ to bring the Act into line with the Constitution. Its decision is legally binding with legal consequences enforceable by the relevant legal institutions. While it has a duty to report to the NPC, it is not subject to its authority. It has supervisory powers over the administrative court, which deals with state officials under the administrative law, with legal consequences. The Office is directly accessible to the public, thereby ensuring that any amendment of the Constitution requires a referendum and other legal requirements.

The Constitutional Office is funded by state budgets and has a permanent and specialized staff. It has the authority to receive petitions and complaints from the public, investigate allegations against corrupt state officials, and has access to all financial information on the officer in question across all state agencies or departments. It may impeach a governmental official who has violated the law or acted against the interests of the people, or is found to be in serious dereliction of public duty. Its staff are appointed or removed by a majority of NPC and SPC members jointly.

Under the jurisdiction of the Office are ombudsmen's offices designated to investigate and discipline the corrupt state officials at any levels under the authority of the Constitution. The differences between this office and people's congresses (at all levels) are as follows:

- The People's Congress supervises only the organs it has established and their personnel, whereas the Office has the supervision of the People's Congress itself.
- The People's Congress supervises finance, elections and appointments of senior state executives, whereas the Office has a focus of exposing and diminishing corrupt state executives.
- The People's Congress hears reports, raises criticisms, and makes suggestions and offers advice, whereas the Office conducts investigations across the national and local levels with law-binding results. (For more about these differences, see Cai 1998: 144–7; Z. Li 1999.)

The Constitutional Office has the final adjudicative power to decide whether any legislation, order and regulations are consistent with the Constitution, as well as to specify the means by which an unconstitutional act committed by a state executive can be rectified. It may respond to courts of any level to clarify Constitution-related issues or concepts as well as to similar requests from the public. Its records may be published, and reviewed by the public, the NPC and the SPC. Most importantly, the Constitution should provide the procedures for such supervision to specify how such supervisory power should be exercised, or how to refer the relevant procedure from other legislation.

Component 2: The Administrative Court

The second component of the remedial model is an Administrative Court, similar to that of the French model. This court is directly under the supervision of the

NPC and the Constitutional Office. It conducts its procedures in accordance with the administrative law, and other relevant court procedures. It will be funded by the national budget and is not subject to the authority of any government or state organs. Its primary objective is to implement relevant administrative laws, and to make rulings on all matters related to the activities of state officials and state organs, as well as various other organizations, in the exercise of their powers. It employs only qualified personnel specialized in public administration and justice or public administrative law.

The especial function of the Court to curb the corruption of public officials, ensuring that legal consequences are exercised by imposing legal penalties on any governmental officials who have violated the law and are found to be in serious dereliction of their public duties. The People's Congress, through its supervision of such a court, will ensure it follows the will of the people, and protect the interests of the people. Lin provides an example of how such relevant legal consequences might be imposed:

> In Germany, for example, its constitution provides that if the Federal constitutional Court finds the Federal President guilty of a wilful violation of the Basic Law or other federal statute, it may declare him to have forfeited his office. After impeachment, it may issue an interim order preventing the federal President from exercising his functions. (F. Lin 2000: 326)

The Administrative Court will have the following procedures. First, the Administrative Court will adopt the procedures followed by the appellate jurisdiction. Secondly, it will establish specific procedures for dealing with corrupt government officials by the NPCSC and the NPC. It should be noted that such procedures are not provided for under the current Constitution (F. Lin 2000: 325). Thirdly, the examination of the exercise of state power by central covenantal organs and local governments will be conducted only when actual disputes or conflicts arise. Taking Italy as a model in this respect, the constitutionality of the actions of the President or ministers is only examined when they have been accused of acting unconstitutionally. As states earlier, Italy's Constitution also allows for relevant rules to be provided for by other legislation, which, I believe, is a good model to follow. Fourthly, there should be procedures by which, upon the request of the Constitutional Office, or of the SPC and other courts, the Administrative Court may review or investigate the conduct of state officials and make a final ruling.

Component 3: Courts Directly under the Constitution

The third component of this remedial model is a court system that is directly under the authority of the Constitution, without being subject to various bureaucratic sub-authorities. The structure of the courts should be simplified. This means an abandonment of the existing judiciary committees, divisional heads, presidents, vice presidents and political-legal committees at local, provincial and state levels.

In this way the remedial model aims to eliminate undesirable interference from all kinds of political and social sources existing in the current system. No extra 'approval' authority will be necessary for the collegial panel decisions, and no unqualified legal personnel will be authorized to make rulings.

The objective of this court system is to implement and interpret the laws and the Constitution. It has the authority to check the legality of power exercised by all state organs and the political parties; to safeguard the procedure and integrity of the law and law enforcement; and to ensure that the protection of people's basic rights is properly implemented. The courts at all levels have access to the Constitutional Office for advice on and clarification of the Constitution, and, as in the existing courts of law, the collegial panels have the authority to make a final ruling (rather than the bureaucrats of the various committees). This is to ensure that all involved abide by the law and follow the legal procedures properly. The SPC, as the highest court of this court hierarchy, has the authority to supervise both the NPC and NPCSC, since it is not impossible for the NPCSC to conduct a fair supervision of its own legislation, nor does it have the authority to conduct supervision of the constitutionality of the Acts of the NPC (F. Lin 2000: 315). The courts of lower levels, however, should have the authority to interpret laws with binding effect, under the supervision of the higher court.

The funding of the courts should come directly from the State Council or the national budget, not the local or provincial governments. This is to limit the government's control over the court.

The personnel of the courts will enjoy the legal protection and immunity from pressure and interference of either governmental executives or congresses. The courts are responsible only to the law and their authority in legal rulings over state officials is binding and final. The courts themselves are to abide by the law, including disciplinary procedures for court corruption and their conduct may be reviewed by a higher court, the Constitution Office, and the NPC. The professional quality of the court system needs to be assured by the criteria and standards existing in the current Law of People's Courts. The collective method of decision-making needs further investigation: it is unfair for the judge whose name is on the case to be responsible for the errors of others. There has to be collective responsibility for a collectively made decision or ruling, though this may need clarification.

The 'request and reply' method will be replaced by a Law Information Desk to respond to any inquiry of any court, by quoting the details of the source of the law in question. This is to avoid the higher courts dictating to courts at lower levels and the consequent confusion of authority and accountability in the decision-making process. Furthermore, the basic courts should have the authority to interpret the Constitution, with advice from the Constitution Office, as they handle more than 90 per cent of cases in China.

In this court system, both the police and procuratorate are subject to the courts' supervision. Their powers are limited to the order of the courts, but are not independent of, or higher than, the courts. This is due to the ambiguous status of the people's procuratorates, under the current legislation, as to whether they should be defined as state organs of legal supervision. Although their supervisory role is similar in nature to constitutional review in theory, they have in practice been closely associated with the police and prosecution. Their original role, as created by Lenin, in which they provided comprehensive supervision of the implementation of law by government organs and state officials, has never been matched by reality. It is argued that it is neither necessary nor desirable to have the procuratorate as another organ with comprehensive legal supervision authority, beside the People's Congress and the people's courts (Cai 1998: 227–9).

Conclusion

Having established that law has a role to play in power check, this chapter has suggested the ways in which the law can facilitate change by setting up the principle of power check and granting the independent status of legal institutions and their staff as legal professionals. The law can also facilitate a structural change by means of the Constitution. I have also proposed a model to deal with corrupt officials and their legal privileges; and to provide a legal forum for people to voice their concerns without fear of persecution or imprisonment.

In a socialist state like China that has, to some degree, retained something of its former feudal mentality, there seems a lack of readiness to adopt a post-industrial philosophy and to take the next step in the Marxist vision of history. The next step would be that, regardless of whether one is following a socialist or capitalist model, the people's supervision of state power must be established, to make that power subject to the people and accountable to the law.

Postscript

There are two major implications of this book in terms of Marx's original vision. First, it has repositioned Marx's vision of the new civil state that is based on democratic values, and that subjects the state power to people's supervision. The vision is a rejection, not an endorsement, of a feudal-style power totality after a Marxist revolution in a socialist state. Any political ideology used as a justification for this arbitrary form of power has been proved futile. Curzon once commented on Soviet jurisprudence that 'Marxism rejected peaceful co-existence in the area of philosophy and ideology' (Curzon 1979: 179). This is not necessarily true. This is because any ideology that justifies its monopoly of power above a common will and scrutiny is a deviation from the original intent of Marx's vision of a people's state. In this sense, it is not only possible, but also natural, that philosophy and ideology coexist. On the other hand, those ideologies that cannot come to terms with this philosophy cannot be called a genuine revolution in Marxist terms – rather it is a mere formality in the name of Marxism – without the true spirit of humanity.

Secondly, this repositioning of power entails a profound historic and cultural change as well. It will be a change in the relationships between persons, in that one individual has no coercive power over another, based merely on one's perception of the ideological beliefs of the other person. It will be a process of social transition of culture and values, from the former power culture and the values associated with that power, to a new notion of 'man' both in terms of his duty and his dignity – his duty as a citizen to ensure that state and public power are ruled by law, and his right as a human to be recognized and protected by law. Furthermore, *all* citizens are to be treated with respect and dealt equally by the rule of the law, including all public power agencies and officials. This conceptual change in the value placed on 'man' will take a long time to evolve, and is a part of the social transformation towards greater political freedom that Marx predicted for the true socialist state.

Historically, this book has suggested that it is unrealistic that a former feudal society with a slave mentality is capable of reaching a socialist state in the purely Marxist sense, without an evolution in the concept of humanity, and a power transfer from the total dominance of one ruling party and its leaders to the will of the people through their assemblies in various forms, by the due process of the law. In this sense, this must be a change not only in the law, but also in a legal culture that has previously been based on master–slave power relationships instead of on humanity or the common good – a culture that is based on the dogmatic control of the human mind against free reasoning. There must therefore be a fundamental change in the concept of man and how man should be treated and have his rights protected by the integrity of the law.

As a certain stage of the historic development, this book has shown that there seems to be a correlation between the strong authority of the ruling power and a weak economy in a former feudal and agrarian society. The current economic progress that has brought prosperity and security to the people of China is expected to bring with it the demand for securing this prosperity and for political stability. As a result, the demand for the accountability of state powers by public scrutiny is expected to increase. As argued, economic growth does not necessarily bring about the idea of power check as a principle and this is where the legal structure can play its role as a legal mechanism for power constraint. This is how law, in the Marxist theory of superstructure, is expected to respond to basic economic and social needs. One of these fundamental needs is to break the feudal-style totality of the state power structure. It is clear that any regime that maintains its power by silencing its critics cannot be ideologically or spiritually healthy or stable. Retaining power by the suppression of the citizens' basic rights as a means of holding on to power supremacy with no sanction of the law must inevitably lead to internal power struggles or to external and violent revolutions with catastrophic consequences, similar to that of the Great Cultural Revolution, as history has already shown. A revolution that keeps the old political and social relationships such as those between the Russian Tsar and the serfs cannot be called a true revolution, for the people have no power over their state and the leaders of the government.

Power must be checked both in principle and in the constitutional structure. There are several reasons why we cannot justify a form of power totality, in the name of the proletarian dictatorship or Marxism. This is an abuse of the vision that Marx and Engels described at the time, and a betrayal to the democratic principles of the revolution. It can be argued that no ideology can be justified without preserving the basic values in humanity. The Cultural Revolution in the 1960s in China is an example where ideology was used at the expense of humanity to preserve a monopoly of state power in the hands of a few individuals. It showed that under a repressive regime of political totality, people's basic rights could not be protected. The written laws had little effect in combating this abuse of power, for the legality of this power monopoly superseded any other means of legal challenge. This study has challenged the legality of power that is ordained by its own authority, but not by the collective will of the people through their representatives. This is against the socialist principle of people's right to supervise or alter their governing body.

Power must be checked even though it will take a long time. History shows us that the monopoly of power by a single ruling entity must come to an end either by gradual and legal processes or by violent movements like the Cultural Revolution. The latter is, I believe, what the current Chinese leadership will strive to prevent. This is why China adopted the rule of law in the first place. The essence of the rule of law, as argued in this study, is to protect people's basic rights; and to submit the dominance of the ruling party to the authority of the common will. The law, as the vanguard, will serve these new values and principles. Law, in its form as an economic regulator, has a similar function in all kinds of states with different political systems or ideologies. However, it has a greater mission – to protect people by restricting the ruling power under the rule of law. This mission would be impossible without an admission by the rulers that no power or party should have overriding authority over the state apparatus and organizations; and that no power should be left unrestricted. This is the precondition if the law is to be able to protect the citizens.

This precondition entails a number of elements, including the principle of power check, the commitment of the ruling party to this principle, the independence of the power check mechanism, and a separation between the Party, government and court system. Most importantly, however, it is the authority of law, including the authority to *interpret* the law, that first needs to be established. This authority has to be independent of the Party and the government, and have direct access to the public and the Constitution. Furthermore, its decision must be legally binding without the order of the Party.

Law, as expressed in the Constitution, should provide a legal forum where, without fear of retaliation, people's rights of supervision over the use of state power are to be exercised; where people's concerns are expressed and dealt with; and where the corrupt officials are punished by the rule of law. This struggle for power check as a principle is yet to be won and the structure of power check is yet to be put in place. Law as a legal forum can provide legal protection of citizen's basic rights and their rights to choose or dismiss their leaders and the government. As an expression of common will, law can also provide a legal structure to restrict state power in a cross-check system. In this sense, law is not only relevant at this critical stage of power transition, but also indispensable in the process of placing any ruling body under the will of the people.

Appendices

Appendix 1: Derbyshire on the Trial of the Gang of Four and the Verdict on the Cultural Revolution

'The historic trial opened on 20 November 1980 with the "Gang" members being charged with plotting to overthrow the party and state leadership and of framing and persecuting over 700,000 officials and leaders, 34800 of whom subsequently died' (Derbyshire 1987: 47). (Western estimates put the true figure of 'Gang'-induced deaths at close to 400,000 (Derbyshire 1987: 47 n.))

'This "show trial" served to end the political careers of the infamous "Gang of Four"'. It also hastened the demise of Hua Guofeng, who was implicated in many of the "Gang"s later misdeeds during his period as minister of public security. It further reduced the standing of the PLA, five of whose former leaders were arraigned before the court. The primary purpose of the trial was, however, to bring to a close an unfortunate chapter in Communist China's history and allow the new administration to make a fresh start, concentrating in a united fashion on its vast modernization programme.'

'Thus, six months after the trial, on 29 July 1981, the CPC Central Committee published an authoritative official verdict on Mao Zedong and the last 20 years of his life, the "Resolution on Certain Questions in the History of Our Party since the Founding of the People's Republic".'

'In this document, Mao's contribution to the building of the CPC and PLA, to victory in the liberation war and the consequent creation of the People's Republic, and to the safeguarding of the nation's independence, unity and security was recognized and praised. He was, however, criticized for becoming tyrannical and obsessed with a misguided leftist line during the last 20 years of his life, culminating in the disastrous "Cultural Revolution". Mao was thus "de-deified" and slavish worship of his thought and writings was now frowned upon. Instead Mao's was seen to be just one of the many contributions to the creation and development of Chinese communist thinking, in what became a new vogue for eclecticism and collectivism' (Derbyshire 1987: 48).

Appendix 2: Mao's Image

During the Cultural Revolution, the image of Mao had an almost magic power over the Chinese people, the power over whether individuals lived or died. The image was adroitly exploited by those in power to intimidate and control the masses. This supernatural feeling was further intensified by Lin Bio's ultra-leftist slogan which bestowed on Mao four great titles – as the people's great teacher, leader, general and helmsman – whose memory would live on for thousands and thousands of years. In this frenzied maelstrom, nobody dared denigrate Mao's image. Mao's words could not be altered, and people had to show utmost respect whenever they mentioned his name, treating him as if he were an emperor or a god.

In one incident, a man singing a song from Mao's *Quotation Book* jokingly changed the words 'you young people, energetic and highly spirited, like the morning sun ...' to 'you old people, stale and withered, in the ending period'. Someone overheard him and reported it to the authorities. The man was later sentenced to jail by the revolutionary committee in his workplace. In another case, a peasant went to buy a Mao's sculpture at the market at the foot of the mountain. To carry the heavy sculpture, he used a rope to hold the sculpture's neck and put it on his back but was quickly arrested before leaving the market. They accused the peasant of being an 'active counterrevolutionary' and sent him to jail that day for five years (Feng 2004: 124).

This power of the image is even better illustrated by an incident that took place in 1969, when military training had become de rigueur among the nation's youth. A high-school training group was walking in a hilly area when a soldier carrying Mao's sculpture made of heavy china slipped over and smashed it to pieces. Everyone was horrified. In Feng's words:

> 'To smash Chairman Mao's sculpture is to lose one's head!' It was the thought in everybody's mind. In no time did the soldier kneel down to the ground, to plead guilty to Chairman Mao, the team head followed; the whole team followed and knelt down asking for punishment. The second team and the third team all followed in a like manner. Each person tried to kneel first, as if whoever knelt first was the most loyal and most firmly dedicated with least hesitation, just like the size of Mao's badges – the bigger the size, the greater degree of loyalty it seemed to suggest. (Feng 2004: 118)

What counted most for these students was their outward show of loyalty and love for their leader, Mao, and how they appeared to others. The loyalty was hollow, however, without true human feeling, and it was based on fear:

> People were all mad then, at that time people's nerves were as tight as the string fully stretched. Worse still, no one cared to get up first, whoever stood up first was most disloyal. What end would it be for this drama? One could not kneel like this forever: under the moonlight, in the open field, a vast dark human

bodies knelt on the earth, no one dared to make a single sound, no one moved and no one looked at others, all facing the pieces of china with a guilty heart. Some even wetted the pants … till the leader found the 'enemy' in front so the whole troop moved on, and yet, no one dared to step on those china pieces on the way. (Feng 2004: 118–20)

Appendix 3: T's Story

Background

'T' was a fitter in a factory in northern China. His 'fault' was to criticize his superior, an action frowned upon as a crime of '*fan shang* – offending one's superior' in feudal times, but at that time viewed as a crime of 'not being in accord with the party organization' (*zuzhi*). T complained about the Cultural Revolution to a close friend when they had a drink, pointing out that when Zhu Yuanzhang became a Chinese emperor he killed all his meritorious officers. This was on 1 March 1968 and the friend reported him. On the following day, a mass meeting was held: T was pronounced a counterrevolutionary and accused of seeking 'class revenge'. Posters were plastered everywhere, declaring him to be a bourgeois to justify the claims of class revenge, which was a crime even more heinous than being a mere counterrevolutionary (Feng 2004: 123).

From the outset, the persecution of T seemed well planned, organized by certain groups of people in power. This was a typical pattern of the time and no written instructions from the top level of leadership were necessary. People, it seemed, were only too eager to suppress others, and showed little respect for other human beings and their rights.

Violence

Their inhumanity was evident in the physical violence that was used against T. They targeted T's head and beat him until he was unconscious, permanently injuring one of his ears and impairing his hearing. They trussed him up with wires and took him to a prison. Although T's class origin was rectified in 1970 as working class and not bourgeois, and he was cleared of being a counterrevolutionary, the military representative and the revolutionary committee members in the factory refused to redress the matter.

Wrongful Imprisonment

This was a result of political class labelling and it had devastating impact on the individuals involved. It was difficult to verify the cases then, and is still difficult today. In T's case the prison staff did not want to be involved in the matter either. As a result, T stayed in the prison for ten years before he was released. This was despite his making more than 20 judicial appeals while in prison.

Total Control

It is noted that in T's case, the same power-holders were able to control T's life before and after his imprisonment. No legal action was possible at the time to challenge the wrongful detention, and no apology and compensation for the loss of his freedom and dignity was ever given. Such an option was nonexistent as far as the Chinese were concerned. It was simply not an issue in the minds of most people at the time. This was shown by the fact that, even after T was released from prison and he sought work in the same factory, the head of the revolutionary committee rejected him. In his words, 'If he wants to come back, I would break his legs first!' Furthermore, when T needed to borrow some money because he had no job and no income, he was refused all help. This shows that the power-holders, in this case, had the power not only to detain T and to determine the length of his sentence, but to control his finances, his income and loans. In other words, the power-holders' control over individuals' lives and livelihood was total. Who gave them such power and control? Would a written law have made any difference? In a political environment such as this, every decision appeared to be based on personal power and not on integrity, character or evidence.

Beneficiaries

During the Cultural Revolution, people's property was taken away and important and powerful positions were occupied by selfish and brutal individuals who became the beneficiaries and major players in this deadly political game. This was shown in T's case when T's home was hit by an earthquake (his previous house had been taken away by activists from the local street committee). These beneficiaries forced those people with a 'problematic' class out of their own properties, so that the power-holders, the so-called revolutionary committee members and their families, could move into the houses and live there instead. This situation was so prevalent in the Beijing that, even today, these people are still living in the places that they obtained during that era even though they had no right to them.

The Function of Political Rhetoric

How did the abusers of the revolution use jargon to achieve their criminal activities? Here is an example which vividly depicts the absurd justifications they used. Victims were also forced to use this jargon in order to have access to family members. The political rhetoric penetrated every corner of private space and there was no escape. There was no such a thing as a 'private matter'. For example, one of T's private letters from gaol displays the kind of rhetoric that prisoners were forced to use in order to pass the prison censorship. As the letter is brief, it is quoted here in full:

> Hello parents,
> Your son did not listen to our respected Chairman Mao, did not follow his instructions, and committed a serious mistake. The revolutionary masses wanted to save me, and took me to the Bureau of Public Security to study. I am now studying at the study class supervised by the Liberation Army, to undertake

> thought reformation. Father, please ease your mind, I am determined to correct my mistake and to be a good person again.
>
> Everything is going well here with your son's studies, so please do not worry. Everyday I study at the Mao Ze Dong's Thought Class led by the Liberation Army leaders personally. Please bring these items to me after you see this letter: soap, toothpaste, pills, underwear, quilt and the mug.
>
> Your son, August 1968 (Feng 2004: 135)

A translation is needed to decode what the prisoner really meant in the letter. He was arrested and imprisoned for ten years without any legal process, and yet he could not tell his family that he was in gaol. We should decode some of his phrases as follows: 'The revolutionary masses wanted to save me, and took me to the Bureau of Public Security to study' means 'I am imprisoned'; 'I am now studying at the study class supervised by the Liberation Army' means 'I am watched closely'; 'I am determined to correct my mistake and to be a good person again' means 'I won't give in'. Forcing prisoners to use this kind of rhetoric seems to have had three purposes: to keep the prisoner in conformity with the state's official line of thought; to eliminate individuality; and to extinguish any free or private thought. The overall effect was to keep the abuser in control through the medium of political rhetoric. Such opportunists also employed rhetoric to justify their abuses of power. This shows how the abuse of power was inseparable from the abuse of rhetoric.

Decoding the Jargon

One example of this can be seen in T's case. Each time he appealed to the superior authority, the reply was the same: 'We may consider the part of "Class Revenge" to be eliminated, and your Class Origin may be changed back to Working Class. However, it is the time to defend the victory of the Great Proletarian Cultural Revolution; these issues will have to wait till later' (Feng 2004: 123–40). Here, 'defend[ing] the victory of the Great Proletarian Cultural Revolution' was a typical rhetorical way of covering up the real inhumanity of those who benefitted during the political turmoil of the Cultural Revolution, which cost the lives of millions of people and caused immense suffering.

Implementing Law

Policies or directives came from the top level of the state to rehabilitate those wrongly accused of being 'political enemies'. However, to issue a policy does not entail a corresponding implementation at the local level. Often such directives met with strong resistance from local authorities and those beneficiaries who held power. For example, in T's case, while he was released because of the change of policy, he still had many obstacles to overcome and a long wait before he was able to reap any benefits from the law. When T went to the housing management office for his accommodation, the office staff wrongly told him that they were not responsible for T's problem. The fact that, no matter how good a law might be, it could be so easily ignored by a local officer is alarming.

Prison Situation

Once a person was arrested as an 'anti-revolutionary', their spouse was termed a 'relative of an anti-revolutionary'. More than 90 per cent of those in prison divorced. There were many cases of suicide, murder or psychiatric breakdown related to divorce. Many spouses were imprisoned for speaking out, labelled as 'active counterrevolutionaries'. Torture was also used in the local Bureau of Public Security, as T himself experienced. According to Feng, the prisons were like warehouses in which the prisoners were treated like stock rather than taking living souls. As the superintendent of the gaol where T was imprisoned said: 'I don't care if you go out or come in. As long as I see the stock list I would let you go. If there is no list, you would have to stay here indefinitely' (Feng 2004: 124).

Summary of T's Lot

T was arrested just 60 days after he was married when his wife was just 20 years old. Her fate changed overnight. Their house was ransacked six times; everything was taken, except the bare boards of their bed, in the name of revolution. The power-holders, the committee chairperson and the military representative, dictated what she should do in every area of her life. Even her baby's name had to be changed three times before they would agree to it. She could sew and do hairdressing to earn some money, but she was criticized whatever she did. If the haircut was no good, she was lazy, and if the haircut was good then it was revisionist. If she used a lunchbox with T's name on it, then it meant she had not drawn a clear line between him and herself, between right and wrong. T's wife and her newborn baby slept on the bare boards in winter and was almost entirely without possessions. Even so she did not tell T everything about the confiscation. Her father was partially paralysed and all her relatives deserted them; the family of four lived on just 17 yuan (= $2) a month from her wage as an apprentice. To get to work, she had to walk for hours while pregnant because she didn't have the money for the bus. Neither did she have money to pay for treatment when her baby had pneumonia, and none of her neighbours dared lend her any money, for fear of being associated with a 'counterrevolutionary' family (Feng 2004: 125–40).

T's father's lot was not much better than T's. T's father-in-law was classified as a capitalist, and was forced to labour even though he was partially paralysed. Once while he was cutting onions, he could not find the knife amongst the big pile of onion peels. This was seen as a deliberate attempt to hide the knife so that he could kill someone in another act of 'class revenge'. The poor old man searched high and low, with tears in his eyes, till T's wife found it under the onions.

Such abuses of power and rhetoric even went so far as to erode societal bonds such as marriage and familial relationships. The pressure placed on T's wife was so great that, even before she went to the court for a forced divorce, the power-holder had already informed the court of her intention. This case shows that the concept of civil liberty in China was not understood. As demonstrated, the Party and the leaders of Party organizations were responsible not only for an individual's work performance, but also for the individual's entire life, including marriage, childbirth, employment, promotion, and even where and how they lived. Needless to say, this kind of power in any organization needs to be challenged.

The situation in which T's wife found herself was very common at the time. The woman as the head of the committee attempted to force T's wife to divorce and to marry a soldier. Her efforts included:

- using T's wife's natural mother (who had sold her due to poverty) to pressure her;
- pressuring her to draw a line between herself and her 'capitalist' father;
- promising her housing, Party membership and remarriage;
- having her followed by a military representative everywhere;
- conducting study meetings to influence her.

The chairwoman marshalled the political rhetoric of the day against her: 'The house is yours pending your revolutionary action,' she was told; or 'This is the responsibility the Party has for you.' T's mother was asked to recall the 'pain under the old system' in the past. 'Only if you divorce can you return to the people's cause, to draw the line. You are our sister of the same class so how can we not care for you? …' (Feng 2004: 145) When the wife hesitated as a result of this pressure, she sought advice from the court, and was surprised to learn that her work unit had already asked the court for a divorce on her behalf, without her knowledge and consent.

The tactics of those who abused their power varied from offering inducements to outright threats. While they may have been on the lower rungs of the social and political hierarchy, the abuses they practiced were just as damaging as those emanating from the top level of the Party machine. In a sense, people like the committee head or the military representative in a local factory were vital links between the top leaders and the ordinary people, and they played a crucial role of implementing political abuses throughout the period of the Cultural Revolution.

Once T's wife decided not to divorce, the factory committee changed its tone and became hostile towards her. The attractive promises of housing and jobs changed into harsh physical punishment. T's wife was then assigned to a team digging trenches. She felt the injustice because she had harmed no living creature in her lifetime, and yet she had to endure such endless suffering. While she was digging an underground tunnel, more damaging posters about her appeared, this time accusing her of being a concubine of her own father.

And as if these physical and mental torments were not enough, an earthquake added to her misery. Her family home was damaged, but no one helped this 'counterrevolutionary' family to rebuild it and nobody helped them to collect the bricks to build a temporary shelter. The worse time was when it rained: her 'bed' became waterlogged and she had to get more mud to cover the shelter. Her father, her son and she, a family of three spanning three generations, huddled together tightly for the night trying to keep warm and dry. The family slept in these cold and wet conditions for several years. T's wife thought of suicide at the time but persevered.

How did people gain advantages from such abuses at the local level? What was their motive for carrying out brutal, inhuman acts? The chairwoman was determined to force through T's wife's divorce and to get her to remarry because from this deal she would be able to maintain her position in the factory committee and even get promoted with the support of the military representative. As for the soldier, he would benefit a great deal by marrying T's wife, a city girl. This would mean that he would not have to go back to his native village for the rest of his life.

Despite a change of the policy from the top, both the chairwoman of the revolutionary committee and the military representative in the factory remained in the new leadership group as the heads of the factory. Thus, the beneficiaries of the turmoil were once again left to pursue their own selfish interests in the name of revolution and the people.

References

Acton, H.B. (ed.) 1972. *Utilitarianism, On Liberty and Considerations on Representative Government by John Mill*. London: Dent Publishing Company.

Alexander, L. (ed.) 1998. *Constitutionalism*. Cambridge: Cambridge University Press.

Anonymous 1966a. Editorial. *The People's Daily*, 1 June.

Anonymous 1966b. Decision on the Proletarian Cultural Revolution by CCP. *The People's Daily*, August.

Anonymous 1993a. A free press vital to constitutional debate. *The Australian*, July, p. 38.

Anonymous 1993b. *The Law Yearbook of China*. Beijing: Law Yearbook.

Interview with Xue. SBS (dir. Anonymous, 2007).

Aquinas, T. 1964. *Summa Theologica Encyclopedia* (A.1). London: Eyre and Spottiswood.

Arendt, H. 1973. *The Origins of Totalitarianism*. New York: HBJ Book.

Arjomand, A. 2003. Law, political reconstruction and constitutional politics. *International Sociology*, 18(1), pp. 7–23.

Beirne, P. and Quinney, R. (eds) 1982. *Marxism and Law*. New York: Wiley Publishing Co.

Cai, D.J. 1998. *The People's Congress System of the PRC*. Beijing: China Legal System Press.

Carpenter, W.S. 1924, 1999. Political thought, in Rosen and Wolff (eds), *Political Thought*. Oxford: Oxford University Press.

Chen, Yunsheng 1988. *Trends of Democratic Constitutionalism*. Beijing: People's Press.

China 1982. *Constitution of the PRC 1982*. Beijing: People's Press.

Current Events. 2005. US: Stamford.

Curzon, L.B. 1979. *English Legal History*. Estover: Macdonald and Evans Ltd.

Deng, X. 1981. Problems on the ideological front, in Deng Xiaoping (ed.), *Selected Works of Deng Xiaoping, 1975–1982*. Beijing: Foreign Press.

—— 1984a. *Selected Works of Deng Xiaoping*. Oxford: Pergamon Press.

—— 1984b. On the reform of the system of Party and state leadership, in Deng Xiaoping (ed.), *Selected Works of Deng Xiaoping, 1975–1982*. Foreign Press: Beijing.

Derbyshire, I. 1987. *Politics in China: From Mao to Deng*. Cambridge: W. and R. Chambers Ltd.

Djilas, M. 1966. *The New Class*. London: Unwin Books.

Draper, H. 1978. *Karl Marx's Theory of Revolution* (vols 1 and 2). New York: Monthly Review Press.

Engels, F. 1892, 1966. On social relations in Russia [pamphlet], in K. Marx and F. Engels, *Collected Works* (vol. 24). Beijing: People's Press.

Feng, Jicai 2004. *A Decade of 100 Personalities.* Chang Chun: Shidai Wenyi Press.

Gerard, Ian 2004. Bail 'betrayal' angers police. *The Australian*, 7 December, p. 1.

Guo, Daohui 1999. Discussion of the phenomenon of disorder in legislation and the measures against such a phenomenon. *Legal Study and Research*, 5.

Hart, H.L.A. (1961). *The Concept of Law*. Oxford: Clarendon Press.

He, H. (ed.) 1992. *The Theory and Practice of the People's Congress System.* Wuhan: Wuhan University Press.

He, Weifang 2004, May. Interview. [Online: All Chinese Lawyers Association website]. Available at http://www.chineselawyer.com.cn/html/ [accessed: 15 January 2010].

Hobbes, T. 1996. *Leviathan.* Oxford: Oxford University Press.

Hu, Jinguang 1998. *Study of Some Issues of Chinese Constitutional Law*. New York: Paragon.

Hu Shih and Lin Yu-tang, 1945, *China's Own Critics: A Selection of Essays.* Paragon, New York.

Hunter, J.D. 1991. *Culture Wars*. New York: Basic Books.

Hunter, R., Ingleby, R. and Johnstone, R. (eds) 1995. *Thinking about Law.* Sydney: Allen and Unwin Pty Ltd.

Huntington, Samuel 1996. *The Clash of Civilizations and the Making of the World Order*. New York: Simon and Schuster.

Jin, Shikai 1993. *The Price of History: The Death Archives of Cultural Revolution.* Beijing: The Great Earth Publishing Co.

Kahn, J. 2005a. When Chinese sue the state, cases are often smothered. *The New York Times*, 28 December.

—— 2005b. Deep flaws and little justice in China's court system. *The New York Times*, 21 September.

Keith, R.C. and Li, Z. 2006. *New Crime in China*. New York: Routledge.

Kolakowski, L. 1978. *Main Currents of Marxism*. London: Oxford University Press.

Landry, P. 2004. *The Common Law: Tradition and Stare Decisis.* Available online at www.blupete.com/Literature/Essays/BluePete/LawCom.htm. [accessed 19 January 2010].

Lenin, V.I. 1917. Imperialism, the highest stage of capitalism. Available online at www.marxists.org/archive/lenin/works/1916/imp-hsc/.

—— 1947. *Lenin, Selected Works* (1). Moscow: Progress Publisher.

—— 1971. *Up Changed: Selected Works of V.I. Lenin* (3). Moscow: Progress Publisher, pp. 139–43.

Li, B. and Xu, B. 1986. *Rights and Duties*. Beijing: The People's Press.

Li, Cunxin 2003. *Mao's Last Dancer*. Sydney: Penguin Books Australia.

Li, Zhisui 1994. *The Private Life of Chairman Mao*. London: Chatto and Windus.

Li, Zhong 1999. *On Constitutional Supervision.* Beijing: Social Science Literature Press.

Lin, F. 2000. *Constitutional Law in China.* Hong Kong: Sweet and Maxwell.

Lin, X. 1983. *A 10,000 Words Letter to Deng*. Hong Kong: Guang Jiaojing Publisher.

Liu, Lansheng 1981. A brief discussion of constitutional supervision. *Social Science*, 3.

Lloyd, Lord of Hamstead 1982. *Introduction to Jurisprudence*. London: Stevens and Sons Ltd.

Locke, J. 1690, 1924. *Two Treatises of Government*, in W.S. Carpenter (ed.), *Two Treatises of Government*. London: J.M. Dent.

Love, N.S. (ed.) 1998. *Dogmas and Dreams*. USA: Chatham House Publishers.

Lubman, R. 1999, 2002. Bird in a cage: legal reforms in China after Mao, in R. Peerenboom (ed.), *China's Long March toward the Rule of Law*. Cambridge: Cambridge University Press.

Mao, Z. 1957a. *On the Correct Handling of Contradictions*. Beijing: People's Press.

—— 1957b. Speech. Chinese Communist Party's National Conference on Propaganda Work. Beijing: People's Press.

—— 1969. *The Highest Instructions.* Beijing: People's Army Press.

Marx, K. 1844. Introduction to critique of Hegel's philosophy, in *Selected Work of Marx and Engels* (1). Beijing: People's Press.

Marx, K. and Engels, F. 1966. *The Selected Work of Marx and Engels*. Beijing: People's Press.

Montesquieu 1731, 1949. *The Spirit of the Laws* (trans. Thomas Nugent). New York: Macmillan.

Morning Sun, dir. C. Hinton, R. Gordon and G. Barme, 2003.

Nathan, J. and Link, P. (eds) 1991. *The Tiananmen Papers.* New York: Public Affairs.

Pan, W. 1945. *The Chinese Constitution.* Washington: Institute of Chinese Culture.

Pashukanis, E.B. 1978. *Law and Marxism: A General Theory.* London: Ink Links Ltd.

Peerenboom, R. 2002. *China's Long March toward Rule of Law.* Cambridge: Cambridge University Press.

—— 2006. *On Law and Democratic Development.* Annals: AAPSS (603).

—— (ed.) 2004. *Asian Discourses of Rule of Law.* London: Routledge.

Perry, M. 1998. What is 'the Constitution'?, in L. Alexander (ed.), *Constitutionalism.* Cambridge: Cambridge University Press.

Phathanothai, S. 1995. *The Dragon's Pearl.* New York: Pocket Books.

Plato 2003. *The Republic* (trans. A. Bloom). New York: Basic Books.

Potter, P. 1991, 1994. Riding the tiger: legitimacy and legal culture in post-Mao China. *The China Quarterly*, 138, pp. 325–58.

Poulantzas, N. 1978. *State, Power, Socialism.* London: New Left Books.

PRC 1990. *Collection of Documents Concerning the People's Congress of the PRC.* Beijing: People's Press.
Pugh, D. 2005. William Hinton on the Cultural Revolution. *Monthly Review*, 56 (10), pp. 33–43.
Rawls, J. 1972. *A Theory of Justice.* Oxford: Clarendon Press.
Raz, J. 1998. On the authority and interpretation of constitutions: some preliminaries, in L. Alexander (ed.), *Constitutionalism.* Cambridge: Cambridge University Press.
Rosen, M. and Wolff, J. (eds) 1999. *Political Thought.* Oxford: Oxford University Press.
Sassoon, A.S. (ed.) 1982. *Approaches to Gramsci.* London: Writers and Readers Publishing C S Ltd.
SBS 2007a. *Hong Kong News.*
SBS 2007b. Interview with Xue.
SBS 2007c. *The Power of Nightmare*. CBBC TV serials.
SBS 2008. *China's Court.*
Songran, W. (ed.) 1987. *Collection of Essays on the Constitution of the PRC* (2). Hong Kong: Chinese University Press.
Spindler, G. 2000. *Legaldate* [online text]. Sydney: Warringal Publishing.
Thompson, E.P. 1975. *Whigs and Hunters: The Origin of the Black Act.* New York: Pantheon Books.
Trevaskes, S. 2007. *The Yin and the Yang of the Death Penalty Debate in China Today.* Griffith Law Seminar Series. Brisbane: Griffith University.
Tucker, R. (ed.) 1978. *The Marx and Engels Reader.* New York: W.W. Norton and Company.
Vyshinsky, A.Y. 1948. *The Teachings of Lenin and Stalin.* London: Soviet News.
Wang, C. and Zhang, X. 1993. *Study of the Theory of Adjudication in China.* Chongqing: Chongqing Press.
Wang, L. 1998. Study of issues relating to the structural setting of the People's Court and reform of adjudication method, in F. Lin (ed.), *The Constitutional Law in China.* Hong Kong: Sweet and Maxwell.
Weber, M. 1968. *The Religion of China.* New York: The Free Press.
Wen, Z. 1994. *The History of Constitutionalism of the PRC.* Zhengzhou: Henan People's Press.
Wilson, C. 1991, 1998. Marx refuted in dogmas and dreams, in N.S. Love (ed.), *Dogmas and Dreams.* New Jersey: Chatham House Publishers.
Xue, Xinran 2007. Interview with Xue. Dateline, SBS, 30 May.
Yardley, J. 2005a. Desperate search for justice: one man vs. China. *The New York Times*, 12 November.
—— 2005b. In worker's death, view of China's harsh justice. *The New York Times*, 31 December.
—— 2005c. A Judge tests China's courts, making history, *The New York Times*, 31 December.

Index

For Product Safety Concerns and Information please contact our EU representative GPSR@taylorandfrancis.com
Taylor & Francis Verlag GmbH, Kaufingerstraße 24, 80331 München, Germany

www.ingramcontent.com/pod-product-compliance
Ingram Content Group UK Ltd.
Pitfield, Milton Keynes, MK11 3LW, UK
UKHW011016180926
475701UK00004B/777
9780367602673